MARIO ANDRETTI  A DRIVING PASSION

*To Stephen
All the best,
[signature]
2002*

MARIO ANDRETTI

A DRIVING PASSION

BY GORDON KIRBY • FOREWORD BY DAN GURNEY

DESIGN BY TOM MORGAN

 **DAVID BULL** PUBLISHING

Library of Congress Cataloging-in-Publication Data

Kirby, Gordon.
    Mario Andretti : a driving passion / by Gordon Kirby ; foreword by Dan Gurney ; design by Tom Morgan.
        p. cm.
    Includes index.
    ISBN 1-893618-12-9
    1. Andretti, Mario, 1940- 2. Automobile racing drivers—United States—Biography. I. Title.

    GV1032.A5 K57 2001
    796.72'092—dc21
    ⌈B⌉   2001037531

David Bull Publishing, logo, and colophon are trademarks of David Bull Publishing, Inc.

Book and cover design: Tom Morgan, Blue Design, Portland, Maine

Printed in Hong Kong

10 9 8 7 6 5 4 3 2 1

David Bull Publishing
4250 East Camelback Road
Suite K150
Phoenix, AZ 85018

602-852-9500
602-852-9503 (fax)

www.bullpublishing.com

Pages 2-3: Mario at speed in Long Beach in 1993. (Michael C. Brown)
Page 4: A portrait of Mario at Indianapolis in 1967. (Joe Farkas)
Page 5: Mario in the Brawner/Hawk en route to victory at Indianapolis in 1969. (Bob Tronolone)
Right: After a tough race at Allentown in August, 1964, the afternoon's frustration is written on Mario's face. He qualified fastest in the Gapco sprint car, but encountered a series of problems and struggled home thirteenth. (Bricker Racing Photos/Andretti collection)
Page 8: Mario's friends and fellow competitors in the ARDC signed his program at the banquet held at the end of the 1962 season. Much of what they wrote in their inscriptions proved to be prophetic. (Andretti collection)
Pages 10-11: Mario won the 1965 USAC Championship with the Brawner/Hawk in his first full year on the circuit. "I knew how to set the car up myself, to really tweak it," he explains. "I used to pre-load the roll bars to create some cross-weight. I won a lot of races with that car, and that concept." (Dave Friedman)

Acknowledgments

This book has been a great privilege and an unqualified pleasure to write and research. Looking at the vast sweep of Mario's career, I must admit that in the early stages I was intimidated by this project. Working with Mario, however, has been an unparalleled delight throughout my career as a racing reporter, and this project only strengthened that relationship. Mario always stood out from the crowd as a driver with a keen eye and sharp wit, an urbane, self-educated man with a sophisticated world view, and deep historical perspective. He is a man of great character with a complex and charismatic yet straightforward manner, and is always able to put people at ease in his presence. His achievements as an individual inspired me to immerse myself in this fascinating challenge of covering and portraying the man's life in racing.

Mario's accomplishments as a race-car driver have become legend and are beyond equal. He was selected by both the media and fans as America's Driver of the 20th Century, and he most surely is that and more after forging the longest and most diverse career in motorsports history, as this book graphically demonstrates.

Many people contributed greatly to presenting the details of Mario's life and career, as well as to the overall production of this book. Most notable are Mario's wife, Dee Ann; brother Aldo; the entire Andretti family; brother-in-law Larry Hoch; his excellent personal assistant, Amy Hollowbush; his lawyer John Caponigro; publicist Patty Reid; his old friend Bruce Craig; Ford's John Szymanski and Sam Scott; Newman/Haas's Peter and Mary-Lin Murphy; Carl Haas's secretary, Sharon Zeeck; Peter Higham at LAT Photographic; Buz McKim at ISC Archives; Kathleen Oreovicz; and my friends Paul and Ann Webb, who helped midwife this project. Thanks also to James Penhune for offering an additional view and valued recommendations in editing the manuscript.

Particular thanks go to Dick Jordan of USAC for providing a complete record of Mario's 322 USAC races and to Bob Tronolone, who provided a meticulously catalogued photography archive that was central to developing this book. I also owe a debt of gratitude to the many people who tell remarkable stories about Mario's life in racing. These include Tyler Alexander, Michael Andretti, Pino Allievi, Nigel Bennett, George Bignotti, Tony Cicale, Jabby Crombac, Chris Economaki, Nick Goozee, Parnelli Jones, Brian Lisles, Jim McGee, Robin Miller, Adrian Newey, Mo Nunn, Brian Redman, Nigel Roebuck, Keke Rosberg, Bobby and Al Unser, and Peter Wright.

Finally, I have to thank, as always, the wide range of photographers and agencies whose excellent work appears in these pages, including Pete Biro, Dan Boyd, Peter Brock, Michael C. Brown, Harley Cluxton, Ken Coles, Bruce Craig, Hal Crocker, Studio Falletti, Joseph Farkas, Jutta Fausel, Art Flores, Dave Friedman, Richard George, Gary Gold, William Green, Bob Harmeyer, Nate Korn, LAT Photographic, Pete Luongo, Pete Lyons, Dan Mahony, Tony Matthews, Sutton Photographic, Barry Tenin, Dale von Trebra, Bob Tronolone, and Paul Webb.

And thanks to my publisher, David Bull, an excellent editor and a consummate professional.

G. K.
April, 2001
Mount Sunapee, New Hampshire

American Racing Drivers Club, Inc.

23rd ANNIVERSARY DINNER AND DANCE

NOVEMBER 17, 1962

LEN DUNCAN - CHAMPION
IN KEN HICKEY OFFY

KAY BROWN 2ND PLACE
IN D-V-OFFY

TONY BONADIES 3RD PLACE
IN BONADIES OFFY

DUTCH SCHAEFER 4TH PLACE
IN BENNETT BROS. OFFY

CARL MILLER - FORD CHAMPION
IN MILLER FORD

DON MORRIS
IN STROPOLI FORD

FAR HILLS INN- ROUTE 202-206 NORTH SOMERVILLE, N. J.

CONTENTS

Foreword by Dan Gurney

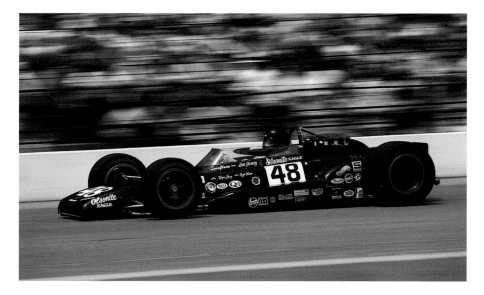

It is always an honor to be asked to write a foreword to a book, but when Mario and Gordon Kirby asked me to write this one, it was especially meaningful. Mario and I go back a long way. Our careers followed similar paths in that we both ventured out and were successful in different branches of motor racing, including Indy cars, Formula One, NASCAR, and sports cars. We were often competitors on the track in the middle sixties. I remember fondly the Indy road-racing series, in which he and I often traded pole positions back and forth until the last seconds of qualifying at places like Sears Point, Riverside, Continental Divide, Indianapolis Raceway Park, and others. We competed against each other briefly in Formula One in the late sixties and touched wheels in long-distance races at Sebring, Daytona, and Le Mans. We also know what it means to haul a stock car around an oval or a road course for 500 miles at a stretch.

Our best memories, however, are of the Indy 500. I have to confess to Mario that I wanted to see a little trail of smoke coming out of the rear of your Brawner-Hawk in the last two laps of that memorable 1969 race. I was hoping Andy Granatelli would kiss me! But you finished first, and I finished second. That was our destiny. Who would have thought that after I retired from driving in 1970 our AAR team would go on competing against you in various venues for the next twenty-five years?

In this honest book, which makes no pretense at political correctness, Mario lays it all out: his early years in Italy, coping with life in a displacement camp after World War II, boyishly dreaming of one day racing a Ferrari, coming to America and learning a new language, the early dirt-track adventures, his arrival as a rookie in Indy in 1965, his marriage to an American girl and the birth of his three children, and a family life that constantly had to take a backseat to a driver's career. Mario talks openly about the people who did him wrong and those who did him right. He shares his thoughts and his grief when his twin brother, Aldo, had a devastating career-ending accident and when some of his rivals died at the race tracks, among them his friends Ronnie Peterson and Gilles Villeneuve. You meet Enzo Ferrari and Colin Chapman, Clint Brawner and Mauro Forghieri, and many other fascinating racing personalities from both sides of the Atlantic, and you see them in a new light from Mario's perspective. But what struck me most of all is Mario's almost superhuman tenacity—not just his determination to get on top and stay there for such a long time, but his steadfast willingness to put himself in harm's way and live in the fast lane.

Mario is a star, not only because of the titles he won, but because he has the aura that surrounds an unusual man, which people sense when they meet him. I used to feel it watching him, a compact boxer-like figure, walking down pit lane before the start of a race, clad in his driver's suit, a matador entering the bullring. There was and is a certain Latin dignity about him that is difficult to put into words. He has aged well and, while he exemplifies the American dream, he also achieved everything for which a successful Italian would like to be known: finely made clothes, a Ferrari in the garage, and a vineyard of his own!

Upon reading the last page of the manuscript, I sat there very moved and a bit stunned. "So this is what he went through," I thought. How much sacrifice, misery, betrayal, and hard work are hidden behind those celebrated championships!

The price we drivers pay in this business and the toll it extracts from the participants are brought home in no uncertain terms in this book. Mario is no wallflower, but a tough hombre: extremely talented, with blinding passion and fierce determination, laced with a great deal of idealism and romanticism. He is a great mixture of the European immigrant and the old American oval-track campaigner with a streetfighter's determination to get to the top. His outstanding ability to discuss the elusive elements of vehicle dynamics with race engineers and chassis-tuning experts mixes the understanding of modern vehicle dynamics with hard-earned, seat-of-the-pants truth. His resilience and sustained passion for driving competitively are breathtaking. Top this off with a business acumen worthy of the toughest Wall Street barons, plus a few Washington politicians and athletes who know what it means to go the extra mile, and you have some sense of Mario's character.

I highly recommend this book to anybody who already is or wants to become a fan of motor racing. Seldom will you get such an honest account of what a racer's life is made of and the price we pay for success in our business. The book is a must-read for any aspiring driver who thinks his chance will never come. If he thinks it is tough in today's racing environment, there's news for you: You have seen nothing yet!

To the older generation, the one that waved Mario on from the grandstands or the pits, this book will be a nostalgic and joyful opportunity to relive the moments of glory and heartbreak, and it will justly reinforce their belief that Mario is one of the great champions of motor racing. So sit down in a cozy chair, and fasten your seat belt: It's going to be a bumpy ride!

Champ, I salute you!

Dan Gurney

Top: NASCAR held a 500-mile road race at Riverside, California, in the sixties. During that period Gurney dominated, winning the event in 1963, '64, '65, '66, and '68. In 1966 Gurney drove the Wood Brothers Ford (shown here) to beat David Pearson. Third-place Paul Goldsmith finished two laps behind. (Bob Tronolone)

Middle: Gurney scored a famous victory in the 1967 Belgian GP on the original 8.76-mile Spa-Francorchamps circuit. Driving an AAR Eagle-Weslake V-12 he became the only American ever to win a world championship Formula One race with his own team and car. He started from the middle of the front row, turned the race's fastest lap, and beat Jackie Stewart by more than one minute. (LAT Photographic)

Bottom: When his schedule permitted, Gurney ran in select Can-Am events driving his "McLeagle", a McLaren M8B powered by potent small-bore AAR engines. Shown here at Laguna Seca in 1969 the car was fitted with a larger 7-liter Chevrolet. He qualified fourth but withdrew from the race with engine problems. (Bob Tronolone)

Opposite: Mario talks with Dan Gurney at Riverside during the Los Angeles Times Grand Prix race weekend near the end of the 1966 season. Gurney's record competing successfully in everything from stock cars to Formula One had made him one of Mario's heroes. (Dave Friedman)

Chapter 1

Chasing the American Dream

As he hammered around the unfamiliar road course at Watkins Glen, New York, Mario Andretti was using all his racing experience to make the most of this qualifying period for the 1968 United States Grand Prix. Although this was his first run at the pole in a Formula One car, the Andretti name was already one to reckon with in a widening range of racing circles. In the previous three years, Mario not only had won the United States Auto Club

Above: In 1941, Mario, who is about a year old in this photo, plays with a pig in Montona, Italy. (Andretti collection) **Opposite:** Mario and Aldo pose with Charlie Clark's sprint car at Langhorne in June, 1956. "We had been here a year," says Mario. "This was a big day for us. It was our first race in America outside Nazareth. We went with my cousin, Carl Benvegnú. He was a very debonair, very handsome man who loved racing." (Andretti collection)

championship twice (in 1965 and 1966), but in 1967 had beaten the best drivers on the NASCAR circuit in stock-car racing's premier event, the Daytona 500. The same year saw Mario extend his reputation to the upper reaches of road racing as he teamed with New Zealand's Bruce McLaren to win the Sebring 12 Hour race in Florida.

Mario had taken his first steps into Formula One racing a month earlier when he tested a Lotus 49 car at Monza, Italy. With the Monza test under his belt, he felt completely at ease in the Lotus. "The Lotus 49B really suited my style," he recalls. "I felt totally at home in it from the first time I drove it."

In addition to his extensive driving experience, Mario's strong memory and a natural gift for engineering made him an unusually quick study when it came to learning his way around new tracks. As he began to master the intricacies of Watkins Glen, he also focused on carrying more speed through the fastest corners. Although Lotus boss Colin Chapman wanted him to come into the pits to change tires, believing fresh rubber would boost his speed, Mario stayed out.

"They had those intermediate, treaded tires they were running at the time," Mario says, "and on the high-speed corners the car would walk around so much." He was convinced his treaded tires would be quickest if they were well worn and as close to slicks as possible. "So I just ran and ran and ran."

Mario's strategy upset Chapman, whose cars were on their way to their third world championship that year. But the great English car builder learned a lesson that day when the F1 novice's plan worked to perfection. "I knew my time was going to come from the high-speed corners," Mario recalls, "and there was a left-hander I was trying to get through flat, and finally I did that."

The lap put Mario on the pole, but Jackie Stewart took it right back. Stewart would win three world championships during the next five years and was battling with Lotus team leader Graham Hill for the 1968 world title. Under the circumstances, Chapman was satisfied to have his rookie driver start from second on the grid, but Mario wanted the pole. Chapman and he argued a little. "I said, 'I'm going out again,' and I just nipped his time. Stewart didn't like that."

"I don't quite know what word to use to describe the feeling of our group," Stewart told *AutoWeek* at the time. "I guess you can say it was a surprise. Not that I, personally, was surprised, because I knew bloody well he can drive any kind of race car and do it quite splendidly."

The versatility that Stewart praised had been demonstrated by Mario in USAC Championship cars, stock cars, and long-distance sports cars, but to beat the world's best in his first time in a Formula One car was something else again. Stewart summed up Mario's debut at the Glen with a remark notable mainly for its understatement: "It was surprising that he goes onto one of our regular road courses for the first time and wins the pole at record speed."

In reality, this was a phenomenal achievement—the first time a driver had taken the pole position for his first world championship F1 race since Guiseppe Farina qualified on pole for the very first world championship motor race in 1950. For Mario, it was only the beginning. In the years to come he would go on to become the second and last American to win the world championship and enjoy one of the longest, most successful careers in the history of motorsports. In an era that spawned a new generation of young, often outspoken, and highly paid sports icons—Muhammed Ali, Joe Namath, Billie Jean King, Pele—Mario also would emerge as an international superstar and become a true household name.

"Above and beyond everything else, he got a group of people

Above: Mario talks with Lotus boss Colin Chapman at Watkins Glen. The Lotus 49B is between them. He won the pole position, creating a sensation. "I wasn't intimidated at all," Mario recalls. "I just loved it. You couldn't imagine how much I wanted to be there and how good I felt." (Sutton Photographic) Opposite: Mario had tested the Lotus 49B at Monza, Italy, a month before his spectacular debut at Watkins Glen in 1968 (shown here). "The 49 was awesome!" Mario says. "I loved driving it. My road-racing experience to that point was in sports cars, which were big and clumsy by comparison, and this nice little Formula One car worked for me immediately. At the Glen I felt so confident." (Phipps/Sutton Photographic)

interested who really didn't follow racing that much. He made them pay attention," says Robin Miller, a former auto racing writer for the *Indianapolis Star* who has covered racing more than thirty years. "Look at all the songs he's been in and all the phrases people use: 'Oh, you're driving like Mario Andretti.' Nobody else in racing is in his league. You can say his name in Tokyo, you can say it in London, and in New York City, and L.A., and everybody knows who he is."

Within the highly competitive and constantly changing world of racing, Mario's legacy as a driver is all but unequaled. "There can't be any argument he must be the greatest all-round racing driver there's ever been," says Nigel Roebuck, *Autosport*'s widely respected Grand Prix editor. "As far as his versatility, probably the only person in history you would think of in those terms is Stirling Moss. I know Stirling never raced stock cars or at Indianapolis, but Stirling had the same uncanny ability in a single day to switch from wholly different types of car and win with all of them."

But unlike many of his fellow superstars in boxing, football, or other sports, Mario remains apparently unchanged by success. "The thing about Mario is that he is so charismatic and so quotable and such a great ambassador with people," adds Miller. "He'll always stop and talk to people and pose for a picture. As famous as he got, he never, ever forgot where he was in 1963 and where he came from."

*   *   *

Where Mario Andretti came from is a remarkable story in itself. While his meteoric rise from local dirt tracks to the international Grand Prix scene would be amply documented, his early years as a refugee and immigrant may have had more to do with forging the characteristics that made him a champion—a love of motor racing and an unswerving determination to overcome whatever obstacles came his way.

Mario and his fraternal twin brother, Aldo, were born in Montona, Italy, on February 28, 1940. Montona is near Trieste, inland from the Adriatic Sea, not far from the border of the former Yugoslavia, now Croatia. Their sister, Anna Maria, had been born six years earlier, in 1934. Before World War II the Andretti family was prosperous. Mario's father, Gigi, managed a group of seven farms, and his maternal grandfather, Piero Benvegnú, owned a small hotel and restaurant.

Gigi's parents died when he was a small child and, after living in an orphanage until he was nine, he was raised by his uncle, who was also a priest, Don Quirino Ghersa, whom Mario and Aldo called their "uncle priest." Under Ghersa's tutelage Gigi grew into a proud and energetic young man. He married Rina Benvegnú and became a successful farm manager.

"When World War II broke out, everything went upside down," Mario says. "Everything the family owned, including my grandparents' hotel and restaurant by the train station, was taken by the state."

Mario believes the Andretti family was lucky to survive those miserable days of occupation. It was a squalid, fearful existence with Nazi soldiers and Communist partisans fighting in the streets. Shootings were commonplace. "It was like anarchy," Mario recalls. "Nazi scout groups would get ambushed by civilian partisans, and then to set an example the Nazis would come into town and randomly grab some young men and mow them down. Two second cousins of mine were nabbed, and they tied them to a pole about a mile and a half from my grandmother's restaurant."

Both youngsters wriggled free of their captors. One was shot dead as he tried to flee. The other escaped and disappeared. He was presumed dead until he reappeared one day twelve years later after serving through Europe and Asia in the French Foreign Legion.

The Nazis also set up headquarters in Mario's grandparents' hotel and restaurant. "They took the place over, and everyone had to shine their boots. They forced the women to come up to their rooms. It was very demeaning. One Sunday, I remember vividly, one of the Nazis threw a grenade out of a window. Aldo and I were playing in the yard, and this grenade popped right behind us. We were lucky not to be hit by any shrapnel. The Nazis behaved like barbarians, and it drove my grandmother almost insane."

Left: The Andrettis in Montona in 1947. From left to right: Mario, Rina, Anna Maria, Aldo, and Gigi. (Andretti collection) **Middle:** Mario and twin brother Aldo in one of the family's vineyards in Montona, Italy, in 1941, when they were about a year old. **Right:** The Andretti family in Lucca, Italy, in 1954, a year before emigrating to America. From left to right are Rina's mother Nonna Tina, Mario, Rina, Anna Maria, Rina's father Nonno Piero, Aldo and Gigi. (Andretti collection) **Opposite:** Montona today, shown in one of Mario's own photos of the village and the surrounding countryside. (Andretti collection)

An aging Lambretta motor-scooter owned by the family priest, Don Renzo Tambellini, was Mario and Aldo's first experience driving a powered vehicle. "We would go with him on his rounds, and when he was taking confession, we would go joy-riding," Mario says. (Andretti collection)

The Andretti family in Nazareth, Pennsylvania, in 1955 with their first family car, a 1946 Ford that Gigi bought for $150. From left to right: Gigi, Aldo, Anna Maria, Rina, and Mario. (Andretti collection)

Mario credits his uncle Ghersa with saving the family. "My uncle priest was a very strong individual. He had a presence, and there was a respect for the clergy that everyone had in those days, even the Nazis." The fact that Ghersa spoke German also contributed to keeping the family relatively safe.

Gigi felt responsible for the laborers who worked on his farms and did his best to help these men and their families survive the privations of war. "There were Slovaks, Croats, and Serbs, and they all worked for my dad, and some of them put very little value on human life," Mario says. "For nothing, for a pack of cigarettes, you could get a knife through the belly.

"My dad was always very generous. He was very alert to taking care of these people. If any of the families or their kids needed something, he took care of it, and because of that he almost had a protective blanket over him. They would risk their lives for him. That's why he came through that unscathed. He was certainly prepared for being killed. A number of times there were rumors that his name was next on the list, but he was spared."

Life after the war was less dangerous but equally tough. It was a struggle just to eat, and the family had lost ownership of its house. In 1945, Montona was ceded to Yugoslavia as part of the post-war political settlement, and the Andrettis spent the next three years under Communist rule.

"In 1948," Mario says, "my dad decided we could no longer live under those conditions. So we packed up a few belongings and left, like thousands of others. We ended up in a camp in Udine, near Trieste.

"The conditions were so crude and appalling," Mario recalls. "There was even a gender separation. For several days I didn't see my mother or my sister. That was the most traumatic time. We were eight years old, and we didn't understand what was going on."

The agreement between Italy and Yugoslavia provided meager financial restitution for those who had lost their property. "I think my father realized $2,800 out of that, and he had close to a thousand acres of land."

From the disbursement camp in Udine, the Andrettis were trucked with a few thousand other refugees to another camp on the site of an abandoned college in Lucca, Italy, where they began to rebuild their lives.

"When we first were given those quarters, our family was in a large room, and our mattresses and pillows had hay in them," Mario adds. "There was no running water, and we spent probably three to four months like that before my dad had a few little jobs and we were able to buy some better things to make it a little more humane."

Things slowly improved. After living four years at the converted college in Lucca, the family was able to expand into two rooms, one exclusively for the grandparents. And by then, there was also running water and a family bathroom. Before then they had bathed using buckets of water.

While living in Lucca, Mario and Aldo's passion for racing was sparked by a friendship with Sergio Seggiolini and Beppe Biagini, who owned a garage where the boys worked parking cars. Seggiolini and Biagini took the Andretti twins to a few local motorcycle and car races, and in September of 1954 they treated the boys to a trip to Monza for the Italian Grand Prix. There they watched Italian hero Alberto Ascari duel unsuccessfully with Argentinian great Juan Manuel Fangio.

Ascari was world champion two straight years, 1952 and '53, driving his Ferrari to victory in eleven of fifteen races. At Monza in 1954, Ascari led much of the race's first half, battling with Fangio's new, streamlined Mercedes-Benz W196 until the Italian's transmission failed.

The following spring Seggiolini and Biagini took Mario and Aldo to watch the Mille Miglia, the day-long 1,000 mile open-road race around Italy, which was held from 1927-57. The boys were transfixed by the powerful sports cars.

"The Mercedes really stood out," Mario recalls. "They had a different sound, and with their silver paintwork, they were beautiful. Compared to the Ferraris and Maseratis, the Mercedes were just incredible, really state of the art.

"The Mille Miglia and Monza capped it off for us," Mario says. "When you dream as a kid everything has grandeur to it, but I remember it as a Catch-22 proposition. I thought, 'Oh man! This is where I want to be.' But it seemed so far away, so totally farfetched, that it would ever happen." From those days the Andretti brothers thought of nothing but racing and even considered starting their careers racing motorcycles

because it would be much cheaper than racing cars.

Meanwhile, Gigi and Rina Andretti had been planning to abandon post-war Italy for a better life in America. Many years earlier, before World War I, Rina's uncle, Tony Benvegnú, had emigrated to the United States and worked in the coal mines of West Virginia. He then moved to Nazareth, Pennsylvania, for cleaner, more profitable work in the limestone quarries and cement mills that surrounded the area. Uncle Tony and his wife, Mary, raised a family of nine children, and he maintained his correspondence with the Andrettis. He helped them as much as he could, sending clothing while they were living in the camps.

Uncle Tony encouraged the Andrettis to come to America and offered the guarantee of a house and job for Gigi, one of the prerequisites needed to obtain a visa. Gigi applied for emigration papers in 1952, but for almost three years heard nothing from the U. S. authorities. "We had almost forgotten about it," Mario says. "Then finally, in 1955, we were approved."

Gigi told his family the plan was to spend only a few years in America. When he had earned enough money, they would return to Italy. "When he broke the news to us, he said, 'We're going to America, but we'll only be there for maybe five years, and we'll come back.' That made it easier to do," Mario recalls.

On June 6, 1955, the family boarded the *Conte Biancamano* in Genoa bound for New York City via Halifax, Nova Scotia. For Mario and Aldo, it was a desolate day. "We loved my uncle priest so much," Mario says. "We had such a tie to him. We said, 'We'll be back.' He was the only one Aldo and I wrote to."

The boys' dream of racing glory vanished with Italy's receding coastline. Racing, they believed, was a European sport, rarely practiced in the New World. Although they had heard of the Indianapolis 500, they knew very little about it. They told friends and family who stayed behind that after making their fortune in America, they would return to Italy to pursue their racing careers.

When the *Conte Biancamano* stopped briefly in Nova Scotia, Mario and Aldo, who had studied English at school, discovered they couldn't understand a word spoken by the locals. A few days later, just before dawn on June 16, 1955, the Andrettis sailed past the Statue of Liberty. As planned, they settled in Nazareth, two hours west of New York

City, just across the New Jersey state line.

"That was the turning point of our lives," Mario says, "and it's what determined my future. You know, you leave your home, lose everything, and go into a refugee camp with a totally uncertain future. Then, all of a sudden, you pursue an opportunity to come to America with so many unknowns, and things start shaping up.

"In every sense we really experienced the American Dream. We're a perfect example of it. We really made a huge positive out of a negative. Many times, when we're toasting at holidays, at Christmas, and so on, we say, 'Here's to Tito!' " Marshall Tito was Yugoslavia's dictator and the man the Andrettis consider responsible for driving them out of their homeland.

After arriving in Nazareth, the family lived with uncle Tony for three months before moving into a rented house just up the road on Whitfield Street.

"Our expectations were not that great," Mario says. "Uncle Tony painted a very modest picture of what to expect. What I really liked was the cars! That's all I cared about. Everybody had a car. Some people had two, and they were all shiny and new."

Gigi Andretti first went to work in Jimmy Taviani's cement plant, then a box factory, and finally at Bethlehem Steel. After a year and a half on Whitfield Street, Gigi bought a small plot of land on nearby Market Street and built a house for his family.

Mario and Aldo were thrilled to find an oval dirt track on the edge of town, which they discovered within three days of their arrival. When they heard the bark of unmuffled engines and feasted their eyes on Nazareth Speedway, the half-mile dirt oval that featured Sunday night stock-car racing, meaning and motivation returned to their lives.

"Man, we were living again!" Mario says with a grin. "There were reasons to look ahead, reasons for hope. It was like we'd never left the Old Country. We were going racing. It was going to be our life, just like we'd always dreamed."

Opposite: The only time Mario saw his hero Alberto Ascari race was at the Italian GP at Monza in 1954. "They used to say he had ice in his veins," Mario says of Ascari. "He was very cool, very relaxed looking. Compared to Nuvolari, for example, who was always wrestling the wheel, Ascari sat back doing his thing. I loved that style, a man totally in control of his car. Watching him, I knew I wanted to be like him." (LAT Photographic) Above: The other major race Mario and Aldo attended was the 1955 Mille Miglia won by Stirling Moss and journalist Denis Jenkinson in a Mercedes-Benz 300SLR. "That was a classic race," Mario recalls. "I clearly remember Jenkinson sitting in the passenger seat struggling to keep his head up, with his eyes wide and his beard sticking out." (LAT Photographic)

Chapter 2

A Fast Start

Because the fifteen-year-old Andrettis' command of
English was rudimentary, the Nazareth school officials decided to enroll Mario and Aldo in the seventh
grade, three grades lower than most students their
age. An agreement was struck with the school princi-
pal that if they made a B average in English, they
would be promoted to the tenth grade. Mario and
Aldo wanted to become fluent in English by the end of
the year, and by Christmas 1955 the goal was achieved.

Opposite: Mario with his first race-car-to-be, a 1948 Hudson coupe fresh from the
scrap heap. "That's the original car as we brought it out of the junkyard," says
Mario. "We stripped it and started from scratch. We took quite a while to build it, because we didn't think we would be able to race until we were twenty-one." (Andretti
collection) **Above:** The Andretti brothers take some practice laps at the old Nazareth
track. "We started building the car when we were eighteen and it probably took six
months before we got it all together," Mario recalls. "Then we said, 'You know what?
We're not going to wait two years. We're going to race it!' " (Andretti collection)

"Both Aldo and I finished with an A in English," Mario says proudly. "And in mathematics we were way ahead because we'd already taken trigonometry in Italy. We were actually bored."

But the school changed principals at the end of the year, and the new man decided that the Andrettis should not be promoted any higher than eighth grade. "I said, 'At this rate I'll be out of high school when I'm twenty-five.' So I quit," Mario recalls.

But a science teacher at the high school, Mr. Weis, urged Mario and Aldo to graduate and suggested they try a correspondence course through the American School in Chi-

cago. Gigi sent $900 to the school, and his boys worked rapidly through the course, earning their diplomas in just two years.

During this time Mario met Dee Ann Hoch, who was two years younger. "Nazareth is fairly small," Dee Ann says, "and we heard about the twins coming into town, and they were our age. All the girls talked about it. Then we met at a dance, and after that I tutored Mario to help him out."

Mario's respect for Dee Ann's teaching skills and her faith and support in his dream of becoming a race driver helped broaden their friendship into a long-lasting romance. "Dee Ann was very smart in school," Mario acknowledges, "and she really helped me learn all the courses. We just got along, and we became a pair. She was very petite and cute as hell, and there was a natural attraction."

Mario and Aldo also worked part-time at Lewis Messenlehner's Sunoco gas station in midtown Nazareth. Messenlehner was married to one of Uncle Tony's daughters and, for the boys, working at the garage was a perfect way to learn about cars and what made them work. They alternated days, each working a full shift every other evening.

"Aldo and I shared everything," Mario says. "We never owned two of anything. We always owned one bicycle and then one car. We had always alternated. It was the same when we went to work. We pooled all our money, gave most of it to Dad, and kept a couple of bucks for ourselves."

The twins were careful to avoid the subject of auto racing with their father, who was totally opposed to his sons having anything to do with the sport. "My dad just did not understand," Mario says. "All he knew about the sport was fatalities. When we came over on the *Conte Biancamano*, every day we got news bulletins, and one day there was this huge story about 85 people being killed at Le Mans."

French racer Pierre Levegh's Mercedes had crashed into the crowd with devastating results during the 1955 Le Mans 24 Hour race. "We were always talking about racing, and he said, 'How can you like this?' He was not going to endorse us going racing by any stretch of the imagination."

In 1959, without their family's knowledge, Mario and Aldo set to work building a 1948 Hudson stock car. They chose the Hudson because most of the drivers at Nazareth were racing '37 Fords. "We felt that if we went to Nazareth with a '37 Ford coupe they'd be years ahead of us because everybody had been running that type of car for so long," Mario says. "But if we went with something different, we've got a chance to find an advantage." Marshall Teague had driven a Hudson with great success in NASCAR and other stock-car races throughout the South and Northeast, and the sleek-looking Hudson had a reputation for handling well.

They built most of the car themselves, in a corner of Evo Taviani's garage. Taviani was a heavy equipment contractor located in Nazareth who provided the workplace, tools, and advice the Andrettis needed. He also went to a local bank with the boys and co-signed a $500 loan so they would have money for parts. Without Evo Taviani we may not have had Mario Andretti, race driver.

"The Tavianis were Italian, and they both liked racing, Jimmy especially. They both helped in different ways," Mario says. "Jimmy used to go-fer for 'Scats' Anfuso in URC [United Racing Club] so he liked the idea of trying to help us. We were so full of piss and vinegar and so excited about it, and we were transmitting all this excitement."

Mario used his guile to get Taviani to do machine work for him on a rapid turnaround. "You couldn't pressure Jimmy, but we always had work we needed in a rush. So I used to play the psychologist. I'd say, 'Jimmy, I've got a job here that nobody can do. This can't be done.'

"He'd say, 'I'm busy! But let me see that.' I'd say, 'It'll probably take a lot of time.' He'd say, 'When do you need it?' I'd say, 'I know you can't do it. We need it tonight, but maybe we're just not going to race. Maybe you can do it in a couple of days.'

"Jimmy would say, 'Look, I can't promise you anything. I'm busy here. But come back in half an hour.' And I would come back, and it would be done!"

The most expensive component was the engine, a six-cylinder Hudson flat-head, which came from J. C. Whitney's catalog and cost $300. "They called it the 7-X. It was supposed to be the hot-tip engine. It was a high-compression motor, and it definitely had good power. It was stout, and we were quick down the straightaways. We had 'em covered."

The enterprising Andretti brothers even attracted a small amount of sponsorship from Frank Tanzosh's construction company that paid for the fuel and tires. "That was our big nut," Mario recalls. "It used to cost us maybe twenty bucks a weekend that we couldn't otherwise afford."

The old Nazareth Speedway was a half-mile, clay track located next to the paved one-mile track that exists today. Automobile races had been held there since the 1920s, and in the 1950s there were regular Wednesday and Sunday night races, run by such promoters as Jerry Freid and Harvey Tattersall Jr.

Mario and Aldo were proud when they made their debut with the Hudson. "We arrived with a car that looked so nice," Mario says. "It was painted red and had nice numbers on it. We had Sala Sport drivers' uniforms. We looked the part."

The unknown Andretti brothers were questioned by the organizers at sign-in about their racing backgrounds. "They said, 'Why should we let you race?'" Mario recalls. "We said, 'We've been racing for most of our lives, since we were thirteen.' We couldn't tell them we had raced somewhere nearby like the Mahoning Valley, for example. So we told them we had been racing Formula Junior cars in Italy since we were thirteen. We figured, 'Who would dispute that?' That's what we told them, and that part stuck. That's where the misconception of me racing at thirteen got started."

The brothers shared the car and a helmet, and Aldo drove the first race. "We had no expectations whatsoever," Mario says. "Aldo went out there, and I was shaking watching him. I really wanted to drive, but I was glad it was him because it was a total unknown."

The starting field was lined up in reverse order of drivers' points standings in the track championship. The idea was the fastest cars and drivers started from the back and had to fight their way to the front. Newcomers with no points were added at the back of the field. "Aldo started last because of their handicap system, and he starts passing cars and passing cars and wins the heat!" Mario says. "We couldn't believe it."

Like most short track races, those at Nazareth comprised a series of qualifying heats from which the top three or four finishers qualified for the feature. There were also semi-final and consolation races for those who didn't make it to try to earn a last-chance berth in the final, or feature, race.

In his first feature, Aldo again started last and came through the field to take the win. "That was an auspicious beginning," Mario says, "and from there on, we were the hot dogs. They laughed at us when we showed up, but we blew their doors off. We did our own motor, and we just did our homework."

Mario also won his first race. Says Aldo: "The first year I don't recall too many second or third places. We either won or crashed."

Even then, at the very beginning, the Andrettis were trying to out think the opposition, an attribute that became woven into Mario's character over time. They asked questions at every turn. One innovation they made was a suspension tuning device bought from Teague. "It was a piece of rubber inner tube molded to fit inside the coil spring, and you could make variable spring rates and cross weight, just by air pressure," Mario says. "That was our secret to really fine-tune the car."

As they began to master the Nazareth Speedway, the Andrettis started venturing to other nearby tracks, including Flemington, New Jersey, and Hatfield, Pennsylvania. Mario won at Flemington, and both brothers immediately showed they could run quickly on unfamiliar tracks.

Mario and Aldo began to gain a small measure of fame in Nazareth, and their successes were reported in the newspaper. But they were able to keep their activities secret from their father because he did not speak or read a word of English. "When we'd win a race it would be in the local paper, and my dad's foreman would

From left to right: Larry Slutter, Bill Tanzosh, David Solt, Aldo, Mario, and Bob Noversel pose in front of Louie Messenlehner's gas station with their first race car. Except for the roll bar, the brothers built most of the car themselves. "Later I learned to weld and I did the roll bars for the other cars I built," Mario says. (Andretti collection)

tell him, 'Hey, Gigi, congratulations! Your kids are doing really good.' Well, the old man thought they were congratulating him for doing a good job at work! He didn't understand what they were saying, and he was never the type of guy to ask, 'What did you say? I don't understand.' That saved us."

Rina Andretti did know what her sons were doing, but she joined in the secret. Mario recalls: "Friends and relatives would say, 'Hey, the boys are doing well.' And she would say, 'Don't tell Gigi.' She knew, but she didn't want us to know that she knew. She was caught in the middle."

At the end of the year, Aldo was badly injured in an accident during a heat race for a 100-lap invitational at Hatfield. The top six finishers in Aldo's heat race would make the feature. "The only thing I vaguely remember was Mario trying to slow me down," Aldo says. "He said I was way out of control. I was running third in my heat, so I was ready to qualify, and Mario was trying to slow me down. And I kind of said, 'To hell with you.' And I lost it. It was just one of those young, rookie mistakes."

The fence at Hatfield was made of heavy wooden planks, and some were warped and curved outward. "I caught one of the planks wrong with the right front, and it just really tore me apart. I never expected it. I thought I was going to just sideswipe it and bounce off the wall, and boy that thing got me and threw me for a ride."

The roof and roll bar caved in, and Aldo's head took a heavy impact that broke his helmet. Aldo was unconscious when he was taken to a hospital. Mario called his mother and lied, telling her that Aldo had fallen off a truck while watching Mario race. "I couldn't deny that we were racing anymore. I told her he just had the wind knocked out of him. I said I was staying with him at the hospital that night, and we would be home in the morning. And she was very quiet on the other end of the phone."

Meanwhile, some friends had loaded the wrecked Hudson on the back of a flatbed truck and driven it back to Nazareth, passing through the center of town. "The word went out like wildfire that Aldo was dead, or seriously injured, and by the next morning between the rumors around town and what my mom had told

him, my dad knew something was up."

When Mario woke up after a night at Aldo's bedside, the doctors told him they needed to see his parents, or they would call the police. "I had to go home and break the news to my dad, and he bounced me around the room like a football. He said, 'I told you this would happen if you went racing.' "

Gigi drove to the hospital, deeply worried about Aldo but believing that his sons had learned their lesson. "In his mind he thought we had gotten it out of our system. Well, little did he know that while Aldo was in a coma, I was trying to stimulate his brain by telling him that I was building a new car." The doctors had told Mario

to talk to his unconscious brother and tell Aldo whatever things Mario believed would provide the best motivation to recover.

Aldo remained unconscious for ten days and required six months to recover fully. "I had a severe concussion," Aldo says. "When I woke up, it seemed like I had to learn most things all over again. I had to learn how to walk again. But, lucky for me, I was young enough and had the desire, and it didn't take long to get it back."

Mario shakes his head dolefully. "That was actually the turning point of Aldo's career," Mario says. "After that, the driving just didn't seem to come to him as naturally as it had."

The '48 Hudson was destroyed in Aldo's accident; only the prized 7-X engine survived. Mario bought a '37 Hudson coupe to replace it and began turning it into a race car. Before the first race at Nazareth the following spring, Mario and the recovering Aldo rolled the finished car into the front court of Messenlehner's gas station to pose for some photos wearing their racing uniforms. They had chosen exactly the wrong moment, as Gigi drove in for a tank of gas.

"I'm puffing on a cigarette," Mario recalls, "which was another thing my dad disapproved of, and he looked over and saw us, and he never stopped at the pump. He just drove right out, and I said, 'Man, we're in trouble now, Aldo!'

"After that my dad thought about disowning us. For three or four months he didn't talk to us, and he made it hell for my mother. That whole year, 1960, was a tough year for us at home. He felt powerless. We had defied him, and he could see we were still going on with racing."

Mario drove all the races in 1960 while Aldo slowly recovered. He won right away at Nazareth and Mahoning Valley, and his reputation began to grow. Finally, Aldo felt ready to drive again. "Aldo was champing at the bit, wanting to get back in, and I got permission from the promoter for him to warm up during intermission at Nazareth. He went out, and he looked pretty shaky, but he drove. The following weekend at Nazareth he said he was going to drive again, and he went out and demolished the car."

Aldo flipped end-over-end and almost hit a bulldozer. The pits were on the backstretch coming off turn two, and Aldo clipped the pit post, flipped into the pits, and totaled the car. He was lucky, escaping with nothing worse than a broken little finger, and Mario went to work building his third Hudson, a '37 sedan.

Mario won his first race in the new car. "Halfway through the feature I was coming through the pack when there was a yellow, and I realized I had no brakes. What happened was that, because of the way we routed the rear brake line, it got pinched when the car was bottoming, so I had no brakes. I figured I'm just going to try to finish and not hit somebody, and I won the race! I won a bunch of races with that car that season."

With these successes Gigi gradually began to change his mind about racing. Mario recalls: "People were patting him on the back when he was at church, saying your boys are doing well, they're winning. So it turned into a matter of pride. He began to think maybe we had been doing the right thing."

During this time Mario worked for Retter Line Incorporated in Easton, builders of Rettermobile Racemasters go-karts. "I never had a steady job," he says. "As soon as I started racing, there was cash flow. We weren't winning much, but I remember at the end of the 1959 season we had a drawerful of cash. A lot of one-dollar bills to be sure, but we always did well.

"I didn't really need a steady job because I was making more money racing than I could doing anything else. My dream was to make a living racing cars, but it seemed too pretentious at the time. But every job I held I couldn't really fulfill because I was busy racing."

At Hatfield near the end of 1960, Mario drove John Yerger's modified, his first race in someone else's car. Before the qualifying heat, Yerger told Mario he had to win the race to earn enough prize money to pay for fuel for the feature! "The guy told me I had to win, no matter what. So I tried."

Instead, Mario lost control and crashed heavily, flipping out of the facility, and tearing the engine from the car. "It was a violent crash, and I was lucky I didn't hurt myself. But having a disaster like that drove home some good sense into me. I realized that being the fastest, bravest guy wasn't what it was all about. I realized you needed to finish races and not get a reputation for being a wild man."

Mario also made a serious career decision. He had won more than twenty stock-car races in Pennsylvania and New Jersey in 1959 and '60, made a name for himself, and learned all he could driving his own cars. But if he was going to reach out and pursue his dream of winning the world championship like Alberto Ascari, he had to move into open-wheel cars. It was time to start pushing and developing his career.

Mario crashed John "Peepers" Yerger's car at Hatfield at the end of the year. "The engine came right out of the chassis. I didn't have a scratch on me, but I didn't take it lightly," says Mario. "I hated the fact that I'd destroyed the man's car. I also hated the fact that it was a huge negative reflection on me, and I made sure it wouldn't happen again." (Bruce Craig collection)

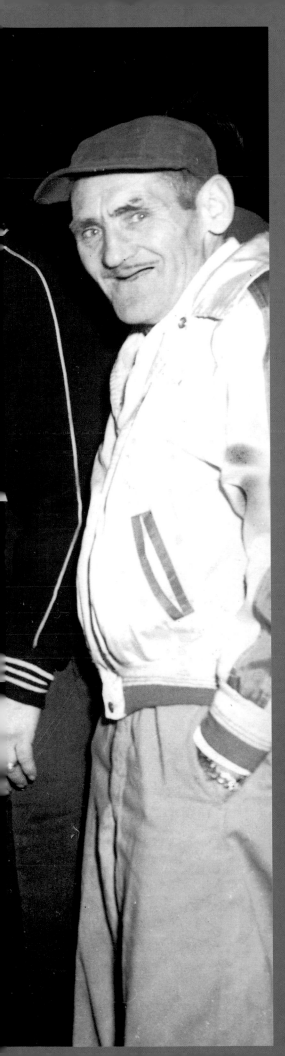

Chapter 3

A Ticket to the Big Time

Now twenty-one, Mario was legally able to compete in officially sanctioned races rather than the independently promoted Friday and Saturday night stock-car races he had run in 1959 and '60. He believed he was ready to handle a sprint car, which was a smaller, lighter, less powerful version of a USAC Championship or Indy car. Sprint cars raced on smaller tracks—half-mile facilities or less. Below sprint cars were midgets and three-quarter midgets,

Above: Mario's Triumph-powered three-quarter midget had been raced successfully by Bobby Marshman. "I drove the TQ in three or four races each weekend, and I never worked on my car at the racetrack," he recalls with pride. "Everybody else would arrive and work, but I would arrive with my car all spiffed-up and ready to race." (Andretti collection) **Opposite:** Mario celebrates his first win in the TQ midget at Teaneck, New Jersey, in February, 1962. Jack Dowie, the car's former owner, is in the left foreground with Nicky Fornoro next to him holding the checkered flag. Mario's friend and protector, Dave Fearing, is between Mario and Fornoro. (Bruce Craig collection)

which were smaller and less powerful. These cars provided the stepping stones to Championship racing.

Mario aimed to race in United Racing Club events. Compared to the nationally recognized USAC, the URC was a humble regional club that organized races across the Northeast and Mid-Atlantic states. But for a low-bucks kid from Nazareth, it was the only way to break into open-wheel cars.

Mario made his URC sprint-car debut in May of 1961 at the Lebanon Valley, New York, half-mile track. The car had been raced with an Offenhauser engine by the 1946 and '47 USAC champion Ted Horn and was known as Beauty. But fourteen years later it was well past its prime. "It had a big Cadillac engine," Mario says, "and no brakes! That car was so heavy, and you couldn't steer it. It was one of the most frustrating days of my life." Still, he had a ride, and he drove the Logan-Cadillac in four more races, two of them at Nazareth. His best result in the car was sixth place in the first race.

As 1961 unfolded, Mario ran twenty URC races driving six different cars. After five races in the Logan-Cadillac, he raced the Brown T-Bird four times, then switched to the Markos-Chevy for a couple of races. His best finish of the year—fourth place—came in the Markos-Chevy at Susquehanna, Pennsylvania, in August. He finished the year driving the Fowler-Dreyer in six races, then started Harry Dee's Chevy-powered car in one race before switching to Charlie Clark's Dodge-engined machine for two end-of-season races.

For Mario, this automotive game of musical chairs was stressful. "You'd show up with a helmet and see what happened," he says. "It was pot luck, but the best thing about it was because there was so much junk in URC there were a lot of owners without regular drivers, so there was always something to drive."

Besides the uneven quality of the cars, there was also an unpleasant side to many of the owners. Mario was often insulted by men who had preconceptions about his slender build. "What is more demeaning than telling somebody, 'You're not big enough. You're not strong enough. You look like a weenie driving my car?' That

was basically the mentality in those days. The cars didn't have power steering, and they thought you had to be big, like a Foyt or Jimmy Bryan. And that really drove me to prove myself." A. J. Foyt and Bryan were both broad-shouldered men from the Southwest who dominated USAC Championship racing in the late '50s and early '60s. Mario was half a foot shorter and fifty pounds lighter than Foyt and Bryan and was heavily derided by many people for being a flyweight who couldn't possibly do the job.

"I can tell you there's not a hell of a lot that I didn't experience in my days. I've experienced rejection in the worst possible way, and I experienced humiliation because the rejection came with incredible humiliation."

The treatment Mario received was essential to the development of his character and career. "I never forgot it, and later, whenever I would see these people, I had no forgiveness for them. To this day, I cannot forgive them, because of what they said and how much they hurt me.

Opposite: At Bedford, Pennsylvania, in August, 1961, Mario chases Bob Hillis. This is John Fowler's Dryer sprinter, an obsolete car that Mario drove unsuccessfully in a handful of URC races in August and September. "I had no chance of doing anything impressive with that car, let alone winning," Mario says. (Bruce Craig collection) Right: Mario's first URC sprint car drive was the ancient Logan-Cadillac at Lebanon Valley, New York, in May, 1961. "That thing was so awful!" Mario recalls. "It steered so hard. It must have had fifteen degrees of caster in it, and there was no adjustment and no brakes! To get it to slow down into the corner I had to pitch it totally sideways." (Bruce Craig collection)

"Certain individuals claim that they were part of my life and career, and yes, they were part of it, but in a totally negative way. I've always believed that behind every negative, there's a positive. As you go through life, you get disappointments because things don't work the way you expect. Or there are stumbling blocks that seem almost insurmountable. But if you have that drive to do it, your passion will get you through it."

By the end of the 1961 season, the URC experience had served its purpose, and Mario decided to make some important changes. First, Dee Ann and he had decided to get married. From the beginning, Dee Ann shared Mario's belief that he was going to be a successful professional race driver, and she now helped Mario convince her father to buy a three-quarter (TQ) midget that Mario had his eye on.

"The car cost $1,200, and I really couldn't afford it," Mario remarks. "The deal I made with Dee Ann's father, Earl, and his partner, Rudy Ashman, was that they would receive fifty per cent of every dollar the car made, and I would operate the car on the other fifty per cent. When they sold the car, all of the money was theirs. How could they go wrong?"

Mario began the American Three Quarter Midget Association (ATQMRA) 1961-62 winter indoor season by finishing third at Hempstead, New York, on November 9. He earned $150 and paid Hoch and Ashman $75. "They couldn't believe it. They didn't think they were going to get anything. It turned out to be a hell of deal because they made money. I didn't, but they did." (Two years later the TQ was sold for $1,750, so the arrangement worked well for Hoch and Ashman.)

On November 25, 1961, Mario married Dee Ann. They lived in his parents' house for about a month, then moved into an attached house they rented from Dee Ann's father. She was now an even more important contributor to Mario's racing program. "I worked at the time in a blouse factory, and my whole pay-

check went to maintain the engine," Dee Ann says.

The engine in the midget, a twin-cylinder Triumph, was indeed a high-maintenance item. It was a 650cc bored out to 850cc. "We maxed it out to run against the Crosleys," Mario says. "There was no size limit for us as long as we didn't get into the cooling fins." It permitted Mario to run a lighter car than most of his competitors, but it required high-octane aviation fuel to develop the power to compete with the more potent four-cylinder Crosley engines run by most ATQMRA front-runners. Because the cars raced indoors during the winter season, officials were quick to black flag cars that blew smoke. The combination of these factors made it necessary to swap the cylinder heads every race to keep the engine burning cleanly.

"I used to rotate two sets of heads. We had to maintain really precise valve guides. On the way to the race track I used to pick up the heads and drop off the used ones, then install the head just before the race. Most of my races were in New Jersey or out on Long Island, and I used to stop at Bob's Motorcycle Shop in Washington, New Jersey."

" It cost me Dee Ann's full paycheck every week just to pay for the heads," Mario says. "That was the only time she actually worked, but every penny that she earned went into keeping the engine fresh."

Dee Ann was so busy during this time that she lost contact with many of her school friends. "I think most of my friends sort of deserted me because I was going one way and they were going another way," Dee Ann recalls.

Mario continued to work part-time for Tim Sheehan. The Retter Line go-kart company had been sold to Sheehan, who reopened the business as the DelWick Company and manufactured golf carts. Sheehan offered Mario a job as a line foreman, and he accepted in his customary fashion, working half the time for the company and the other half on his race car.

Above: Mario drove the Magnotta midget just once, at Owego, New York, in August, 1962 when the Mataka brothers decided not to enter their car in the race. He finished fifth despite the wrong rear-end gear and a serious leak that blew oil from the crankcase all over the driver. "I was covered in oil," remembers Mario. "The car was run on a shoestring, but it handled really well." (Bruce Craig collection) Opposite: "The two years with the Matakas were very, very good for me," Mario reflects. "The competition was as tough as it could be, and the Matakas prepared a very good car. I learned a tremendous amount racing with them." (Andretti collection)

Top: In July 1963, in the middle of a busy summer racing the Mataka midget in ARDC, Mario won a race in his own TQ midget at Pinebrook, New Jersey. He is seen here on the outside, avoiding a collision on his way to victory. (Bruce Craig collection)

Bottom: Flat-out in the Mataka midget, Mario shows the aggressive style that was beginning to attract the attention of USAC team owners. By the summer of 1963 Mario was maturing into one of the hottest prospects on the East Coast, proving himself a winner on all types of oval tracks: dirt, paved, flat, and high-banked. (Bruce Craig collection)

Opposite: Mario poses at the wheel of the Mataka-Offy before the first road course race of his career at Lime Rock, Connecticut, on July 27, 1963. He beat established ace Mark Donohue, who piloted a unique rear-engine, Cooper-based midget. "Mark Donohue was not pleased!" Mario recalls. (Bruce Craig collection)

Between November of 1961 and March of 1962 Mario ran twenty ATQMRA indoor races. He made the top three seven times and scored his first TQ win at Teaneck, New Jersey, in February 1962.

"That was the first time I saw Mario race, and he had a style that was different," says Chris Economaki, the venerable editor emeritus of *National Speed Sport News*. "He drove watching the right front wheel within inches of the fence. He drove looking at the outside retaining fence. I only saw one other guy drive like that, a guy named Tony Wilman, and the guys that didn't like Mario said he was 'fence shy,'" a derogatory term that ridiculed Mario's very effective technique of using all the track rather than hugging the inside wall.

Dee Ann drove to all the races with Mario, but in those days women weren't allowed in the pits or garage at any type of automobile race. So she would go off on her own and watch from the grandstands.

"That was just the way it was back then," Dee Ann says. "You know, 'No women in the pits.' It didn't bother me. There was nothing I could do for him in the pits anyway, so I just went and watched and enjoyed it."

Mario couldn't have been happier with Dee Ann's view. "I liked her independence at the races," he says. "She let me do my thing and concentrate. She was never one to be demanding or distract me from my work, and she was that way throughout my whole career. If you notice there are very few podium photographs when she was there. She was close but not overwhelmingly close, which I thought was a great way to support me and let me do my job properly."

One or two friends usually accompanied Mario and Dee Ann to the races and helped as an informal crew. ATQMRA President Jack Dowie, who had sold the TQ to Mario, also would help by making sure his tire pressures were correct and assisting with push starts.

ATQMRA competition was tough because between twenty-five and thirty cars would show up for most races with only sixteen starting places available for the main event. Usually, there were three qualifying heats, two semifinals, a consolation, and then the late night feature. Drivers at the top of the point standings had to start from the back, in time-honored short-track, reverse-starting-order tradition. "So it was easy to miss the show," Mario says, "and I could not afford to do that. It meant that if I was fourth or fifth and there was somebody in front of me on the last lap of a heat, I had to spin 'em."

At Hempstead, a Long Island power track where the twin-cylinder Triumph was outperformed by the Crosleys, Mario found himself in fifth place in his qualifying heat, one position short of making the feature. "So I had to spin out Tony Bonadies. And that was the wrong guy to spin because he was a big guy from the Bronx and had his sons and the whole family there, so the word went out that I was going to be killed."

Dave Fearing, a scion of the St. Regis paper family, was with Mario that night. He was a large, imposing man who loved towing Mario's car to the races and enjoyed acting as Mario's protector.

"So I said to him, 'Dave, these guys want to kill me,'" Mario recalls. "'Get the trailer ready, and we're booking it out of here.' Then I saw them coming. We were tying everything down and trying to get out of there when they arrived and started beating the heck out of Dave and threw him over a fence! We got out of there OK, but we were pretty roughed up. Ah, those were the days!"

Following the indoor winter season, Mario ran four outdoor ATQMRA races in May and June of 1962. He finished in the top three in each race and won at Wall Stadium in New Jersey. He also drove the Blair-Chrysler sprint car in four URC races during those months, but had no success.

Then, in July, Mario got the first big break of his career. Bill and Ed Mataka, who were friends of Jack Dowie's and had been watching Mario's progress, decided he was ready to run on the American Racing Drivers Club (ARDC) midget circuit. When they asked the twenty-two year old Mario to drive their highly successful Kurtis-Offy, he was overjoyed.

"I had admired their car, but I was almost intimidated by it. I wondered if I could really handle something that good, but right away, it felt comfortable. The car had power, and it really hooked up."

The Mataka brothers celebrate their first win with Mario as their driver at Hatfield, Pennsylvania, on September 1, 1962. Mario's friend and supporter Frank Boeninghaus, wearing a USAC cap, stands proudly behind him. "Frank just loved motor racing," says Mario. "He was a saint." (Andretti collection)

The Matakas' invitation was helped along by Frank Boeninghaus, a paving contractor from Piscataway, New Jersey. "He was like an angel for me, and he was a saint of a man. He loved racing so much. He went to the Mataka brothers and said he would sponsor me, so they put his name on the car. That was the biggest break of my racing career."

Mario made his ARDC debut with the Matakas' midget at Danbury, Connecticut, a paved half-mile track. "I had been used to dirt primarily, except for indoors, but this was an asphalt track. It was totally different, and I liked it. I really developed a feel for it right away."

Mario was first alternate for the feature at Danbury, but thereafter qualified for twenty-one features that year for the Mataka brothers. He scored his first win at Hatfield in September and was in the top three in three other races. Despite missing the first third of the season, he finished fourteenth in points.

"The Mataka brothers were great mentors for me because they really were mindful of my youth and exuberance. They knew I had the potential, but they also knew I could easily kill myself. They really tried to restrain me in the right away."

A case in point was the season-ending race on the fast, banked half-mile track at Thompson, Connecticut. "I finished third in the race, and I was all over the other guys in the corners. I'm going by in the corners, and they're passing me again on the straight. So I finished third, and we're driving home, and I said, 'Man, we need more power! These guys are blowing me off.'

"And they said, 'We'll let you in on a little secret. We just wanted to teach you a lesson. We backed off the throttle.' I almost jumped out of the car! I could not believe it.

"I said, 'Think about it. You tried to kill me. Don't you realize I tried to make up for what was lacking?' We had a rhubarb like you can't believe! But I understood their side as far as being mentors and taking care of me. They thought by not giving me full throttle, I wouldn't go so fast, and I wouldn't get hurt."

Big things happened in October of 1962. Mario and Dee Ann's first child, Michael, was born. Mario was now a family man with a son and the added responsibility of raising, caring for, and educating his children. Then the Matakas hired Mario for the full 1963 ARDC season. During the winter season Mario once again drove his own TQ Midget in the ATQMRA. He ran eight ATQMRA races between January and March, winning once at Hempstead.

The ARDC season began at the end of March at Oldbury, New Jersey, and Mario drove forty-six races in the Mataka midget that year. He won five races, finished in the top five in twenty-four other races, and finished third in the championship standings.

"To beat Len Duncan or Dutch Schaefer was like having Jackie Stewart or A. J. Foyt or Richard Petty finish second to you. It was an accomplishment."

Mario believes the ARDC drivers and teams from those days were the best in the business. "Whenever USAC sprints would come to the East Coast," Mario says, "our eastern hot dogs in sprint cars could never match them, not even come close. But whenever USAC midgets or any USAC drivers would come and run ARDC, they would never beat them. So that was one way to evaluate myself as a driver in the bigger picture."

One of the many lessons Mario learned in ARDC was how to manage attempts at intimidation. His teacher was Len Duncan, a veteran driver. "I was running second," Mario says, "and Duncan was running third in a heat, and he was hitting me and hitting me and even broke my exhaust. Finally, I spun. I got restarted and knew I didn't have a chance to qualify, so I took a shot at him.

"I went across the infield and nailed him right against the wall. I swore at him and said, 'Don't ever do that again!' I almost got barred. He and I had to qualify

Opposite: Two weeks after making his USAC debut at Allentown, Mario started his second USAC race aboard Charlie Sachs's sprint car at Williams Grove, Pennsylvania. Here he poses with car owner Sachs before going out to qualify seventh and finish thirteenth in the feature. (Andretti collection) **Above:** For the first time in his career, Mario lines up beside A. J. Foyt (in the foreground) for his USAC debut at Allentown in September, 1963. Mario had driven John Werglund's Chevy-powered sprint car a week earlier in a URC race at the same track. "Bobby Marvin was killed in this car the week before I first drove it," he says. "He burned right in the cockpit and I saw it. That was really, really awful." (Bruce Craig collection)

through the semis and consi [consolation race], and we both made the main. This was Friday night.

"The next night, I won the race, Len Duncan finished second, and he never touched me. He came to victory lane and said, 'Hey kid, good job. You didn't think I was going to touch you, did you?' And I said, 'I knew you weren't!'

"It was a moment of reconciliation in some respect and a great moment for me because I had the respect of the venerable old man. I've loved that man ever since. The guy drove until he was seventy."

As Mario was making his mark in ARDC, the sport's cruel realities were all too apparent. This was the era before any serious consideration was given to safety. Equipment such as proper roll bars or cages, fuel cells, fire suits, and shoulder harnesses didn't exist. Many ARDC veterans were killed during those years.

"Sooner or later, even guys with thirty years experience, it would catch up to them. Dutch Schaefer for example. Nobody thought he would be killed. He was just going to go on and on, and it really hit me when he was killed. Tony Bonadies as well. I realized I was closer to that possibility than I thought."

On July 27, 1963, Mario entered his first road race, which was held at Lime Rock, Connecticut. Road-racing ace Mark Donohue drove a special rear-engine midget built by F1 team owner John Cooper for Ken Brenn who was from New Jersey. Brenn was in the construction business and owned some of the best midgets in ARDC.

"I used to drool to drive for him, but I never drove one of his cars. Nobody, not even the Matakas, would freshen up the engines every week, but Ken would. His stuff was always totally fresh and immaculate.

"For Lime Rock, he got Donohue to drive his car, and the only one that challenged him in that race was me. I pushed him so hard. I flew over the curbs. I had the car up on two wheels most of the time."

Donohue's leading-edge midget featured a two-speed gearbox. Mario's car used the traditional single-speed transmission designed strictly for oval racing, known as an "in-and-out box," which connected the engine directly to the differential. This proved to be a real disadvantage for Mario because his car was over-revving on the long front straightaway, and he was floating the valves. He was forced to ease out of the throttle to preserve his engine.

"The whole race I'm right on him, pushing him," Mario says. "Toward the end, about two laps to go, he drove off the course and got a puncture. It was the right rear, which is not the dominant tire at Lime Rock, but it slowed him down just enough that coming off the last corner I got underneath him, and I won the race! I held it down this time all the way across the line. I didn't care if the valves came out of the exhaust. I felt like Fangio!

"I badly burned my left elbow because there was no guard covering the exhaust. On all of the oval tracks, we ran the other way, but this was mainly right-hand corners, so my elbow got burned. But, God, did I feel good that day!"

Tragically, there was a dark side to that afternoon. "I started right behind Bill Randall, and he was killed right in front of me. He jumped over somebody's tire at the start and went end over end.

"I'll never forget it. It was a really hot July day, and before the race, Bill was cooling off in his beautiful black Mercury. He called me over to join him and I sat in the air conditioned car with him for about a half hour. Then we went out and—boom—he was killed.

"In those days, you'd lose four or five drivers each year. It was a normal thing. You just didn't know who, but you knew that some of us would be gone."

A month later, on Labor Day weekend, Mario scored another famous victory, winning three races in one day for the Mataka brothers. He won his heat, a match race, and the feature at Flemington, then drove to Hatfield, about seventy miles away, where he again won his heat, the match race, and feature. A second feature was also run at Hatfield that night from a previous rainout, and Mario won that race as well.

"After the last race I won that night, Chris Economaki, who was the track announcer, said, 'Mario, you just bought your ticket to the big time!'"

Above: Mario, flanked by Aldo at the far left, poses in Frank Anfuso's "Fuel Activator Special." In 1961 and '62 Anfuso had steadfastly refused to offer Mario a ride in the URC sprint car—even after Mario invited him to be best man at his wedding. In October 1963, Mario finally drove Anfuso's car in two URC races and finished third and fourth. "After that he was begging me to drive," Mario remembers. "I told him I wouldn't drive for him again if I had to quit racing tomorrow. I had made my point." (Andretti collection) Opposite: This page from Mario's scrapbook includes an assortment of credentials and banquet invitations from his 1960-62 racing seasons. (Andretti collection)

Twenty-Second Anniversary
DINNER DANCE

at the FAR HILLS INN, Route 202, North of Somerville Circle, N. J.
Saturday, November 17, 1962 at 8:00 p. m.
Donation $5.00 per person   N° 70

Twenty-Second Anniversary
DINNER DANCE
at the FAR HILLS INN, Route 202, North of Somerville Circle, N. J.
N° 71   Saturday, November 17, 1962 at 8:00 p. m.
Donation $5.00 per person

1961
Driver

Maceo Andretti

Name

1962
Driver

Mario Andretti

Name

Nazareth, Pa.

Address

65   *Harry D. Johnson*
President

INCORPORATED

Sportsmanship   *Showmanship*

P.R.O.S.
*Professional Racing
On Speedways*

Dedicated to the Betterment of Racing

ANNUAL LICENSE   STOCK CAR DIVISION

WHEEL CLUB INTERNATIONAL CORP.
MOTOR RACINGS SOCIAL CLUB

YEAR
60   THIS IS TO CERTIFY THAT

Motor Racings Social Club

1960   This is to certify that

MARIO ANDRETTI

Is a Member of   **ALLENTOWN, PA.**

Chapter No.   **106**

WHEEL CLUB INTERNATIONAL

Subject to the Constitution and By-Laws of the Local Chapter
and National Board of Wheel Club International.

Signed   *Mario A. Andretti*

Expires Dec. 31.   Title

ALL STARS STOCK CAR RACING CLUB
1960

Chapter 4

No Second Chances

Mario's goal for 1964 was clear. He wanted to race USAC sprint cars and, ideally, Championship cars as well. "I was becoming one of the forces to be reckoned with," Mario says, "and I was ready to push forward. So what's the next step? I wanted to be in Champ cars. And '64 seemed to be a threshold."

Mario started the new season in February with his first visit to Daytona's Speedweeks. He drove Bruce Homeyer's new midget in three NASCAR-sanctioned

Above: Dee Ann, Mario, and Michael, who's less than two years old, pose with Rufus Gray's Gapco sprint car in 1964. Mario ran fifteen USAC sprint car races for Gray and finished third in the championship that season. (Andretti collection)
Opposite: Mario notched a fifth-place finish in Charlie Sachs's sprint car at the Reading, Pennsylvania, half-mile track in March, 1964. This was the first of two USAC sprint-car races Mario drove for Sachs early in 1964 before moving to Rufus Gray's car for the rest of the USAC sprint-car season. (Bruce Craig collection)

night races run at the old Daytona Municipal Stadium on Wednesday, Thursday, and Saturday before Sunday's Daytona 500.

Many of the top USAC drivers were in Mario's pits, working on his car. A. J. Foyt, Roger McCluskey, Parnelli Jones, Don Branson, Johnny Rutherford, and Bobby Marshman all were there, making it look as if Mario was the hottest of young prospects.

"I didn't know these guys," Mario says with a shrug. "That's when I first met them. The reason all these drivers paid attention was because the Konstant Hot car belonged to Bruce Homeyer, a very prominent car owner. It was a beautiful Willard Coil car, absolutely state of the art, that Mel Kenyon won the national championship with later on. Roger McCluskey was driving for Bruce Homeyer, and all the hotshots were there. They were all checking the crossweight, making sure my set-up was right. That really intimidated the field."

He finished second in the first race, was fourth after a spin in the second race, and then won the finale. It was an auspicious beginning to a season that launched Mario into a whole new world.

At the end of March, Mario drove Charlie Sachs's URC sprint car in the year's opening USAC East Coast sprint-car races, at Reading, Pennsylvania. After winning his heat, Mario finished fifth at Reading and was a disappointed tenth two weeks later at Williams Grove. Mario was eager to get into a better car and had been talking to Rufus Gray about driving Gray's Gapco-Chevy USAC sprinter. He also agreed to make his Champ-car debut in Doug Stearly's USAC roadster.

"It was not a car that was going to win," recalls Mario, "but Stearly knew I wanted to move forward, and he asked me if I wanted to do Trenton. And I said, 'Of course.'"

Five days before the Trenton race, Mario and Dee Ann's second son, Jeff, was born on April 14, and the next day Mario became an American citizen. His family life was changing as rapidly as his racing life, and there were inevitable sacrifices.

"I think I really missed out on something in my life in the sense that I wasn't really one to hold the kids and change their diapers," Mario admits. "I probably only held them in my arms twice when they were babies. Of course, I loved my kids, but I was so busy in my career. So Dee Ann took care of them properly and allowed me to go flat out. At the time, it worked. I was probably overly focused to some degree, but that was the way it was.

"The fact that I was never home never became an issue. The understanding we

Below left: Mario gets ready to win with Bruce Homeyer's midget at the Daytona Municipal Stadium in January, 1964. In the background are USAC stars Roger McCluskey, A. J. Foyt, Parnelli Jones and Don Branson. "That was a nice midget, a great car," says Mario. "Mel Kenyon won the national championship with it the next year." (Andretti collection)
Below middle: In his first outing in a USAC Championship car, Mario (No. 28) spins Doug Stearly's roadster to avoid the No. 37 car during practice at Trenton in April, 1964. He had never sat in the roadster, let alone tested it, prior to this opening practice session at Trenton. Rodger Ward is passing Mario in A. J. Watson's rear-engine car. (Andretti collection)
Below right: In his June, 1964 USAC Champ dirt car debut, Mario tries to pass Bobby Marshman on his way to ninth place at the infamous Langhorne, Pennsylvania, mile. Mario's gloves were torn and hands bloodied from wrestling Lee Glessner's car, which lacked power steering. "My arms were giving out at the end because at Langhorne you just didn't rest," he says. "You were working the wheel the whole time." (Bruce Craig collection)

Mario (top) runs the high groove at New Bremen, Ohio, in the Gapco sprinter, going around the outside of Mickey Rupp and another car. In three USAC sprint car races at New Bremen that summer he finished second twice and was third once. (Bruce Craig collection)

had was that Dee Ann could travel with me whenever she felt like it, and when it was comfortable to have the kids with us they would come too. Before I got my first plane [in 1968] we did a lot of driving. Sometimes she would take the station wagon and meet me at some of the sprint-car races and then drive home, just to be there on the weekend."

Trenton, on April 19, was the second USAC Championship race that year. It followed Phoenix and preceded Indianapolis. Mario sat in Stearly's car for the first time that weekend, ten minutes before practice started. "I didn't know where the switches were. I didn't know what the procedures were or any of the protocol. I could have been more demanding and said I needed to test, but I was afraid to lose the ride. I was afraid to ask for even a seat adjustment.

"I'd been intimidated before, like in sprint cars when some car owners had told me I was too small and frail-looking to handle the car. 'Where's your blanket?' one guy asked me. They thought I didn't have the strength. In those days everyone believed you had to be like Hercules to drive those things."

"Stearly said, 'How do you fit?'" Mario recalls. "And I said, 'Oh, good!' I didn't dare complain about not fitting the car because I was afraid they would have just said good-bye. After my time in URC, I didn't want to have a stigma about being too small. But you talk about being fed to the wolves. I was thinking, 'Oh my God!'

"I could reach the pedals, but I was much too small for the seat and was too far away from the steering wheel, but I didn't dare ask for any changes. So I went out there, and the car was just rattling all around me. It was as if I wasn't even strapped in."

Brother Aldo was trying to resurrect his own career in local stock cars and re-

mained as fiercely determined to race as Mario. Aldo also had married and had three children, Carolyn, Mark, and John. Aldo was at Trenton that day, doing anything he could to help his brother in this important first step into the big time.

"I watched some of the practice to see where the other guys were backing off on the front straightaway," Mario says. "I had never run that speed on a mile so I wanted to see where they were backing off. I sent Aldo over to the back straightaway, and I asked him to stand somewhere that I could see him that would give me a reference point for the third turn.

"And, of course, Aldo wanted me to win so if Rodger Ward was backing off at a certain place Aldo moved up another ten or fifteen feet. He wanted me to go deeper, so I went in there, and there was no way! I was losing the back end, and I came in and said, 'How do those guys do it?' And then Aldo admitted he went real deep!"

Much to his embarrassment, Mario spun twice in the warmup before qualifying sixteenth. In the race he had to spin to avoid Ed Kostenuk's spinning car, which was hit by Ward. Mario recovered and drove on to finish a distant eleventh.

After the race Ward, who was an Indy 500 winner and USAC champion in 1959 and 1962, buttonholed Mario and upbraided him, telling him he should go back to pumping gas rather than trying to race Champ cars. It wasn't a good day, and it also happened to be the first time Gigi Andretti had come to watch his son race.

"He knew I was winning in midgets and sprints, but he didn't know anything about categories of cars," Mario says. "He figured he was going there to watch me win. Well, I wasn't winning that day. It was my debut, and it was a bit precarious. So he said, 'Hey, what happened?' But from there on he became my staunchest supporter."

After Trenton Rufus Gray asked Mario to race the Gapco sprinter in place of top USAC sprint-car ace Jud Larson (ironically, Larson was too big for the car). Mario considers this one of the biggest breaks of his career because it provided him with the platform to step into Champ cars full-time. The Gapco drive came as the month of May—Indy 500 time—rolled around. Mario decided he would travel to

Above: Mario drove Charlie Alfater's USAC sprinter just once, at Salem, Indiana, on July 4, 1964. He filled in for Alfater's regular driver, Mickey Shaw. The next day Mario was back at the wheel of the Gapco sprint car at Eldora. He finished sixth in both races. (Bruce Craig collection) **Opposite:** In the pits at a USAC sprint car race in 1964, Mario pauses with Jim Hurtubise (left), Johnny Rutherford (middle), and Jimmy Maguire (right). Hurtubise was at the height of his career in 1964, and was rated by many observers to be as good as Mario, Foyt, and Parnelli Jones. (Bruce Craig collection)

Before the start at Milwaukee in August, 1964. Parnelli Jones is on pole in a factory Lotus-Ford with Rodger Ward beside him in A. J. Watson's first rear-engine car and A. J. Foyt starting third in another factory Lotus. Mario is back on the inside of the fifth row in Dean's roadster, which he raced to third place behind winner Jones and second-place Ward. (Andretti collection)

Indianapolis and spend the month nosing around the Speedway's garage area and settling in with Gray's team for the series of spring and summer sprint-car races in the Midwest.

When Mario asked his boss, Tim Sheehen, at the DelWick Company for the month off, Sheehen, who had given Mario plenty of vacation time over the previous two years, suggested that Mario should decide what he wanted to do with his life, work at DelWick or drive race cars.

"That was the year I realized fully that this is my career, and I don't need to work for anyone doing anything but racing," Mario says. "But it took until then for me to really feel that I could do that, and I never looked back."

Up to this point Mario was still racing only for prize money, forty per cent usually, without a salary. But after Mario quit his job, Gray started sending weekly checks for $175 to Dee Ann at home in Nazareth. Gray's business was making nuts and bolts for the aircraft industry and, unbeknownst to Mario, he put him on the company payroll.

Mario's scheduled first race in the Gapco sprinter was rained out at Salem, Indiana. He finished fourth at the next event on May 3, at New Bremen, Ohio, where many of the Champ-car drivers racing at Indy that month also were driving sprint cars. One of them, Chuck Hulse, ran into the Gapco's tail at the start of the feature race, crashed hard, and suffered a broken back.

Hulse had been driving Champ cars that year for Clint Brawner's high-profile Dean Van Lines team. Al Dean's Long Beach, California-based company, Dean Van Lines, was one of the nation's largest trucking companies, and Brawner's team was one of the best in the business. With the legendary Jimmy Bryan the team had won seventeen races from 1954-57 and captured the 1954 American Automobile Association (USAC's predecessor) and 1956 and '57 USAC championships. Now that Hulse was injured, Brawner and Dean were looking for a replacement. One highly respected observer who recommended Mario to Brawner and Dean was Chris Economaki.

Above: Jim McGee, Mario, and master mechanic Clint Brawner pose with Al Dean's roadster in the summer of 1964. The trio would become one of the most potent combinations in USAC Championship racing over the next five years. (Andretti collection)

"I was instrumental, to some extent, in Mario getting that ride," Economaki says. "Brawner asked me who the comers were from the east, and I told him about Mario. Brawner later said he took Mario on my recommendation."

Jim McGee, Brawner's chief mechanic, approached Mario and asked him to come to their Indy shop to get fitted to the car. "I was very excited," Mario says. "Here was a chance with one of the top teams." Mario's hopes for starting in the 500 were dashed, however. "Brawner said, 'You're not ready for Indy.' He was so right, but I was very disappointed."

Brawner told Mario he would have to wait until after a race at Langhorne, Pennsylvania, in late June to drive his car. He believed Langhorne was too dangerous for such a spirited and inexperienced youth. Brawner hired the more experienced Bob Mathouser to drive his car for two races, Langhorne included, and told Mario he would start driving the Dean Van Lines car at Trenton in July.

Mario bided his time by walking around the garages at Indy, seeing if anything else was available. "It was great to be there at the Speedway and to have car owners interested in talking to me about driving for them. I wasn't one of the big names, but I was known as a comer. People were talking about me as a guy on the way up. The bad old URC days seemed a long way behind me."

One day, fellow drivers Bobby Unser and Johnny White recommended Mario to Mickey Thompson, and Thompson told Mario to come to his garage the following morning. "I tossed and turned that night. Something was telling me, 'Clint Brawner knows better. If he says you're not ready, he's probably right, and you shouldn't botch it. You've got a ride with a top team,' I said to myself. 'Cultivate that, get this year in, get a feeling for it, and really go for it next year.'

"So I purposely slept until eleven o'clock and didn't even go to the Speedway, because I didn't want to face the situation. I think Mickey Thompson forgot about it and, in retrospect, that was the best thing that could have happened. I would not have been able to do anything revealing in Mickey Thompson's car. He only ran Indianapolis, not the full season, and taking that drive would have been a huge mistake."

Above: Mario raced Bob Nowicke's midget in one USAC race at DuQuoin, Illinois, on Labor Day weekend in 1964. He didn't finish, and was classified seventeenth before racing the Gapco sprinter at Winchester, Indiana, the following day. He then returned to DuQuoin for the next day's Champ dirt car race in Dean's Epperly dirt car. (Bruce Craig collection) **Previous pages:** At the California State Fairgrounds at Sacramento in October, 1964 Mario runs hard in Dean's Epperly dirt car. He is followed by Parnelli Jones (No. 98), Rodger Ward behind Jones, and Chuck Booth (No. 65). Mario finished eighth in this 100-mile race, the last of five dirt track races on that year's Championship trail. (Dan Mahony) **Opposite:** A portrait of Mario in 1964. (Bob Tronolone)

Mario stayed to watch the race from the old Tower Terrace grandstands, where he had a perfect view of the fiery accident at the end of the first lap that claimed the lives of Speedway veteran Eddie Sachs and Thompson's driver, Dave MacDonald.

"That accident was just the worst, but it didn't discourage me in any way. I look back now, and I'm amazed by how drivers accepted the fact that potentially we were not going to survive. It really isn't part of the thinking process today, and thank God. But in those days it was. You never really felt like you were settled in life."

The day after watching that year's Indy 500, Mario finished second in the Gapco sprint car, at New Bremen again, and was second-fastest qualifier at Terre Haute, Indiana, a few weeks later. He also had driven Jake Vargo's midget at Zipps Speedway in Indiana the night before the 500 and would drive it again in June at Eldora, Ohio, and Toronto.

On Doug Stearly's recommendation Mario was offered a car by Lee Glessner for the June 21 Langhorne event. This would be Mario's first drive in a "Big Car," as the Championship dirt cars of the 1940s, '50s, and '60s were known. Glessner's car was prepared by retired East Coast sprint-car legend Tommy Hinnershitz.

"I had never raced at Langhorne, but I had been there and had watched several fatalities," Mario says. "I knew that place claimed more lives than Indy. Preparing for that first time made me feel as though I were a soldier on the front lines facing battle the next day. That was the only time in my career that I remember on the night before the race I felt that maybe I wouldn't come back. Those are things you never forget."

Langhorne's D-shaped configuration featured the notorious 'Puke Hollow' turn, one of the most fearsome on the circuit and one that had claimed many lives, including the great Jimmy Bryan in 1960.

Unlike those of most of the front-runners, Glessner's car lacked power steering which, Mario says, made his job even more difficult. "Going into Puke Hollow you had to pitch it in there, throw it sideways into the cushion, and give it full power, and you were lock to lock three or four times. With power steering it was no big deal, but without it, it was hard work. I could handle a few laps like that, but I knew it was going to be tough doing a hundred laps in the race.

"The man who probably saved my life that weekend was Tommy Hinnershitz. He was a racer's racer. If anybody knew the dirt, it was him. I was very lucky he was

my chief mechanic for that race."

Hinnershitz watched Mario take the car out to the edge of the track in practice and cautioned him on his braking points because he knew Mario would press even harder in qualifying. "Kid, you're doing good," Hinnershitz told him, "but when you're qualifying, on the backstretch, no matter how good a feel you think you have, back off by the pole."

"He knew I'd be carrying that much more speed coming out of turn two in qualifying," Mario says, "and sure enough, he was right, because I just barely made it. That was the maximum. Had I gone ten feet past the pole I would have gone out of the ballpark for sure."

Mario qualified eighth and hung on to finish ninth in the race, passing Brawner's substitute driver, Bob Mathouser, late in the hundred miles. "I was the highest-finishing non-power steering car, and my hands were like hamburger. I had so much adrenaline going I didn't feel it until the end of the race, but that was the worst I've ever torn up my hands."

Typically, the dirt surface broke up badly late in the race, and deep ruts formed in the track, particularly through Puke Hollow. "You really had to power through there. That 100 miles seemed like two days, but when I passed Bob Mathouser, that made me feel a lot better. That I was proud of. I was so focused, and I had so much desire that desire superseded reason. I wanted it so bad. I said I was just going to get it done."

The week after Langhorne, Mario finished second to Don Branson driving the Gapco sprint car at Indianapolis Raceway Park. He led much of the race but in the end was outfoxed by the veteran Branson. At Williams Grove three weeks later, Mario spun just one lap after passing Foyt for the lead and was hit by Branson, taking both drivers out of the race. Branson gave Mario a stern lecture. Then, Clint Brawner, who was there as a spectator, came over to warn his young charge that any more wild driving would cost him his ride. These were critical days in Mario's career, and he was confronted by a tough question that often faces aggressive young racers. Should he hang it out the way he naturally preferred or try to contain himself and drive more conservatively?

Mario made his debut in Brawner's roadster at Trenton the following day, and he worked his way up to sixth place before spinning on some oil and stalling. He lost two laps and quietly drove home in eleventh place. The Trenton race was followed by a Firestone tire test at the track that proved to be eventful.

"We had the wider tires because it was the beginning of the low-profile tire revolution," Mario recalls, "and I could drive it through the corners, but I couldn't keep the car going straight on the straightaway. I was doing fairly decent times, but not as fast as I should."

Brawner had fitted the new lightweight car with rack-and-pinion steering gear, a system that had recently been adopted by all the European rear-engine car builders. Those cars, however, used four-wheel independent suspension rather than the straight-axle design of Brawner's car. The combination of rack and pinion and a straight axle created a tremendous amount of "toe steer" as the wheels went up and down. The new roadster was evil to drive and required constant steering corrections.

Mario complained, suggesting Brawner and McGee put more caster in the front end. "They said we already have eleven degrees of caster, and I said, 'Yeah, I know, and it steers really hard.' " [Toe-in is the tiny amount the front wheels point in toward each other to assist the ease of turning. Toe-out is the opposite, with the front wheels pointing slightly apart. Caster is the angle of the front uprights from vertical. Negative caster tends to make the steering lighter; positive caster makes it heavier.]

Rodger Ward was also at the Trenton tire test, driving A. J. Watson's car. Brawner asked Ward to run some laps in his car to compare the veteran driver's opinion with their rookie's impressions. "Ward went out there, and he was two seconds slower than me," Mario says. "He came in and said to Brawner, 'This kid is either the bravest guy I've ever known or the stupidest bastard I've ever met. You can't drive this car straight. This is a dangerous car. You shouldn't even run it.' That, of course, was a blessing for me."

Ward's run in the car convinced Brawner that his steering innovation didn't work, and it also built his confidence that Mario could judge car set-up properly. Brawner installed the normal steering gear for the next race in Milwaukee, and Mario finished third. What was also significant about Mario's third at Milwaukee was that his was the highest-placing front-engine car. Winner Parnelli Jones scored the second USAC victory for a Ford-powered rear-engine car, and Ward was runner-up in a similar Offy-powered machine.

Twelve months earlier Scotsman Jim Clark had scored the first win for a rear-engine car in Championship racing at Milwaukee. By August of 1964 the rear-engine revolution had arrived full force as most of the field consisted of rear-engine machines. Mario's performance in an outdated roadster competing against the ground-breaking rear-engine machines emphasized his driving talent. By this time, it was clear that he was an exceptional driver who was capable of making up for deficiencies in equipment, something very few drivers can do.

There were five more Championship races in 1964: three dirt events at DuQuoin, Illinois, the Indiana State Fairgrounds in Indianapolis, and Sacramento, plus two paved tracks at Trenton and Phoenix. Mario's best finish in those five races was eighth at Sacramento, although he qualified Brawner's roadster third among the rear-engine brigade at Phoenix.

In the remaining USAC sprint-car races that season, Mario had been equally competitive. At Allentown in August he started from the pole but was clipped by Foyt at the start and spun. Restarting last, he tore through the field, thinking only of catching and passing Foyt. He made it all the way to Foyt's bumper, having passed Branson for second in the closing laps, before the car failed him. Mario's deep desire to succeed occasionally drove him to the point of recklessness, and he admits he was probably lucky he didn't catch Foyt.

"I was in a blind rage. I was driving like a madman. I even ran Bobby Marshman off the track, and I know that if I had caught Foyt I would have bumped him for sure. The crowd and press went into hysterics over my performance that day, but I wasn't proud of myself. I was a menace to the other drivers, and that is absolutely not the way to be."

Mario had a particular rivalry with Foyt that Brawner tried to defuse. "Clint thought I was going to kill myself in a race car. He used to tell me just to do my thing. 'Don't worry about beating Foyt,' he would say. 'The only way you're going to beat Foyt is if a jealous husband shoots him.' That fired me up, and the first race that I won and Foyt finished second, I said, 'Hey Clint, he's still around. Nobody shot him!' That was all-important to me."

After finishing second in the Gapco sprinter at New Bremen the day after his wild drive at Allentown, Mario finished second again two weeks later at St. Paul, Minnesota. He went on to score his first USAC win in Gray's car at the high-banked Salem half-mile track on October 4, beating Branson and Larson. Branson and Larson were fighting for that year's USAC sprint-car championship, and Mario's victory helped him finish third in points behind the two veterans. It had been a very tough but extremely pivotal season for him.

"1964 was a very traumatic year for me because of all these firsts I experienced in the big time," Mario says. "I knew I had to do it. There would be no second chances."

The last USAC Championship race of 1964 was held at Phoenix in November. Parnelli Jones in a rear-engine Lotus-Ford and A. J. Foyt (No. 8) in a rear-engine Hallibrand-Offy share the front row with Mario (No. 7), who started third and was the fastest roadster in the field. (Andretti collection)

Chapter 5

A Very Big Year

When Mario agreed to drive for Al Dean and Clint Brawner in May of 1964, there had been talk about a two-car team in 1965 that paired Mario with the returning Chuck Hulse. Mario wanted no part of a two-car team, and after his strong half-season in 1964 he gave Brawner the ultimatum that it was either him or Hulse, not both of them.

"I had never been a fan of two-car teams," Mario says, "and I just didn't believe Clint had the resources

Opposite: The new Ford-powered Brawner/Hawk was an immediate success when it made its debut at Indianapolis in 1965. "I really began to understand what that rear-engine car wanted, and in the hands of Clint Brawner and Jim McGee we really got it working," Mario explains. "The Hawk helped launch my career because I became a competitive factor right away." (Joe Farkas) **Above:** In this Firestone publicity photo Mario and Brawner hold one of the first fuel cells above the Hawk. The fuel cell at that time was a metal fuel tank lined with a rubber bladder, which made it less likely to rupture in a crash. It was an important safety innovation of the day. (ISC Archives)

to run two cars equally. I knew 1965 was going to be a very big year for me. I had to win races, and I believed the only way that could happen was in a one-car team."

Chief mechanic Jim McGee agreed. McGee had been high on Mario from the start, and the pair was quickly in sync. With McGee pushing them, Dean and Brawner chose Mario.

"The first actual contract I had was with Dean Van Lines for 1965," Mario recalls. "Al Dean offered me a contract for $3,000. Up until then I always drove for forty per cent, never more, never less."

Signing with Dean and settling in with Brawner and McGee was what he had been seeking. "I felt like I had a home, and the beautiful thing about that association was we started testing. All of a sudden we became the test team for Firestone, and that was huge for me. I was craving those miles, and all of a sudden I had a feel for the car, and I felt so prepared going to a race. All these other doubts were out the window. Those miles were gold for me. I was doing every test Firestone wanted, so we put on a lot of miles.

"Everything was done in-house of course. McGee and his crew were doing the engines, as well, so it was an incredible workload on them. But they could see the value to it, and they knew how much I wanted it. They were regularly working until two or three in the morning to freshen the top end of the engine or pull the block and put in new rings. It was a big workload on them and great effort on their part that benefited us all."

It was during this time that rear-engine car design all but replaced the traditional front-engine roadster. Although Brawner had built a new lightweight roadster for 1965, he also built a rear-engine car based on a Brabham tube-frame chassis he had borrowed from chief mechanic Denny Moore. During the winter Brawner and McGee built three rear-engine chassis using the 1964 car as a template. "One car was for Denny Moore with an Offy, and two were for us with Ford engines," McGee says. Famed Champ dirt car and roadster builder Eddie Kuzma was hired to fabricate all the sheet metal and bodywork.

Brawner and most other established team bosses thought the aluminum monocoque chassis used by Lotus and Lola were flimsy. The more traditional tubular chassis, Brawner believed, would be stronger, safer, and easier to set up for each track.

Called Brawner/Hawks, the new cars were different from the original Brabham because they were equipped with proper fuel cells rather than traditional gas tanks. These were located on either side of the cockpit as low and far to the outside as possible to produce a lower center of gravity.

Brawner didn't want to start the season by combining an essentially rookie driver and a completely new type of car. Neither Brawner nor Mario had any experience with rear-engine cars, so Mario drove Brawner's lightweight roadster in the first two races while the first rear-engine car was completed.

Mario qualified third at the Phoenix season-opener behind a pair of rear-engine cars driven by A. J. Foyt and Rodger Ward. In the race, Ward and Mario soon passed Foyt, and Mario was chasing hard after Ward when the latter had to spin to avoid Johnny Rutherford's spinning car. Mario passed Ward and took the lead, staying in front for the first time in his Champ car career for 63 laps until he had to spin to avoid hitting Rutherford, who had spun again.

Mario recovered to finish sixth while Don Branson, also driving a traditional front-engine roadster, inherited the victory. That was the last time a traditional roadster would win a Champ car race. Front-engine Champ cars would continue to win on the dirt through 1970, but would never again win on a paved track.

"That was a great race for me," Mario says. "It really pumped up my confidence. Until that race I'd shown a lot of promise, but I hadn't actually done any leading, and when that happened it made me feel ten feet tall. Now I knew I could do it."

At Trenton the following month, Mario again mixed it up with the rear-engine brigade. He qualified fifth, but was soon chasing early leaders Foyt and Jim McElreath, who were both in rear-engine machines. Foyt dropped out, leaving

Above: Mario qualified the Hawk on the inside of row two and finished third in the Indy 500 behind Jim Clark and Parnelli Jones. Mario also won the race's Rookie of the Year award. "At that time there were no aerodynamic aids," he notes. "The car was very sensitive. Brawner reinforced the original Brabham chassis so it was stiffer, which is what you needed for the ovals where good weight transfer is important." (Bob Tronolone)
Opposite: At Terre Haute, Mario tries too hard to tame the unwieldy 1965 Gapco sprint car. "I think I might have hit the wall," he concedes. "Rufus was a good guy and he and his crew worked hard to improve the car, but it was just awful. It was a shame. I was lucky things were going so well in Champ cars." (Bruce Craig collection)

Mario to battle fiercely with McElreath.

"I was all over him," Mario says. "I just didn't have the power, and that roadster didn't have the brakes of a rear-engine car. A couple of times I got alongside him in turn one. I had my inside front wheel off the ground and almost as high as his head. I could have put my wheel in his cockpit. I was that close to him." Finally, McElreath put lapped cars between them and was able to pull away. Mario had to settle for second, his best Champ-car finish to date.

Then came the month of May at Indianapolis, Mario's rookie year at the Speedway. In those days, there were no fewer than three weeks of practice at Indianapolis, with the track opening on May 1. But the brand-new, Ford-powered Brawner/Hawk wasn't ready until the middle of the second week of practice. Pole day in 1965 fell on May 15, and Mario didn't get onto the track until May 9. An engine failure on his first day cost more time.

"I'm a rookie, and I'm waiting for my new car," Mario recalls. "I've never sat in it, never driven a rear-engine car, and it had never turned a wheel. I mean, I was dying. But when we got out there, it was a piece of cake."

Mario first had to complete his rookie test, but after just one day of practice he was ready for another test that required drivers to complete a series of laps at pre-determined speeds supervised by USAC observers. He cruised through it without any drama, taking immediately to the track and car.

"I went out and started standing on it, and I was right in the top-five times that day. I think I was third quickest, actually, and we said, 'We're in business.'

"I was lucky because the car was so good. It really didn't need any serious sorting out. To me, as a driver, it felt good right away, and the more I learned, the more I enjoyed it. With a roadster you felt every crack in the road, every little dip, and it all upset you. When I got in the rear-engine car, everything was absorbed. It was so much more forgiving. Then I started really hustling it, getting it out of shape, drifting it, and the lap times really came. The overall performance was there. I didn't have to slide the car as much because I had the grip.

"The braking seemed like it was twice as good. Even though I had a lightweight roadster it was still heavier than a rear-engine car. So you felt it in braking and in putting power down. The roadster always had the tail out. With a straight axle you could never get it going exactly straight under power. But with the rear-engine car it stuck, and you could put the power down earlier. There was no doubt that the rear engine was the way to go."

The four-wheel, independently suspended rear-engine cars were also much more adjustable or tunable than the roadsters which had straight axles and therefore lacked any adjustment to wheel camber (the perpendicular angle to the road) or toe-in. The only thing that could be adjusted on a roadster was to shift the balance of the car's weight across its four wheels from corner to corner, called cross-weighting.

"The rear-engine car had independent suspension so you had cambers, toes, roll bars, and springs to work with," Mario says. "With the roadster you were locked in. The measure of your speed was how much you hustled it and how much you slid it without wasting time. You would drift it everywhere. It was a powerslide

69

"Colin said, 'When you think you're ready, call me.' Those words were imprinted in my mind. I said to myself there and then that I had some serious work to do because my ultimate goal was to get into Formula One."

everywhere, and you couldn't help yourself because you couldn't adjust the car."

At Indy Mario drew an early place in the qualifying line and set new one- and four-lap records in his rookie qualifying run, averaging 158.849 mph for the four laps. Right away however, Mario was beaten by Jim Clark in the factory Lotus-Ford, and then both were beaten by Foyt, who was driving a 1964 Lotus-Ford he had bought from Clark's boss, Colin Chapman. Before the day was over Dan Gurney made it an all-Lotus front row as he also beat Mario, knocking him back to the inside of the second row. The Hawk lacked power because Brawner had been very conservative with his fuel mixtures.

"I was forty horsepower down," Mario says. The disparity between the teams was in the fuel mixtures they used. "Most people were running ten per cent nitromethane in their methanol in the races, but I couldn't get Clint to do that. He was afraid it would burn the engine down. The other competitors were running twenty to thirty per cent nitro for qualifying. If we had done that, maybe I could have sat on the pole there in my first year. If I had at least ten per cent nitro I think I could have put it on the pole because I wasn't that far off."

Mario describes Brawner's parsimonious nature. "He didn't want to spend the money. In those days we were testing so much for Firestone that we had brand-new engines, but Brawner would run cracked crankshafts in the race car if he could get away with it. McGee would tell me to just go out and blow it up, and we'd get a new engine. McGee made sure we wouldn't run junk like that."

As engrossed as Mario was in his first experience at Indianapolis, he was looking ahead to his dream of racing in Formula One. "In the back of my mind I wanted to be impressive to Chapman and Clark," Mario recalls. "They took notice that I qualified on the second row, and I don't remember when it was exactly, but I was talking with Colin and Jimmy, asking all kinds of questions. Jimmy was having a banner year in Formula One, and I said to them, 'That's what I'd really love to do.' And Colin said, 'When you think you're ready, call me.' Those words were imprinted in my mind. I said to myself there and then that I had some serious work to do because my ultimate goal was to get into Formula One."

Only six front-engine cars made the field in 1965. Mario's objective in his first 500 was to finish. He let the leaders go in the early laps and fell back a few places. He later realized he could run a little quicker and was soon back to fifth behind Clark, Foyt, Gurney, and Parnelli Jones.

Clark dominated to win easily in his third start at Indianapolis. Foyt and Gurney dropped out with transmission and engine problems respectively, and Jones

kept Mario at bay despite running out of fuel as he took the checkered flag. Brawner and McGee tried to get Mario to go after the fuel-starved Jones in the closing laps, but he was too exhausted to try. Their inexperience with the new car had caught up to them, and he had to settle for third.

"What killed me in the race," Mario says, "was the car got looser and looser because it was burning all the fuel from the left-side tank first, then the right-side tank. So when I was midway through the fuel load the car was bicycling because I had all the weight on the outside."

By the end of the race Mario's hands were badly blistered from fighting the car. He also got very hot because the cockpit was improperly ventilated, so he was completely spent. "It's too bad we didn't know the beast any better for the first race, but we still finished third. It was a miracle that the thing ran all day with no experience at all."

Meanwhile Brawner protested Jones, claiming he was push started in his final pit stop. USAC threw out Brawner's protest, declaring Jones had used his clutch to restart the car rather then the muscle power of his crewmen. Brawner was livid, but Mario wasn't concerned. He had won his share of $42,500 for finishing third, earned the track's Rookie of the Year award, and was leading the USAC championship standings entering the season's fourth race at Milwaukee the following weekend.

With practice beginning at Milwaukee only four days later, there was no time to re-engineer the car. Mario therefore fought the same problems that were magnified and made more difficult on the smaller, one-mile Wisconsin oval. He qualified twelfth and finished a distant fourth, helped by a high rate of attrition.

The open weekend before the next race at Langhorne allowed Brawner and McGee to do some work to both the fuel and cooling systems. Langhorne was newly paved, and with the Hawk now handling better than ever Mario won the pole and finished second to McElreath after leading a few early laps.

Next came Trenton, but Mario missed the race because a driveshaft broke in practice, and he lost a wheel and crashed. Although Mario was unhurt, the car was

Opposite: In August, Mario finished fourth at Milwaukee in Ray Nichels's Zecol Lubaid 4 USAC Late Model stock car. He raced the car twice at Milwaukee that month and also on the dirt at Springfield and DuQuoin. It was a busy time: "One weekend there was a stock-car race on Friday and a Champ dirt car race on Saturday at Springfield, and then a Champ car race at Milwaukee on Sunday." (Bruce Craig collection) Previous pages: The dramatic difference between old and new technology becomes clear as Mario duels at Milwaukee in August with Foyt's front-engine dirt car. Foyt famously ran his dirt car after his rear-engine Lotus failed to arrive. Incredibly, the Texan qualified on the pole and finished second. Mario qualified third but failed to finish because of an engine failure. (Bruce Craig collection)

Mario made his sports-car racing debut in the No. 18 Ferrari 330LM fielded by Luigi Chinetti's North American Racing Team at Bridgehampton, New York, in September. This was a USRRC event. Jim Hall leads in the No. 66 Chaparral, with Bob Johnson in the No. 91 Cobra and George Wintersteen in the No. 12 McLaren M1A following. The Ferrari's safety equipment was vestigial at best, says Mario: "The seat belt was just a lap belt, and it was sewed to the removable cushion just to get by scrutineering. The roll bar was just a bent piece of tube with the base pop-riveted to the aluminum floor." (Pete Luongo) **Opposite:** Mario drove this Lola T70 Can-Am car in the Los Angeles Times GP at Riverside in October. "That car really under-steered," he recalls. "There was a tiny little chin spoiler on the front, but it wasn't much. Lola needed to learn more about aerodynamics." (Andretti collection)

too badly damaged to be repaired in time.

The first road race for Champ cars in almost thirty years was held the following week. The track was Indianapolis Raceway Park, an oval with an infield road course, and Mario again qualified on the pole. This was only his second road race, following his midget victory at Lime Rock in July of 1963.

Mario's car had a two-speed, speedway-style gearbox at IRP while his primary rival Foyt had a much more effective four-speed Hewland transmission in his Lotus. "It was the first and only road race of the year, so I don't think too many people were too concerned about going for four speeds," Mario adds. "But Foyt was smart. He had a Lotus, and he knew you could easily put a four-speed box in it. So he had a distinct advantage there, even though the course was simple."

Foyt's superior gearing enabled him to outpace Mario by almost ten mph on the main straightaway, but Mario was able to stay with him on the rest of the course. At one point Mario spun while leading, but was able to catch back up to Foyt and score his first Champ-car victory when Foyt ran out of fuel when he began the last lap.

"To win a road race really meant a lot to me because that was always my passion, so it was ironic and very meaningful that my first Champ-car win came on a road course. My car was very awkward; it didn't shift right. I made do, but it was difficult at best. We were so lucky to win because Foyt had an insurmountable advantage with four speeds. One good thing about that Brabham design was you could pitch it and slide it around. The car was really well balanced, and it really suited my style. I also knew how to set it up, and that paid off. If I had had a Hewland four-speed, I would've been long gone."

The victory solidified Mario's lead in the USAC standings, which provided a points cushion that allowed the team to race the lightweight, Offy-powered roadster one more time in the next race on the high-banked Atlanta speedway.

"We did that because I didn't think the suspension on the rear-engine car was strong enough," Mario says. "The uprights and spindles on the Hawk weren't up to it on a track like that."

Mario qualified eighth and finished second, well behind winner Johnny Rutherford, after Foyt and most of the other front-runners had dropped out. That was Mario's last race in a roadster. There would be no more wins in the remaining nine races, but Mario added three more seconds, a couple of thirds, and a fourth. He clinched his

first USAC championship at Trenton in September with two races to run.

McGee believes the Brawner/Hawk generated a substantial amount of downforce from its wide, flat bottom, although neither he nor Brawner had any idea in those days. "At that time," McGee says, "A. J. Watson and Colin Chapman were building those skinny, cigar-shaped cars, and Watson used to laugh at our car. He called our car a bathtub.

"The oil and water radiators were in the front, and we used to run tubes down the side of the car to transfer the oil and water from the radiators to the back of the engine, and they acted like little skirts. With that big, flat bottom, I bet at 200 mph we generated 1,000 pounds of downforce."

Chris Economaki says Brawner and McGee introduced aerodynamics to Champ-car racing without knowing it. "The art of aerodynamics actually began with the Dean Van Lines Special," Economaki says. "They built a cover for the Hewland transmission hanging out the back to make it a little sleeker, and Mario went out and found the car didn't want to turn. So they put little chin spoilers on either side of the nose to bring the nose back down. That was the beginning of the aero era in racing, all through happenstance."

At Phoenix, the last event of the season, Mario took his third pole of the year and led most of the race, holding off a challenge from Foyt. With just eight laps to go, Mario brushed wheels with a lapped car and damaged his car's rear suspension. He had to slow down and nurse it to the finish, which allowed Foyt to pass him and win.

Mario Andretti had truly arrived. He had beaten Foyt for the title by more than 600 points and was the first rookie to win the national championship since Johnny Parsons in 1949. At twenty-five, Mario was the youngest champion ever and would remain so for thirty years, until Jacques Villeneuve won the 1995 Championship Auto Racing Teams (CART) title.

"Timing was the key to what happened in my career, like being able to jump from sprint cars into one of the top three teams in Champ cars. Even then there were a lot of good teams, but there were only three or four teams that were doing all the winning, and you had to be with one of them.

"So I was lucky that I was with one of those teams. It was not the best team maybe, but for me it was the best because I found myself with McGee and Brawner. It was a perfect balance. Here you had a young guy that really identified with me and understood me, and a crusty, older guy with lots of wisdom who understood how to cool me down."

Back in September, Mario had made his international sports-car racing debut the week before he sealed the USAC title at Trenton. It happened at the beautiful Bridgehampton road course on Long Island, where he drove a Ferrari 330LM for Luigi Chinetti's North American Racing Team, once again at Economaki's recommendation.

"I told Luigi Chinetti about this young Italian, and he was more interested that he was Italian than how good he was," Economaki says. "So he brought a Ferrari to Bridgehampton for Mario to drive."

This was the third road race of his career, and Mario admits he wasn't really up to it. "I had no idea what Bridgehampton even looked like. I arrived there, and just because I had a reputation I was supposed to be the hot dog and know everything. The onus was on me to get it done, and God, Bridgehampton was a hell of a course—very

demanding, the first corner alone. I don't know how I got it done, but I never crashed."

During practice, Mario stopped in the pits a few times, just to relax for a few minutes and try to catch his breath. "I knew I'd gotten away with this one or that one, and I'd come into the pits to think about it and try to do it better."

In the race Mario got up to third behind Pedro Rodriguez and Walt Hansgen before the clutch failed.

"There was no prize money to speak of in those races. At Bridgehampton I was paid $1,000 appearance money, and Luigi was pretty happy with what I did, and he asks, 'How many kids do you have?' I told him two, and he wrote me a check for $2,000! I never forgot that. What a gentleman. I always had great respect for Luigi." Chinetti later invited Mario to co-drive a 4.4-liter Ferrari 365P2 with Rodriguez in the following year's Daytona 24 Hours and Sebring 12 Hours.

At the end of October, Mario had another road-racing opportunity when he was invited by Riverside promoter Les Richter to drive a Lola T70 Can-Am car in the Los Angeles Times Grand Prix. He was teamed with Jackie Stewart, but was a second a lap slower than the Scotsman and was driving over his head to do it. In fact, Mario crashed in qualifying and didn't start the race. "I was trying too hard and misjudging my apexes. I was just not ready. I hit Graham Hill in the back end going into turn nine and really felt like a fool.

"I didn't feel like I was in real harmony with the car. I felt that I needed miles. In those days I would jump into any situation. It was all heart and the will to do it that got me through it. Of course, you didn't have the luxury to go testing."

The next day Lola boss Eric Broadley called Mario. "You have a lot going for you," Broadley said, "but you need to get experience. You need miles."

"I said, 'You're so right,'" Mario recalls. "That was really what told me that I had to learn how to road race. Winning IRP with a two-speed gearbox was one thing, but there was no finesse. It was just a do-or-die situation. The experience at Riverside really sent a loud and clear message to me that I needed to learn how to road race properly.

"That's when I figured I had to get into long-distance racing. I had Chinetti's offer of the Ferrari ride at Daytona and Sebring in 1966 and at that time Ford was really trying to win Le Mans. I was already part of the Ford team. So I told the guys at Ford that's what I wanted to do."

Left: Driving Al Dean's USAC dirt car at the Sacramento 100-mile race in October, Mario finished third. (Bob Tronolone) Opposite: Newspaper clippings from Mario's scrapbook show he was getting plenty of good publicity in 1965. (Andretti collection)

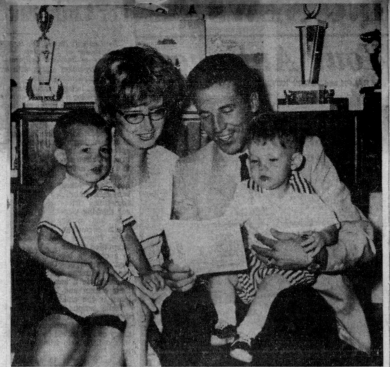

ENTERED AT LANGHORNE — Mario Andretti of Nazareth is shown at the wheel of the Dean Van Lines Special which he will drive at the newly paved Langhorne Speedway on Sunday. Andretti drove the car to a third place finish in 1965 Indianapolis 500.

RACING STAR AT HOME — Mario Andretti looks over the latest copy of the United States Racing Club news sheet with his family in Nazareth after learning that he holds a 500-point lead in the National Championship point race over his nearest competitor in tomorrow's 100-mile race at the new Langhorne Speedway. His wife, Dee Ann, holds their son, Jeff, while son Mike sits on his father's lap.

—Easton Express Photo

Andretti Tries To Increase Point Lead At Langhorne

By THOM SHRIVER

Several important questions will be answered Sunday afternoon at the new Langhorne International Speedway when the inaugural event for the recently refurbished speedrome is run off.

Uppermost in the minds of local championship car racing fans is whether or not Mario Andretti of Nazareth can increase his slim 100-point lead in the USAC Championship standings.

Parnelli Jones, Andretti's closest challenger will not be driving in the 100-mile race Sunday but will be at Langhorne in an advisory capacity with the Agajanian-Hurst Racing group.

Jones, who finished one spot ahead of the young Italian in the 1965 Indianapolis 500, will be replaced in the rear-engine Ford Agajanian-Hurst Special by George Snider of Bakersfield, Calif.

Al Gerber and Irv Fried, co-promoters at Langhorne, will also be facing an acid test Sunday when the first race is run on the newly paved "D" shaped one-mile track.

Langhorne has been a dirt track since it opened in 1926. To many fans the switch from dirt to asphalt amounts to an unpardonable sin.

The promoters explained that their reason for the switch was the sudden drop in the size of the fields running in the annual classics. The advent of the fragile rear-engine championship racers was responsible for the smaller fields. The new breed of car is lower and cannot take the beating that goes along with racing on a dirt track.

More than likely, three-quarters of the field of 22 cars that start the 100-mile grind Sunday will be rear-engine machines.

Bobby Unser, Albuquerque, N. M., was the first driver to sign to run the race and will be piloting the Vita-Fresh Orange Juice Special, entered by Gordon Van Liew of Houston, Tex.

Unser, seven time winner of the Pikes Peak hill climb, drove the STP Ferguson Novi car at "Indy" this year but dropped out on the 69th lap with mechanical malfunctions.

Roger Ward and Don Branson will drive as a team in rear-engine Fords. Ward will have a battle on his hands trying to prove himself after failing to qualify for the "Indy 500" this May. Ward's teammate, Branson, is the current one-mile and 100-mile record holder at Langhorne and will also have to go all out to hold on to his record as the old marks are expected to fall.

All-time great A. J. Foyt, who has won the National Championship four times, has yet to make a good showing this season and is not listed in the top 12 of the USAC point standings. Foyt will drive a rear-engine Ford powered car.

Chuck Stevenson will lead the conservative element driving a front engine Offenhauser roadster, while Billy Foster, the popular Canadian pilot, will drive a rear-engine Ford.

Other drivers who will be out in time trials competing for one of the 22 starting slots include: Lloyd Ruby, who started the rear-engine revolt several years ago at Trenton; Joe Leonard, who finished second in the recent Milwaukee 100 miler; Red Reigel, who is popular in local sprint car events; Len Sutton, Rodger McCluskey, Ronnie Duman, Gig Stephens, Gordon Johncock, Bob Mathouser, Bill Eldridge, Jim McElreath, Bob Harkey and ever popular Bud Tinglestad.

Andretti will drive the same rear-engine Ford powered Dean Van Lines Special with which he won third spot in the 1965 "Indy 500."

Little publicized after the noise was over at "Indy" this year was the fact that Clint Brawner, chief mechanic of Mario's car, received the highly coveted "D-A Lubricant Mechanical Achievement" award for his work on the Dean Van Lines Special.

Andretti will take practice run tomorrow afternoon at Langhorne and then head for the Reading Fairgrounds for the Saturday night sprint car races. Sunday he will take time trials at 12:30 p.m. trying for a top starting spot in the 100-lap event which will get under way at 3:15 p.m.

An official dedication ceremony will be held prior to the start of the main event.

Racing Is 'Tough Racket' But Rookie Star Likes It

"The cars and equipment can all very easily go the 100-lap distance with no troubles and I expect the race to be a sprint from start to finish. . ."

This is how Mario Andretti, the pride and joy of Nazareth, described his feelings about the 100-mile championship race tomorrow at Langhorne.

Andretti has already driven on the one-mile, newly-paved track and said: "Its gonna be a hairy one. The race at Langhorne will be the most demanding one in the country. There is only one short straightaway and no two of the turns are the same.

Asked about his chances of finishing the season with USAC Championship point crown Mario replied: "I feel optimistic about it. We want to keep finishing and break into the winner's circle if we can. The equipment is good and is capable of many wins this summer."

Andretti, who still has the remains of heat and wind burns on his knuckles from the Indianapolis 500, said further that the biggest problem that he encountered so far this year in the Dean Van Lines Special was with insufficient ventilation in the cockpit.

He went on to describe the cockpit of the car during the 500 race as "a living hell." "My feet were burning up but there was nothing I could do. I could hardly stick my foot out into the air while going 150 miles an hour. I did stick my hand up in the air in the straightaway sometimes to try to cool it off but I still got blisters all over my hands."

Andretti finished third in the 500 and was named the top rookie driver.

Andretti, whose wife and family will watch him race Sunday at Langhorne, plans no special strategy for the race but said he will go all out from start to finish. He said his biggest competition would come from: "the regular boys. . .You can never count out Don Branson or Jim McElreath, and also Lloyd Ruby who has been running good."

Parnelli Jones is second in the point standings but will not be racing Sunday and Jimmy Clark, who is third in the point battle will also be out of the competition Sunday.

This leaves Gordon Johncock as Andretti's closest challenger although there aren't enough points in the offing to put Johncock in the lead should he win.

Andretti will also be in competition tonight at the Reading Fairgrounds where he will drive a sprint car and try to keep a high point standing in that branch of motor racing.

The young Italian said he "never had the desire to stay in stock car racing. I'm not knocking stock car racing but I always had my sights set on the top. Many people say that I came up too quick but I can remember going to a lot of races and not getting a ride and I also remember many very lean years. I may lack a certain little amount of experience but I take little chances and so far I have had good luck.

"It's a tough racket," he went on, "but I like it."

Chapter 6

Widening Horizons

In 1966 Mario drove fourteen different cars in fifty-one races. He won fourteen of those races driving four different cars, a phenomenal achievement. Few drivers in their entire careers have raced such a wide range of cars. Over the next few years Mario would establish himself as the most complete driver in the sport's history. The level of diversity across racing disciplines Mario attained during the late sixties simply doesn't exist today because contracts prohibit drivers from racing

Above: Though largely unchanged for 1966, the Hawk was fully developed and understood by Mario, Brawner, and McGee. Mario dominated practice and qualifying at Indianapolis, beating Jim Clark to the pole by two mph, only to have his engine blow early in the 500. Even so, he went on to win seven races with the Hawk and take his second straight USAC title. (Andretti collection) **Opposite:** Le Mans was the first of four races Mario drove for Ford's overpowering factory team in 1966 and '67. Mario is in the pits with his close friend and co-driver, Lucien Bianchi, in their GT40 Mk II. Bianchi would also be Mario's teammate at Daytona and Le Mans in 1967. (Joe Farkas)

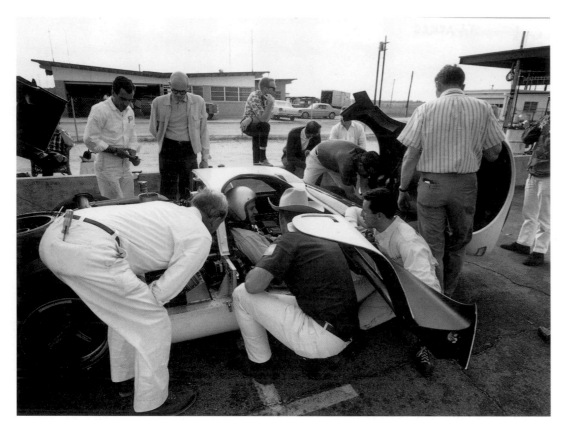

following week he was at Riverside, California, for the NASCAR Motor Trend 500 stock-car race, driving a Bill Stroppe Ford Fairlane. He started 25th and finished 16th after being involved in a crash with 31 laps remaining.

In February, Mario co-drove a NART Ferrari with Pedro Rodriguez to a fourth-place finish behind a trio of Ford Mk IIs in Daytona's 24-Hour race. The Ferrari was the only car to challenge the fleet of four factory Fords, beating one of them across the line. "It was my first real long-distance race," Mario says. "It gave me good experience in road racing, dealing with slow corners and handling the gearbox."

Three weeks later, on February 26, two days before his 26th birthday, Mario made his first start in the Daytona 500, driving Smokey Yunick's Chevrolet Chevelle.

"Smokey just called me—I was getting calls from everywhere with invitations to drive—and that was a joy to me because I had choices. It was very exciting to be invited to drive in these big events. But with Smokey it was almost a nightmare.

"That car was an unbelievable handful, but I didn't know any better. It had a good motor in it, but it didn't handle a damn! Donnie Allison took a look at the set-up and told me Smokey was way off. I only realized how bad that car was later when I got into the Holman-Moody Ford." The Daytona experience ended early in a multi-car crash.

The USAC Championship season opened three weeks after Daytona on March 20 at Phoenix, where Mario qualified the Dean Van Lines Brawner-Ford on the pole and set a new track record. In the race he came under intense pressure from archrival A. J. Foyt, and during a ferocious duel they side-swiped each other while lapping a slower car. The collision ended the race for both of them, although Foyt was able to limp along a little further. "I guess both of us were a little stupid," Mario says. "It was one of those racing accidents that happen when you're running hard like that. Nobody was to blame."

The following week, Mario flew to Sebring for the 12-Hour race held on March 26, again teaming with Pedro Rodriguez in the NART Ferrari they shared at Daytona. This time the Ferrari was plagued by mechanical trouble and, with about two hours left in the race, Mario was involved in a bizarre accident when his car went into a wild spin because of gearbox problems.

The Ferrari's wheels locked, and it spun off the track before coming back across

so many different cars and series. Top F1, CART, and NASCAR drivers are paid huge salaries, and their sponsorship agreements make it virtually impossible to drive for other teams in different categories.

At that time, however, Mario's growing relationships with Ferrari and Ford Motor Company helped him branch out into both long-distance sports cars and NASCAR stock cars, and his amazing 1966 schedule was essential fuel for his burgeoning career.

"From day one," Mario says, "I never wanted to be categorized as a stock-car driver or a midget driver or sprint-car driver. I didn't want people to say that was my specialty. I wanted to be versatile, an all-arounder.

"I used to particularly follow Dan Gurney and Foyt, because they were both into everything. They were the ones I looked up to. Even in those days, there were not that many drivers who ran a lot of different types of cars. Dan was the guy I really admired because he raced everything: Formula One, sports cars, stock cars, Indy cars. He really inspired me."

Mario's agreements for these drives were usually done with a handshake for forty per cent of the prize money. "I never really did a lot of negotiating. I thought everything would fall into place. That was not part of my worries."

Mario's remarkable season got under way on January 9, when he drove Bob Higman's Offy-powered midget on a one-time basis at an indoor race in Fort Wayne, Indiana. He was second in his heat and dropped out of the feature. The

Above: Mario raced a lot of sports cars in 1966. He co-drove this 4.4 liter V-12 Ferrari 365P2 with Pedro Rodriguez in the Daytona 24 Hours and Sebring 12 Hours. The pair finished fourth at Daytona behind a trio of factory Fords; at Sebring they were involved in a tragic accident with Don Wester's Porsche. (Harley Cluxton) **Opposite left:** In February, Mario drove Smokey Yunick's Chevelle in the Daytona 500. This was his only experience with the legendary car builder. "Smokey was so secretive," Mario explains. "He would not let me go in his shop. He would not let the mechanics open the hood any more than six inches, and he would not let me idle the car because he said it created carbon in the combustion chambers." (Andretti collection) **Opposite right:** Mario drove Bill Stroppe's Ford in his first NASCAR stock-car race at Riverside near the end of January, 1966. "I think I got into Gordon Johncock early in the race and bent the fender," he says. The race ended for him in a crash on the 154th of 185 laps. (Bob Tronolone)

the road into the path of Don Wester's Porsche 906. Mario recovered and went on, but Wester had to take evasive action and ran off the track, striking and killing four spectators who had wandered into a restricted area. Mario was able to drive his car to the pits, but it was withdrawn after a refueling fire.

"It was a bad first time at Sebring," Mario recalls. "I didn't know anything about what happened to Wester or the spectators until later. It was terrible."

The next day Mario was in Reading, Pennsylvania, to race Wally Meskowski's Wynn's sprint car for the first time. He had agreed to race USAC sprinters for Meskowski in 1966, teamed with Johnny Rutherford. This was the sixth of the fifteen different cars Mario would race before the year ended. Mario was fifth at Reading and finished seventh and eighth in the next two USAC sprint races, both at Eldora, Ohio, in April.

At the next USAC Championship race at Trenton on April 24, Mario was again on the pole with a new track record. He led more than half the race before cutting a tire on some debris. The pit stop to change the tire dropped him down in the field, but he had worked his way back to fourth before the race was stopped by rain.

Mario headed to Indianapolis next for the month of May. He dominated practice and qualifying and took his third straight pole of the year. He set a new record of 165.899 mph on his four-lap qualifying run and was challenged only by Jim Clark, who was almost two mph slower. No one else was even close. Foyt and Gurney were the fastest second-day qualifiers, so they were back on the seventh row.

The month seemed too good to be true and, sure enough, things turned sour on race day. First, there was a sensational accident at the start. As Mario and Clark accelerated away from the green flag, Mario's friend Billy Foster lost control when his car's nose cone fell off. The ensuing melee involved half the field, eliminating eleven of the thirty-three starters and resulting in a red flag for an hour and a half. Fortunately, nobody was seriously hurt.

When the race was finally restarted, Mario's engine was running on only seven cylinders. He was able to stay ahead of Clark and the rest for a handful of laps before the engine started smoking and he retired from the race.

"Some days the only place to stay is in bed—with the covers over your head," Mario wrote in his regular column in the next day's *Indianapolis Star*. "When I pushed down on the throttle it was just like putting my foot into a tub of Jell-O. You talk about surprises. I felt like General Custer standing there counting the Indians."

Mario's luck turned around at Milwaukee the next weekend as he took his fourth pole and track record in a row, then motored to the finish without any trouble to score his first win of 1966.

He repeated the trick—pole, new track record, and victory—at Langhorne the next weekend and did it again on the high-banked Atlanta superspeedway at the end of June. During this three-race span he led more than 500 consecutive laps, another record.

Mario's speed was helped by the fact that the fuel distribution problems that had unsettled the car in the previous season had been solved. "I had two electric pumps, and I could actually move the fuel around. I could run a 300-mile race without stopping, and the car had the same balance all the way. It was incredible."

Between Langhorne and Atlanta, Mario flew to France for his first crack at the Le Mans 24-Hour race. He had been added to Ford's roster of drivers after his

Top: At the off-season Group 7 race in Nassau, Mario ruined the nose of this Can-Am Lola fooling around before the race started. "I was doing doughnuts and I crashed the nose in the parking lot," he admits. "We didn't have another one." (Dave Friedman) Above: Mario flipped Ray Nichels's Dodge Charger in turn two at Mosport in a USAC stock-car race. Here he presses on through Moss corner, with the damage caused by the crash visible on the car's roof and rear quarter panel. (Dale Von Trebra) Right: In 1966 Al Dean produced this twenty-page brochure detailing the history of his race team. Photos and complete results of all the Dean Van Lines cars and drivers were provided, including Dean's first driver Bob Sweikert; Jimmy Bryan, who won three championships with the team in 1954, 1956, and 1957; and A. J. Foyt, who started his Champ car career driving for Dean in 1958 and 1959. (Andretti collection) Opposite: Ford's fleet of eight 7-liter Mk IIs and their driving teams line up in the pits at Le Mans. Although Mario and Bianchi dropped out with an engine problem, the Ford team finished one-two-three, with Bruce McLaren and Chris Amon winning narrowly from Ken Miles and Denny Hulme. (Joe Farkas)

The Dean Van Lines Special

Driver:
Mario Andretti
1965 USAC Driving Champion

Chief Mechanic:
Clint Brawner
1965 Mechanical Achievement Award

Owner:
A. E. Dean
1965 USAC Championship Car

Sponsor:
Dean Van Lines, Inc.
Long Beach, Calif. 90801

THE DEAN OF
AMERICAN MOVERS

A RECORD OF CHAMPIONSHIP COMPETITION
1953-1965

impressive performances at Daytona and Sebring in Chinetti's Ferrari. His inclusion in Ford's massive Le Mans effort was another step in his fast-developing career.

"It was a first-class program, put together really well, and I was with some of the best drivers of the day," Mario says. "Exposure to the top road racers was really what I was looking for. I needed to learn more about road-racing technique, hairpins in particular. There was also an extensive test program, and I don't think there was a single test I was not involved in. I loved that and needed that and got thousands of miles of seat time that was invaluable. I learned the discipline of taking care of the equipment. It was training I could not have received anyplace else, and I embraced it in the best possible way."

No fewer than thirteen Fords started at Le Mans in 1966. Eight of them were the new 7-liter Mk IIs; the other five were less powerful GT40s. Mario co-drove with Belgian ace Lucien Bianchi, but their car fell out on Saturday night because of a dropped valve. Only three of the Fords made the finish, all of them Mk IIs, but they came home one-two-three with New Zealanders Bruce McLaren and Chris Amon in the winning car.

Back in the States, Mario drove Cotton Owens's Dodge on July 4 in the Firecracker 400 at Daytona. He dropped out early because of a blown engine. Four days later in Marne, Michigan, he won a USAC midget race driving for Myron Caves. A string of sprint-car races followed, with the first of five wins for Meskowski coming at Cumberland, Maryland, at the end of July.

Mario had swept the pole position for the first six Champ car races of 1966, but Lloyd Ruby ended that streak at Indianapolis Raceway Park in July. There Mario qualified second and spun as he tried to pass Ruby on the start.

Indianapolis newspaperman Robin Miller was at IRP that day as a young fan. "Mario spun out on the first corner on the first lap and then came storming back through the field and beat everybody," Miller recalls. "There probably weren't 10,000 people there, but that's all they were talking about. You had the sense that this guy was something special because he had such bravado.

"I remember one time at Salem or Winchester he had a huge lead, and his crew was out on the straightaway screaming at him to slow down because he was way ahead. At that point in his career, there was no throttle control. It was wide open."

Next came Langhorne in August, the year's second Champ car race at the track. On

his first qualifying lap Mario set a new track record, but tried too hard on his second lap and crashed heavily. He was uninjured and was able to jump into Billy Foster's spare car for the race, getting up to seventh place before the engine burned a bearing.

"That was one time I was just a little too brave," Mario says. "I did a 29.07 on my first lap, and I was sure I could break twenty-nine seconds. I just drove it in too deep. I was lucky to get out of that one unhurt."

Two weeks later, at Springfield, Illinois, Mario drove Brawner's front-engine dirt car to second place behind Don Branson in the first of four dirt Championship races that year. At Milwaukee the following weekend, Mario again won from the pole in the rear-engine Brawner/Hawk, beating Gordon Johncock after a race-long battle. The next day, Mario was at Oswego, New York, where he won another USAC sprint-car race, and five days later, at the start of Labor Day weekend, he won again for Meskowski at Eldora, Ohio.

Mario failed to finish the USAC Championship dirt race the next day at DuQuoin, Illinois, but at the Indiana Fairgrounds five days later, on September 10, he won the Hoosier 100 Championship dirt car race and took the points lead from Johncock. Foyt was on the pole for the Hoosier 100 and led most of the way, but with three laps to go the Texan's brake pedal broke, allowing Mario through to win. Two weeks later Mario scored a dominant victory at Trenton in the Brawner/Hawk. He qualified on the pole and led all the way despite a few anxious moments

ILLUSTRATED SPEEDWAY NEWS

AUTO RACING'S LEADING PUBLICATION

Pictorial Section

ISSUE: AUG. 16, 1966

MARIO ANDRETTI AT THE WHEEL OF THE JIM ROBBINS SPECIAL LISTENS CLOSELY AS BILLY FOSTER EXPLAINS THE CONTROLS. AFTER SETTING A TRACK RECORD AT THE LANGHORNE, PA., ONE MILE SPEEDWAY, ANDRETTI CRASHED THE DEAN VAN LINES CAR AND DECIDED TO DRIVE THE ROBBINS CAR. HE STARTED 20TH AND WORKED UP TO SIXTH SPOT UNTIL MECHANICAL PROBLEMS FORCED HIM OUT ON THE 34TH LAP.—C & R PHOTO.

This clipping from Mario's scrapbook shows him with his close friend and fellow racer, Billy Foster (left). Together they bought a Can-Am McLaren in 1966 and Foster drove it in a few races. The caption explains how Foster gave Mario his car to use after he had crashed his Brawner-Hawk in qualifying at Langhorne. Previous pages: A USAC drivers' meeting was an informal affair in 1966. Jim McElreath is in the foreground, with Mario in the middle, wearing sunglasses. Next to him is Bobby Unser (who has a cigarette in his hand). Al Unser is on the other side of Bobby. (Andretti collection)

when he ran out of fuel and had to pit with eight laps remaining.

At the California State Fairgrounds in Sacramento on October 23, Mario drove Brawner's Offy-powered dirt car and led most of the way only to have his transmission fail with four laps to go. He was classified in tenth place, but collected enough points to wrap up his second USAC title. With only one race remaining, it would be impossible for either Jim McElreath or Johncock to beat him.

Mario finished the year with a pair of wins in Phoenix. On November 20, he drove the Brawner/Hawk to victory in the season's final USAC Championship race at the one-mile Phoenix International Raceway after a serious duel with Parnelli Jones. Seven days later, he won the season-closing USAC sprint race on the half-mile Manzanita dirt track in Meskowski's Chevy-powered sprinter.

It had been a remarkable season for Mario. He was the USAC champion for the second year in a row. He finished second to Roger McCluskey in USAC's sprint-car series and had begun to make his mark in both long-distance sports-car racing and NASCAR and USAC stock-car racing. At the end of the year at Ford Motor Company's annual motorsports dinner, Mario was presented with the Ford Award for the Ford-affiliated person who had done the most for racing that season.

"I was having a great time from a satisfaction standpoint," Mario says. "I felt like I was expanding my knowledge and my horizons at the same time. I was learn-

ing more about what makes things tick."

At the end of the year Mario was vigorously recruited by Goodyear with a tempting offer. Goodyear had entered the sport in 1964 and already had lured Foyt and other top stars away from Firestone.

"At the end of 1965," Mario says, "Bill McCrary of Firestone handed me a check for $100,000 and said, 'This is for doing the job for us.' He didn't say this was a contract for next year or anything. He just gave me $100,000 as a bonus. So I felt indebted, but I didn't have a contract with Firestone.

"Then about January of 1966 I got a call from Larry Truesdale at Goodyear, and he said Goodyear was prepared to give me a three-year contract for $250,000 a year. I went to Dee Ann and said, 'Holy mackerel, what do we do?' Three quarters of a million dollars you couldn't fathom in those days. I said to Dee Ann, 'Whatever happens out of this, we're OK. We have some stability now.' She agreed, and she left it up to me and my manager, Chuck Barnes. So I called Chuck, and we went to Akron together. We were picked up at the airport by the Goodyear limousine, and we went into Goodyear first, and they confirmed their commitment to me. We said we have an obligation to go to Firestone because we've been with them so long. Then we went to Firestone in the Goodyear limousine."

Firestone countered with a four-year offer at $200,000 per year. "We felt like we could not negotiate. We felt we owed a loyalty to Firestone. So we went back to Goodyear and said we couldn't go through with it, and they were very gracious. After that Firestone was totally committed because they had a huge investment in me."

Above: A dropped valve early in the race ended Mario's run at Le Mans with Lucien Bianchi. Although only three of the 13 cars fielded by Ford made the finish, those three won the prestigious event in a resounding one-two-three sweep. (Dave Friedman) Left: In the last two Can-Am races of 1966 at Riverside and Las Vegas, Mario rounded out his remarkable year by driving this Mecom Lola T70 powered by a Ford four-cam engine. He was an early DNF in both races. (Bob Tronolone)

Chapter 7

Winning NASCAR's Biggest Prize

Becoming a peerless road racer and competing on
the international Grand Prix circuit remained a
deeply rooted goal for Mario, and to that end he was
eager to hone his road-racing skills. Being part of
Ford's sports-car program at the end of 1966 provided the perfect learning environment. As with his
1966 drives outside of the Dean team, Mario had no
formal contract. "I felt that I was contracted because Ford was supplying engines for the Indy car.

Opposite: Mario savors his startling Daytona 500 win in victory lane with the trophy
girls, Miss USA and Miss Firebird. Chris Economaki stands by, ready to conduct the
post-race interview for ABC's *Wide World of Sports.* (Bruce Craig collection)
Above: In 1967 Mario drove in seven USAC stock-car races with Bill Stroppe's
Daytona 500-winning Holman-Moody Ford. He's pictured here on the Mid-America
Raceways road course in Wentzville, Missouri, where he qualified second but encountered trouble in the race. (Dave Friedman)

But there was never a proper, let's-sit-down-and-negotiate contract."

To prepare for the 1967 Daytona 24 Hours and Sebring 12 Hours, Mario and Bruce McLaren worked closely during the winter as part of Ford's exhaustive sports-car testing program. McLaren was considered to be one of the sharpest technical drivers in the business. He had been the lead driver for the Cooper Formula One team from 1962-65, then started building and racing his own F1 and Can-Am cars.

Ford's effort operated at an intensity that was otherwise unknown in those days. The team completed a couple of twenty-four hour simulation runs at Daytona, which gave Mario plenty of seat time. "Between stints, they'd say, 'Go back to the room, and get some sleep.' But I never would. I would stay right there watching, absorbing like a sponge.

"Doing all that testing for Ford and co-driving with Bruce was perfect for me. It gave me the knowledge and the opportunity to really work on my skills as a road racer, and I was beginning to feel very confident in my road-racing abilities. Bruce was probably my best mentor, without his even realizing it. I knew he wasn't the quickest guy in the world, but he was very technical. I thought I was quicker than him, but what I needed to learn was how to negotiate hairpins and slow corners."

Mario spent plenty of time studying McLaren's technique during testing. "I would go out to the corners and watch his apexes, where he'd pick up power and where he was shifting. That taught me more than anything."

As the 1967 season began, Mario's good friend Billy Foster was killed in a crash during qualifying for the NASCAR race at Riverside on January 30. One of Foster's brake drums exploded as he entered the fastest turn on the course. His car hit the concrete wall at almost full speed.

In the qualifying line immediately before Foster's death, the two drivers had needled each other as usual. Ironically, Foster told Mario he was crazy to keep racing sprint cars when he had achieved so much success in Championship cars. Sprint cars, Foster said, were just too damn dangerous. "You should stay away from them," he told Mario. Minutes later, Foster was dead.

The sixties was a decade of terrible casualties for racing drivers in all categories and formulas. For Mario and Dee Ann, Foster's death emphasized the reality that at any time Mario could be killed. "In the beginning I was very naive," Dee Ann recalls, "and I got friendly with this person and that person. But later on I stayed away from people because we lost so many friends. I'd look around and say, 'Who's going to be missing from our community?'"

"You have no idea how fortunate I feel I've been," Mario says. "Foyt, the Unsers, and I were spared big time. It could have gone the other way so easily for any of us in a couple of different situations. In those days, a driver would never say, 'Oh, this isn't safe.' Anybody in the business would look at him like he was crazy. It took a little while for everyone to accept safety."

One week after Foster's death, Mario was back in Daytona for the 24 Hours. After qualifying his Ford Mk II fifth, he dropped out of the race early because of clutch failure. All six Fords suffered transmission problems, which enabled Ferrari to score a one-two-three sweep with its factory cars. After all the testing and preparation, Ford's racing department was deeply chastened by the loss.

The next event was the Daytona 500 in which Mario drove a Bill Stroppe Ford run by Holman-Moody. Mario didn't like a car with the understeering characteristics preferred by NASCAR drivers, and he flew in the face of accepted practice by setting up his Ford with an extremely soft anti-roll bar to make it oversteer.

"None of them would dare run a very light bar because they were afraid the car would get too loose," Mario says. "We put the smallest bar they had on my car. In fact, I think we had to get it made. We put it on, and the car hooked up like crazy. Donnie Allison and some of the other NASCAR regulars told us to throw away that little bar, but it worked for me."

After qualifying an unspectacular twelfth, Mario took the lead for the first time on the 21st of 200 laps, and right away it became obvious to everyone in the packed grandstands that he would be hard to beat. It wasn't what the largely southern crowd had paid to see.

Above: Hoping to tip the race to NASCAR regular Fred Lorenzen, Ford's NASCAR crew held up Mario's car on the jacks. Lorenzen beat Mario out of the pits and assumed the lead. (ISC Archives) Opposite: Closing in on a stunning victory in the 1967 Daytona 500, Mario chases Richard Petty's Dodge (43) and Cale Yarborough's Ford (21). Hard on Mario's tail is Dick Hutcherson (29). Mario used an unconventional suspension set-up and driving style to win the race. (Joe Farkas)

Above: The Chaparral 2F driven by Jim Hall and Mike Spence posed the greatest challenge at Sebring, setting the fastest lap with Spence at the wheel. Here the Andretti/McLaren Ford Mk IV has passed the Chaparral, which has just suffered a blown engine. (Joe Farkas) **Opposite above:** Mario's Ford Mk II exits the International Horseshoe at Daytona during the 1967 24-hour race. All six Fords ran into transmission or drivetrain troubles and were routed by Ferrari, which swept the first three places. (Dave Friedman) **Opposite below:** The driveline failures in the Daytona 24 Hours prompted Ford to introduce the new Mk IV for Sebring in March, ahead of schedule. Mario and Bruce McLaren drove the new car to an impressive debut victory. It was Mario's first long-distance sports-car win—and also one of his toughest. (Dave Friedman)

Mario's racing line used all the track, diving down to an apex and letting the car slide, tail out, up the banking on the exit of the corners. The NASCAR drivers thought he was crazy. Chris Economaki was ABC's pit reporter that day, and he remembers it well. "Mario put his left front wheel practically on the apron going into the corner and the right rear wheel was almost brushing the wall on the exit," Economaki says. "He was powering clear across the track, twice a lap. It was incredible! Nobody would run with him. They said, 'Look at him. He's going to lose it. He'll never make 200 laps,' but he did it, comfortably in the end."

David Pearson was the only driver who was able to match Mario's pace, but even he found it difficult to draft Mario because of Mario's unique line. Just after the halfway point, Pearson suffered a blown engine, leaving Mario on his own.

Mario's teammate was NASCAR regular Fred Lorenzen, whose speed and movie-star good looks brought a glamorous new style to the circuit. Lorenzen appeared to be the man Ford officials and most people in the grandstands wanted to win that day. This became clear to Mario during his final pit stop.

"I was leading and came into the pits first," Mario says. "Lorenzen came in and pulled into his pit stall right in front of me. I sat there up in the air, and my crew didn't release my jack until he had accelerated totally clear of the pits! It was never really confirmed, and I can't point fingers, but they made sure Lorenzen went out first from the last stops."

By the time Mario hit the ground he was seven seconds behind, but he quickly caught and passed Lorenzen for the lead on the 168th of 200 laps. Passing Lorenzen was one thing, but getting away from him was something else. "Lorenzen was the master of the draft," Mario says. "He latched onto me, and it took me a little while to figure out a way to break away from him." With twelve laps to go, Mario and Lorenzen came up to lap Tiny Lund's car. Lund waved Mario by on the outside, but Mario instead dove to the bottom of the track and passed Lund on the inside. Lorenzen went high and lost contact with Mario and any chance of making a last-lap slingshot pass.

When a caution flag came out with just two laps to go, Mario held a half-lap lead. He cruised home a delighted winner. "The way that race unfolded, having to catch and pass Lorenzen, was important in putting a premium on that victory and my performance that day."

Mario's Daytona 500 victory was a classic in motor racing history, but it didn't sit well with many hardcore NASCAR fans. Stock-car racing in those days was a southern sport, devoid of Yankees or foreigners. An Italian-born, open-wheel racer was about as far away as possible from the NASCAR ideal, and the feelings of many in the South at the time were reflected in a satirical column titled "All Dixie Mourns Andretti's Win."

For the 12 Hours of Sebring in March, Ford rushed to introduce its new Ford Mk IV, hoping to avenge its loss to Ferrari in the Daytona 24 Hours. It was a gamble, but the new car ran faultlessly in Mario and McLaren's hands. It was a hot, windy weekend, and paper and debris clogged the Ford's air intakes, making the cockpit brutally uncomfortable.

"Between stints, I would just about get myself ready to drive again. I spent half the time in the trailer with the shower trickling over my head. That was probably the most physical race I had in my life. If you look at some of the photos in victory lane, my eyes were sunk in my head about an inch. I was really spent."

Mario and McLaren led almost all the way to beat teammates A. J. Foyt and Lloyd Ruby by twelve laps after the second-place Chaparral 2F, shared by Chaparral builder Jim Hall and Englishman Mike Spence, dropped out. "We fought hard with the Chaparral and, luckily, the Chaparral blew its engine, but we were in front of them when they blew. That was a good win and a hard-fought race."

The USAC Championship season got underway the following weekend in Phoenix. During practice Mario crashed heavily in the Brawner/Hawk, and without a back-up car he appeared to be through for the weekend. He got a brief reprieve from his friend Lucien Bianchi, who was making his USAC debut at Phoenix. Bianchi loaned his own car to a grateful Mario—who crashed on his qualifying run when the suspension collapsed.

Three weeks later at Trenton, Mario led from the pole to score a virtually unchallenged win. The Trenton victory put Mario in a confident frame of mind for the month of May at Indianapolis where, once again, Mario and Brawner's team believed it was ready to win and, once again, Mario proved himself the man to beat as the month unfolded. For the second year in a row he was on the pole with a new track record, pushing the mark up to 168.982 mph.

Above: Mario was on the pole for the second year in a row at Indianapolis, and set another new track record. Inspired by Jim Hall's Chaparral Can-Am and sports cars, McGee and Mario added chin spoilers to the Hawk's nose. "That was the first time anyone put any kind of aerodynamic device on a single-seater," Mario notes. (Joe Farkas) Opposite: Raymond Firestone, chairman of Firestone, presents Mario with his pole awards at the 1967 Indy 500 drivers' meeting. Arguably the greatest race on the international racing calendar, the Indy 500 drew an eclectic mix of drivers. Two-time F1 world champion Jim Clark (in jacket and tie) is to the extreme left behind Mario. Next to him is USAC's Johnny Rutherford, with NASCAR's Cale Yarborough seated behind him. Beside Yarborough are USAC's Carl Williams, NASCAR's LeeRoy Yarbrough, and F1 superstars Jackie Stewart and Jochen Rindt. Partially obscured by the microphone is Graham Hill. (Andretti collection)

But lurking on the outside of the second row was Parnelli Jones in Andy Granatelli's STP turbine known as "Silent Sam" or the "Wooshmobile." The car's General Electric turbine engine was bizarrely quiet, thus its nickname, and immediately proved to be more powerful and more efficient than the much lower-revving conventional, multi-piston V-8 and four-cylinder engines used by everyone else.

Jones qualified the turbine at 166.075 mph, but Mario reckoned the turbine could run all day at that speed. Mario knew that with the reduced nitro content in his race fuel mixture, compared to his qualifying mixture, he would be at least five or six mph slower in the race. He was not alone in his misgivings. All the drivers were grumbling before the race that the turbine would make their cars obsolete if it wasn't restricted.

Indeed, Jones and the turbine dominated the race while Mario was almost immediately in trouble. His clutch was slipping, and after fading down the field, he had to pull into the pits, which was where he was sitting when rain stopped the race. It kept raining, so the conclusion of the race was postponed until the following day.

This gave Clint Brawner and Jim McGee a chance to fix their car, and Mario took the restart from the back, six laps behind the leaders. For a while he put on a good show, but then he felt a vibration, heard a whirring sound, and slowed just in time to watch his right front wheel part company with the car. That brought an end to another frustrating month in Indianapolis, though his instincts and rapid reactions had prevented a bad accident. Meanwhile, Jones's turbine was four laps away from scoring a crushing victory when a bearing in his gearbox broke, which handed Foyt a lucky win.

Things didn't improve for Mario at Milwaukee a few days later. He crashed during practice while trying to avoid Carl Williams's car, which had lost a wheel. The Hawk was too badly damaged to qualify, so Mario had to miss a race for the second time in four events.

Mario then flew to France for the Le Mans 24 Hours, where he again teamed with Lucien Bianchi in one of the fleet of Mk IV Fords. Bianchi and Mario had become good friends, and whenever Mario and Dee Ann were in Europe they used to visit him at his home in Belgium. At Le Mans that year, Mario and Bianchi fought for the lead in the early stages with the other leading Fords, a pair of Ferraris, and a lone Chaparral.

"That could have been a pretty interesting second, for sure, and maybe first, because I was so much quicker than Foyt," Mario says. "I busted my ass putting time between us because Lucien would go against [Foyt's teammate] Gurney, and

Top right: Ford's impressive phalanx of Mk IIs and Mk IVs line up in the pit lane prior to the start of the Le Mans 24 Hour race. The winning Mk IV of Dan Gurney and A. J. Foyt is in the foreground. This would be Ford's final appearance at Le Mans. (Joe Farkas)

Bottom right: At Le Mans Mario again co-drove with Lucien Bianchi in a Ford Mk IV. Here Mario chases eventual winner A. J. Foyt through the esses approaching Tertre Rouge as dusk approaches. Later in the race, Mario had a massive accident at that corner because of improperly installed brake pads. (Joe Farkas)

Opposite: Mario drove A. J. Watson's new, four-cam Ford-powered sprint car in three USAC sprint car races in July, two at Oswego, New York, and one at Eldora, Ohio. He won both races on the fast, paved Oswego Speedway in the car's debut, and was fifth on the dirt at Eldora. (Bruce Craig collection)

Dan would be quicker than Lucien, but I was miles quicker than Foyt. I had a stint in the wet against Foyt, and I put a lap and a half on him."

For a while, Mario and Bianchi were right there with eventual winners Gurney and Foyt, but they ran into brake problems. The Mk IV Fords were equipped with beryllium brake discs that would warp under heavy use. Mario had discovered in testing that the brakes wouldn't deteriorate beyond a certain point, and with judicious use the discs would go the distance.

"I knew about the problems we had with the brakes, which was easy to deal with, but Lucien didn't. He wasn't part of the test program so this vibration bothered him, but you just had to deal with it. The Mulsanne Straight [section of the course] would totally cool down the brakes."

Nevertheless, Bianchi came into the pits early in one of his stints to ask for a change of brake pads. Seeing this, Mario insisted on getting back into the car, and Bianchi readily acceded. With eighty gallons of fuel on board, Mario charged back onto the track. "I was going over the hill just before the Dunlop Bridge," Mario recalls, "and I downshifted and braked, and the car just turned right. It was so heavy with a full load of fuel—there was so much weight on the wheels—it just jerked the wheel right out of my hands. It turned right, head-on into the wall." He later learned that the right front brake pads had been installed backwards.

The car bounced back onto the track and triggered a multiple accident as two more Fords spun to try to avoid clouting Mario's crashed car, including one driven by Roger McCluskey. Luckily, everyone scrambled out, and there was no fire, but Mario had suffered a couple of broken ribs and badly bruised shoulders from his shoulder and chest harness.

McCluskey jumped out of his crashed Ford and ran to Mario's aid. Ford's racing bosses had told their drivers that in the event of an accident they should avoid any French doctors and wait for the team's American doctor to arrive. In a virtual "Keystone Kops" routine, McCluskey threw the ambulance's keys into the woods and carried Mario away from the French medics until Ford's doctor was located.

Broken ribs or not, Mario had two races scheduled the following weekend. There was a USAC stock-car race at Mosport, Canada, on Saturday and a Champ car race at Langhorne the next day, and he fully intended to compete in both. In practice at Mosport, Jim Hurtubise's car blew an engine directly in front of Mario, who spun on the oil and crashed hard. The race was rained out, and Mario received some medical attention.

The promoters at Mosport, Doc and Charlotte Feinberg, took Mario to the Toronto Maple Leafs' physiotherapist, who taped Mario's torso. From there Mario headed to Langhorne for Sunday's Champ car race. "At Langhorne during the race it was so hot," Mario says, "and all this tape came loose, and I felt like my whole inside was falling out."

Mario hung on to finish third behind Ruby and Al Unser, but it was a tough few weeks. Some friends suggested that maybe Mario should sit out a few races and allow himself to heal properly. But the thought never entered his mind. "There was no way I was going to lay around, feeling sorry for myself. I wasn't hurt that badly, but I was seriously sore for a few weeks."

The next weekend, on June 25, Mario was at Pike's Peak for another career first. From 1965-69, the Colorado mountain climb was a race on the USAC Championship car circuit, and Mario took his first run up the hill that summer in a Chevy-powered 1962 Lotus 24 F1 car owned and operated by his friend Bobby Unser. On race day, the car's front suspension broke, but Mario nursed the Lotus to the top and finished fourteenth.

His string of bad luck continued through a pair of soaking-wet Champ car races at Mosport the following weekend, the Firecracker 400 NASCAR race at Daytona on July 4, and a USAC stock-car race at Milwaukee. At Mosport he spun out of the first race, then came from the back of the field to finish eleventh in the rain-shortened second race. He failed to finish at Daytona and was fourth at Milwaukee. At the Daytona and Milwaukee stock-car races, he was a victim of mechanical failures.

Mario's disappointing season began to turn around with a pair of victories in A. J. Watson's new four-cam Ford-powered USAC sprint car at Oswego, New York, on July 16. The next weekend Mario won the Indianapolis Raceway Park USAC Championship race for the third year in a row, then won the first of two heats in the postponed USAC stock-car race at Mosport the next week. "When I crossed the finish line at Mosport, I felt something break loose," he says. "Just like that, I felt the pendulum swing the other way. My luck had changed."

Following his Mosport stock-car win, Mario scored Champ car victories at Langhorne at the end of July and in early August at the St. Jovite, Quebec, road course, where he won two separate 100-mile races. At Springfield, Illinois, the next weekend for the first dirt Champ car race of the year, he finished second to Foyt, then won on the pavement at Milwaukee the next day in the Hawk. Championship leader Foyt finished ninth.

In September, Mario finished second to Foyt on the dirt at DuQuoin, Illinois, then beat him in the Hoosier 100 a week later at the Indiana State Fairgrounds. Mario's Hoosier 100 victory pulled him within sixty points of Foyt. Back in their rear-engine cars at Trenton, Mario and Foyt qualified one-two, but Mario crashed while battling with Lloyd Ruby. Although Foyt spun to avoid hitting them, he recovered and went on to win.

"That was quite a year," Mario says. "Both Foyt and I had our ups and downs, and so did the Unsers. We were all capable of running up front at almost every race, but none of us could really put together a string of strong finishes."

Foyt won again on the dirt at Sacramento on October 1 with Mario second, but neither scored any points three weeks later at the Hanford, California, paved oval. Mario then won the penultimate race at Phoenix on November 19, pulling within 340 points of Foyt. While Mario beat Al and Bobby Unser across the line at Phoenix,

Foyt crashed after colliding with Jerry Grant's car.

The season closer was on the road course at Riverside, and although the place held bad memories for Mario after Foster's death there ten months earlier, he ran at the front, battling for the lead with Gurney. Foyt's car was knocked out of the race when he collided with a spinning Al Miller, but Goodyear desperately wanted its man to beat Firestone-sponsored Mario to the title, and had worked out a deal for Foyt to take over McCluskey's car if he encountered trouble.

McCluskey obliged, and Foyt was able to salvage fifth place. For a while it looked like Mario was home free, but he had to stop for fuel while leading with just four laps to go and fell to third. Foyt won the championship by 80 points, 3,440 to Mario's 3,360. "When I ran out of fuel, it just killed me. I had the championship in my hands, and then it was gone," Mario recalls.

Nonetheless, a panel of twelve top motorsports writers named Mario "Driver of the Year." He earned more votes than Foyt, who had won the Indy 500 and Le Mans, as well as the USAC Championship, and NASCAR champion Richard Petty, who had won a record twenty-seven stock-car races, including ten in a row.

"It's funny," Mario says. "I won 'Driver of the Year,' which was a tremendous accolade, but that wasn't a year I felt good about. Billy Foster had been killed, Indy turned into a disaster, and I lost the championship at the last minute. I always said, you can have 1967. I just wanted to move on."

There was more unhappiness in December, when Al Dean passed away after a long battle with cancer. Dean had been a friend and mentor for Mario, as well as his boss, and Dean always said he wanted the race team to continue after his death. But when the lawyers went through his will they discovered Dean had changed his mind and decided to sell the team.

Mario, Brawner, and McGee sat down and discussed what to do, and in the end Mario determined to dig deep into his pockets and buy the operation. In 1968, he would be an owner/driver. "I really didn't want to do it," Mario says. "But it was the only solution. There were no other teams that appealed to me, and I wanted to continue working with Clint and McGee because I believed they were the best."

Top left: The Honker Can-Am car was a Ford project built by Holman-Moody, which Mario drove in three 1967 Can-Am races. The car required a tremendous amount of work in many areas. Here the Holman-Moody mechanics modify the windscreen with a heat gun and a pliers clamp in an attempt to reduce wind buffeting around Mario's head. (Pete Lyons)

Bottom left: Mario and the Honker in action at Bridgehampton. "That was probably the worst car I ever drove," he says. "There was nothing about it that was right." After his first discouraging run in the car Mario suggested to sponsor Paul Newman that they switch roles—put Mario's name on the car's nose and have Newman drive it. (Pete Lyons) **Opposite:** Accompanied by Dee Ann and Michael, Mario attends a May, 1967 fan appreciation dinner in Bethlehem, Pennsylvania. At four and a half, Michael is already a seasoned racing fan. (Andretti collection)

Chapter 8

The Reluctant Team Owner

Mario's regimen underwent a big change for 1968, largely because he became a reluctant team owner. "I was paying the bills, and the whole program came together late because of Al Dean's death," Mario says. "We were behind the eight ball from the start." That he was able to step up to the task at age 28 after only four years in Champ cars was a stunning testament to how far Mario had come—both personally and financially—in the dozen years he had

Opposite: Aboard the turbo Offy-powered Hawk at Hanford in November, Mario qualified second and finished third behind A. J. Foyt and Bobby Unser. With two races to go at Phoenix and Riverside, Mario led his friend Unser by a slender thirty-nine points in the USAC Championship. (Bob Tronolone) **Above:** The new turbocharged four-cam Ford engine would take a lot of development before it worked effectively or achieved a basic level of reliability. Here Mario proudly displays the new engine in the back of his Lotus-based car. The 1968 season was Mario's first and only year as a team owner, and the car was sponsored by Overseas National Airways. (Joe Farkas)

lived in the United States. To make traveling more efficient, he bought his first airplane, a Piper Navajo.

It was a challenging time to become a team owner. Since the arrival of the rear-engine car in 1963, a multi-faceted technological revolution had swept through USAC Championship racing. After decades of stability, the cars changed dramatically between 1963 and 1970. There were major developments in tire design, spurred by a tire war between Goodyear and Firestone. Ford's challenge to Offenhauser introduced turbocharging, and with it came massive increases in horsepower. During the same period, wings, aerodynamics, and a new god named Downforce arrived on the scene. Lap speeds began to climb at an astonishing rate.

Two further significant developments appeared: turbine engines in 1967 and four-wheel drive in 1968. USAC attempted to control the spiraling rise of new technology by reducing the turbine's air inlet diameter from 20 inches in 1967 to 15.999 inches in 1968 and 10 inches for the 1969 season. USAC banned four-wheel drive outright at the end of 1969.

A profound change also had taken place in the forums in which USAC performed. Dirt-track racing, usually on one-mile state fairground tracks, had been the staple of the USAC Championship series and had comprised more than half the schedule, but that began to change as some dirt tracks were paved and a handful of new paved ovals were built. USAC also had begun to reintroduce road racing to the Champ car schedule in 1965. During the next few years the number of races rapidly ballooned from the customary twelve or thirteen races per season to eighteen in 1965, twenty-one in 1967, and twenty-eight in 1968. No fewer than six road courses were on the 1968 schedule, and three of these were two-race events, making nine of twenty-eight races on road circuits.

Costs soared because there were more races to run, and teams now needed a speedway car, a dirt car, and a road-racing car. If a team wished to remain competitive, it had to buy or build new equipment every year.

Ford had decided to pull out of long-distance racing after winning Le Mans with Dan Gurney and A. J. Foyt in 1967. Consequently, Mario drove only one sports-car race in 1968, the Daytona 24 Hours in an Alfa Romeo T33. He also ran just three stock-car races, all in NASCAR, and without any success.

The expanded Champ car schedule was another factor in Mario's revised pro-gram. With so many races and so much responsibility, he had to focus almost entirely on Champ cars in 1968 to the complete exclusion of sprint cars for the first time in five years.

Finding sponsorship was one of the new duties Mario faced for 1968. With the help of Chuck Barnes, he signed Overseas National Airways, an executive charter jet service based at New York's Kennedy Airport. ONA paid Mario $150,000 to sponsor his team that year. "The Overseas Airways sponsorship covered the incidentals. It was the icing on the cake for us. Firestone's support was ninety per cent. It was almost everything we needed."

Meanwhile, Clint Brawner and Jim McGee were busy building new cars to accept the new and much more powerful turbocharged Ford engine. Ace sheet-metal specialists Eddie Kuzma and Wayne Ewing built two new monocoque Hawk chassis. "We had Kuzma build a skinny, Lotus-type tub with all the Brabham pick-up points on it," McGee says. "We used the Brabham suspension, uprights, and hubs."

Mario also bought a Lotus 38, one of three "Soft Alloy Specials" chassis built for Lotus in 1966 by subcontractor Abbey Panels. "That car never had a good feel," Mario recalls. "When we first ran it with the big suspension offset, I said, 'There's no way I can hustle this thing. Jim Clark must have been a magician.' "

Ford's new turbo engine wouldn't be ready until Indianapolis, so Mario raced a Hawk with a naturally aspirated Ford in the first four races. He didn't finish in two, but was second in the other two and qualified among the top three in all four, taking the pole at Trenton. But Bobby Unser won three straight races prior to Indianapolis, the last two with a turbo Offy engine.

The new Lotus turbines made their debut at Indianapolis. Colin Chapman had designed a stunning, wedge-shaped 4WD car called the Lotus 56 for STP sponsor Andy Granatelli's turbine. Jim Clark first tested the car at the Speedway in March with promising results. But, tragically, Clark was killed in a Formula Two Lotus at Hockenheim, Germany, in April. Clark's death was a huge blow to the sport and to Lotus boss Colin Chapman, who had formed a

Chased by a small pack of paparazzi, Mario arrives at Monza in August to test the high-winged Lotus 49B in preparation for the following month's Italian Grand Prix. He was delighted to discover that the 49B suited his driving style perfectly. But because FIA rules forbade competing in two events within a 24-hour period, he was not allowed to start the race. (Andretti collection)

close bond with the quiet Scotsman during their eight-year partnership.

Englishman Mike Spence, who had been Clark's Lotus F1 teammate from the end of 1963 through 1966, took over the unenviable task of trying to fill the great Clark's shoes. An excellent driver, Spence quickly settled in at Indianapolis and was lapping as fast as anyone, only to lose control and crash hard. On impact the right front wheel came back, hit Spence in the face, and killed

him. Spence's death came exactly one month after Clark was killed. Chapman left for England, insisting he no longer had the stomach for racing, although he would return for qualifying and the race.

Meanwhile, Granatelli cajoled Mario into taking a few laps in the Lotus 56. Mario was impressed. He ran easily at 168 mph, substantially faster than he had run in his own car, and found the turbine a pleasure to drive. Granatelli urged Mario to give up his car and race a turbine, but Mario wouldn't do it. "I had too much invested in my own program," Mario says, "and everyone was working their tails off, trying to get my car going. There was no way I was going to walk away from Brawner and McGee or from the guys at Overseas Airways. They'd put their faith and money behind me, and I had to stay with it."

The original version of the turbo Ford churned out almost 800 horsepower, but it was barely controllable—all top-end power and no torque. Regulating the turbocharger and wastegates also proved difficult. These problems continued in qualifying. Then, on the morning of pole day, Mario's engine blew.

Removing and reinstalling the complicated turbo Ford normally took the best part of a day, but Brawner and McGee got the job done in two-and-a-half hours. Mario went out and produced the fourth-best time of day despite his engine developing a heavy oil leak on his fourth and last lap.

Joe Leonard won the pole in a Lotus turbine with 1966 winner Graham Hill starting beside him in another Lotus turbine. Championship leader Bobby Unser was on the outside of the front row in his turbo Offy-powered Eagle.

At the start, Leonard took the lead, with Unser beating Hill into the first turn. Mario passed Hill in the first turn and was taking a run at Unser going down the backstretch when he realized his engine wouldn't last the opening lap, let alone 500 miles. "The thing fried itself going into turn three because the wastegate had stuck. I saw the pressure going up and up. It almost went right off the gauge."

Sprint-car ace Larry Dickson put Mario's backup car in the field on the final day of qualifying and agreed to hand the car over to Mario if necessary. But the engine in the second car was equally unhealthy, and after a handful of laps Mario pulled into the pits with a burned piston.

"That was one year too soon for the turbocharged Ford," Mario says. "The engine was certainly not ready to race. I was compelled to go with it; otherwise Ford would have pulled their support. I should have had an Offy in there. If I had, I would have blown them all away, Bobby included, because that Eagle was no match for our car."

Unser went on to earn his first Indy 500 victory and his fourth consecutive win of the year after Leonard's turbine suffered a broken fuel pump while leading with just nine laps to go.

At Milwaukee the next weekend, Mario raced the proven, naturally aspirated Ford and did so in most of the remaining races that year. He was second at Milwaukee and second again in both 100-mile races at Mosport the following weekend.

Above: The 1967 Lotus-based car Mario ran at Indianapolis in 1968 was powered by the new turbocharged four-cam Ford. "That was not a good car," he explains. "Aerodynamically, it made lift instead of downforce. They took a Lotus tub and copied it, but it was too flexible." After Indy, Mario abandoned the car and engine, reverting to a Hawk with a normally aspirated Ford engine for most other races in '68. (Bob Tronolone) Opposite: Mario drove one of his Hawks at Pike's Peak in 1968. The car's ride height was raised and it was fitted with dirt-track tires. Here he negotiates "The Ws" high above the tree line on his way to fourth place. This was the second of three times he ran Pike's Peak. (Andretti collection)

Top: Mario qualified fastest and finished fourth in the last of four late-season Championship dirt car races at the California State Fairgrounds in Sacramento at the end of September. Here, he battles furiously with Bud Tingelstad, Bill Vukovich, and Gary Bettenhausen. (Bob Tronolone) **Middle:** Mario drove George Bignotti's Indy Ford-powered Lola T70 in the Bridgehampton and Elkhart Lake Can-Am races in 1968. "We had a smaller engine than the Chevrolet people—McLaren and Hall—but Mario drove the hell out of it," Bignotti says. "He'd pass them all in the corner and they'd blow him off down the straightaways. We weren't too successful, but we had a good time." Mario qualified seventh in both races but failed to finish either one. (Pete Biro) **Bottom:** Mario had another one-off Can-Am drive, this time in a Lola T160 at Stardust Raceway in Las Vegas. He qualified fifth and struggled home twelfth, many laps behind. (Bob Tronolone) **Opposite:** Yet another combination Mario raced in 1968 was this turbo Offy-powered Hawk. He won his first race with the car in that configuration at Trenton in September: "We put that Offy in there and I won flag to flag." The same combination would take him to second at Michigan in October and third at Hanford, California, in November. (Bruce Craig collection)

He also took the Hawk to Pike's Peak, but the car wasn't really suited to the mountain climb, and Mario finished fourth while Unser won in his own, front-engine, Chevy-powered, hill-climb car.

A Championship dirt-car race at Nazareth on the next weekend in July was the first time Mario had raced in his hometown in seven years. The entire family turned out at Nazareth, of course, including Gigi and Rina. "My parents were huge supporters by then," Mario says. "My dad went to quite a few races, and he was there with bells on. He knew I was a force to be reckoned with that weekend. Michael and Jeff had been to many sprint-car and dirt-car races, so coming to Nazareth was just another race for them."

Mario finished second to Al Unser, who scored his first of five wins in a row that day. Mario was second to Al in both races on the IRP road course the next week, then scored his first victory of the year at the St. Jovite, Quebec, road course in August, winning both ends of the two-race event. In September, he won on the dirt at DuQuoin and finished second to Foyt in the Hoosier 100.

Finally, Mario, Brawner, and McGee decided to forsake the troubled turbo Ford V-8 for a four-cylinder turbo Offenhauser. The first race with the new engine was Trenton on September 22, and Mario won easily. "That car was dynamite. It hauled ass with the turbo Offy in it," McGee says.

Mario agrees: "We knew the turbo Offy was the way to go, and that race convinced us all around."

All the time Mario was whittling away at Bobby Unser's points lead. As his season improved, Unser's deteriorated. Through a hectic stretch of fifteen races in June, July, and August, Unser won only at Pike's Peak. After Trenton in September, Unser had 3,301 points to Mario's 3,018.

Toward the end of the season, while they were locked in a fierce battle for the USAC title, Mario and Bobby Unser made their Formula One debuts together. Mario remembered well his first meeting with Colin Chapman and Jim Clark at Indianapolis

in 1965, when Chapman invited Mario to call when he felt ready to try Formula One. "So I called Colin, and he said we'll do the last two races of the season at Monza and Watkins Glen." Unser agreed to drive the same races for the BRM team.

Two weeks before the Italian GP, Mario flew to Monza to test the latest Lotus 49B F1 car. "I went right out and set a record for Monza testing. I felt so good! I felt like I was born in that car." There was a problem, however, because the Italian GP was the same weekend as the Hoosier 100 USAC Championship dirt race, and F1's sanctioning body, the Federation Internationale d'Automobile (FIA), had a rule that prohibited drivers taking part in two races within twenty-four hours.

The Monza organizers told Mario the rule would be waived, but there were protests from the Italian press. Even the Italian parliament debated the matter, with one legislator describing the Americans' schedule as "the edge of folly." Another claimed Mario and Unser were "risking the safety of the other drivers and the public."

The Hoosier 100 was on Saturday, so Mario and Unser spent the weekend flying back and forth between Italy and Indianapolis. They qualified at Monza in the first practice session on Friday morning, then flew back to the United States. Mario had been fastest, although he lost spots during Saturday's final practice and qualifying. "I caught a good draft from Bobby, then tried to pull him, but he couldn't keep up because the BRM was so slow. He qualified way back, but my time was still good for seventh on the grid."

On Saturday, Mario finished second to Foyt in the Hoosier 100 while Unser dropped out early because of a broken water pipe. As soon as the race was over, they turned around again and flew to Monza, arriving early the next morning. But instead of being met at the Milan airport by a helicopter, as planned, they found a Lotus mechanic waiting for them in an Austin Mini-Minor.

"We jumped into this Mini-Minor," Mario recalls, "and I asked, 'What's going on?' Well, the mechanic didn't know. He starts driving, and we're hauling ass. I'm

sitting in the front, and Bobby is in the back, and Bobby says, 'Hey, we need to go faster!' He says, 'Hey Wop, you drive.' And he grabbed the guy and jerked him out of the seat. I had to grab the steering wheel and take over."

After a furious drive, they arrived at Monza's main gate without any credentials. "The police stopped us, and I told the guy, in Italian, that we were drivers. Of course, he didn't believe us. I told him we didn't have the time to mess around, and the guy pulled his gun. I said, 'Bobby, shield me!' And I gassed that thing and took off for the garage." Unser cursed the policeman in English and Spanish and gesticulated wildly at the man in uniform, who understandably was flustered by the pair of Americans.

When they got to the paddock, Chapman told them they wouldn't be allowed to start the race. Ferrari had lodged an official protest to stop the two from racing. Mario argued, but it was no use. "I said, 'Let a doctor give us a physical, because we're fine.' And Colin said, 'No, they won't let you run.' And they wouldn't. They had our cars on the grid almost to make it look like we never made it, to make us look bad."

At the U. S. Grand Prix at Watkins Glen a month later, there were no such distractions. Mario qualified on the pole in his F1 debut, which astonished the regulars who were contesting the entire series.

"Again, the timing was right," Mario says. "I was lucky because the Lotus 49 was the car of the moment. It would be like a rookie going into a Ferrari or McLaren today. It suited my style because I felt immediately in control and very much at home. It was light and forgiving with a beautiful little gearbox. You could drift it. It was like a dream. Right away I was at the limit. That's when I truly fell in love with a Formula One car. I felt, 'This is where I belong.' "

Mario led the race from the start, but didn't contest an outbraking attempt by Jackie Stewart at the end of the first lap. "I didn't know how to judge the braking,

so I let Stewart go by. I thought I would follow him and see what he was doing."

Mario could follow fairly easily and says he would have done so for most of the race. "I probably would have used that as a learning experience. I really needed it because I had no judgment in those cars."

Mario's car was fitted with an old engine, a lightweight transmission, and a smaller rear wing than the other Lotus, driven by Graham Hill, who was battling with Stewart for the world title. With most of the team's effort directed toward Hill, Mario knew the likelihood of his car making the finish was slim. Sure enough, a number of problems afflicted it, and he finally dropped out.

"They had a split nose on that car, and there was a clip that held it together that unhinged," Mario says. "That affected the car, but not that badly. As it dragged along the ground, it was wearing the wing out, but then the damn clutch started slipping, and that was the beginning of the end."

Mario believes his car suffered from Chapman's reluctance to spend enough for parts. "With me coming in as a third driver at the Glen, I am certain there weren't enough fresh parts to go around. I'm sure my clutch was worn out to begin with, and I guarantee you I didn't have a fresh engine. Maurice Phillippe was engineering my car, and the night before the race he was changing CV joints. He had to put another used one in so he tore it apart and repaired it." Despite the disappointment Mario had shown what he could do in an F1 car, and Chapman and Enzo Ferrari both were interested in hiring him for more races.

The next weekend witnessed the opening of the brand-new, high-banked two-mile Michigan superspeedway. Even in 1968 the track was fearsomely quick—too quick, everyone thought. "Every lap is a drama in itself," Mario told the press. He qualified the turbo Offy-powered Brawner/Hawk on the pole at 183.67 mph with championship rival Unser qualifying second.

Unser took the lead at the start with Mario chasing him until their fuel stops halfway through the 250-mile event. Mario stayed out a lap longer than Unser and ran out of fuel as he came into the pits. That cost him some time, but Unser's

Opposite: At the start of the United States Grand Prix at Watkins Glen, Mario takes the lead from the pole while teammate Graham Hill tries to force his way by Jackie Stewart's Matra (No. 15). Following immediately are the McLarens of Denny Hulme and Dan Gurney (No. 14), and Jacky Ickx's Brabham (No. 4). (Sutton Photographic)
Above: Not long into the race, the split nose on Mario's Lotus came apart and the right front wing dragged along the track. The problem didn't seriously affect Mario's lap times, and he continued to run in second place until his clutch started to fail. (William Green)

engine soon blew up, allowing Mario to finish second behind Ronnie Bucknam. Unser had jumped into Mike Mosley's car and was able to come back to finish third, but Mario had edged ahead of Unser in the championship. At the 1.5-mile Hanford, California, oval a few weeks later, Mario qualified second and finished third behind Foyt and Unser after a fierce battle among the three.

That meant Mario went to Phoenix two weeks later with a thirty-nine point lead over Unser. He took his eighth pole of the year, but early in the race Foyt slid on some oil, hit the guardrail, and bounced into Mario's path. Mario was unhurt in the crash, but Foyt had trouble getting out of his car, and his right hand was severely burned. Mario ran back to the pits and jumped into George Snider's car, which he drove to third place while Unser again commandeered Mosley's machine after his own broke a connecting rod. In the closing laps, the suspension of Mosley's car began to collapse, and Unser scraped home in ninth place.

With one race to go, Mario led the championship by 308 points. The final race at Riverside was more than 300 miles and worth 600 points. If Unser won, Mario could take the title by finishing fifth. If Unser was second, seventh place would do the job for Mario.

For the Riverside road course, Mario switched back to a normally aspirated Ford engine, which was more responsive, if less powerful, than the turbo Offy. He qualified second, behind Gurney's stock-block Ford-powered Eagle, with Unser back in ninth place. For a while Mario led the race before settling into second behind Gurney. Then, his engine failed.

Thus began an incredible thrash for Mario. First he took over Joe Leonard's Lotus turbine, but only a lap and a half after rejoining the race he was caught out by fading brakes, crashing with Art Pollard's car. Parnelli Jones rushed Mario back to the pits on his motorcycle so he could jump into Lloyd Ruby's car. Some cockpit padding was required before Mario could rejoin the race and, despite problems reaching the pedals, he was able to finish third.

But all of these efforts proved fruitless because Mario received only a portion of the points earned in Ruby's car. Unser finished second behind winner Gurney and

won the championship by just eleven points—4,330 to Mario's 4,319—in the tightest contest in USAC history.

After winning the USAC title in 1965 and 1966, Mario had now been a championship runner-up two years in a row. "There were a lot of second-place finishes that year. Indy was worth 1,000 points in those days, which put Bobby way ahead of me, but I damn near beat him."

But there was great satisfaction for Mario in the successful start of his Formula One career. "Doing those F1 races in '68 was very productive for me," Mario says. "That was a very pivotal year in that respect. It gave me a great taste of Formula One immediately, because that Lotus 49 really suited my style so well. Doing those two races for Colin that year got me started on the road to the world championship."

Left to right: At the championship-deciding Rex Mays 300 at Riverside Mario raced the latest version of his Lotus-based car, powered by a normally aspirated Ford engine. Midway through the race the engine blew, and he returned to the pits to take over Joe Leonard's Lotus turbine to try to win the championship. (Barry Tenin)
2: Now in Joe Leonard's Lotus Turbine, Mario prepares to rejoin the race. This stint lasted only a lap and a half before fading brakes caused him to tangle with another Lotus Turbine driven by Art Pollard. (Barry Tenin) 3: Parnelli Jones hustled Mario back to the pits on his motorcycle. Here Jones, Mario, and Clint Brawner discuss the situation, trying to determine if there is another car that he could take over. (Pete Luongo) 4: Jones, Brawner, and Mario wait in Lloyd Ruby's pit after Ruby's team owner Gene White, also a Firestone man, agreed to put Mario in Ruby's car. (Pete Luongo) 5: Ruby pulls into the pits as his crewmen prepare to refuel his car. Mario stands at the far right, ready to climb in, while McGee prepares to jam the cockpit with whatever padding is needed to help Mario fit into the larger Ruby's seat. (Pete Luongo) 6: Refueling completed, seat padding in place, Mario is buckled in and ready to go. He rejoined the race to finish third behind Gurney and Bobby Unser. But he didn't earn enough points to beat Unser to the title in the closest USAC championship battle in history. (Pete Luongo)

Chapter 9

A Milestone Year

As 1969 began, demand for Mario's driving skills was
once again strong enough to attract multiple offers.
Enzo Ferrari had asked him to run the Sebring 12
Hours and Monza 1000Ks in a factory Ferrari
teamed with the company's lead driver, Chris
Amon. At the same time, Colin Chapman wanted
Mario to drive a third Lotus in three F1 races.
Chapman also agreed to supply Mario with a
brand-new Lotus 4WD "wedge" Indy car. "Colin

Opposite: Mario returned to the tried-and-true Brawner/Hawk for the 1969 Indy 500
following his crash in the fragile Lotus 64. He qualified the car in the middle of the
front row between A. J. Foyt's Coyote-Ford and Bobby Unser's Eagle-Offy. Despite a
few mishaps in the pits Mario scored a memorable win. (Bob Tronolone)
Above: Mario jokes with three-time World Champion Jack Brabham (middle) and
Goodyear's racing boss Leo Mehl in the pits at the Nurburgring. Brabham's team
raced on Goodyear tires from the time Goodyear entered racing in 1964, and Mehl
and the taciturn Australian were close friends. (Jutta Fausel)

wasn't really hot on the idea of handing over one of his new cars to someone outside Team Lotus," Mario recalls. "But I had some leverage. Chapman was worried he wouldn't be able to make a deal with Ford for 1969 [because in 1968 Chapman had turned his back on Ford to race turbine engines]. I told him I could deliver Ford's new turbo cam V-8, which was now ready to win races, if he would supply me with one of his new cars."

In the middle of winter, Mario and Jim McGee flew to England to take a look at their new Lotus 64. McGee stayed to help complete the car while Mario flew home to bad news. Firestone was cutting back, he was told. It would continue to supply and develop tires, but there was no sponsorship for Mario's or any other team.

Suddenly, Mario needed considerably more sponsorship income than Overseas Airways could afford. Unfortunately, most major companies had committed their annual budgets months earlier. Mario approached Andy Granatelli, who controlled the budget for STP, the manufacturer of an engine oil additive, and Granatelli offered to buy the team. "Most people think Granatelli owned STP," Mario says. "He didn't. He was an officer of the company, but he had broad powers, and he was one of the few at the time who understood the power of marketing for a product that you could do without.

"Firestone had been basically financing my team. I could have gone out and promoted some sponsorship, but I didn't like that. My sights were elsewhere. I wanted to race. I had Formula One in my head and I soon realized I really didn't want to own my own team. I didn't want the responsibility of being a team owner.

"So I asked Andy if he wanted to buy my team and I would drive for him, and he didn't blink. We made the deal."

It took six weeks of negotiations with Granatelli before an agreement was reached. "Every time we'd send him a contract," Mario says, "Granatelli would send it back just filled with changes." Granatelli eventually agreed to purchase the team and to pay Mario $50,000 for the year, plus his usual forty per cent of all prize money. There were bonuses of $25,000 apiece for winning the Indy 500 and the USAC title. Mario also retained all rights to run the team himself with Clint Brawner and McGee.

"Andy had absolutely nothing to do with anything we did in 1969," says McGee. "In fact, we wouldn't even let him come in the garage. Mario did a good business deal with Andy that was based on money for results, so Mario cleaned house."

"It's true. That was the deal," Mario says. "We knew we had a good thing among ourselves and could run the team very effectively. We didn't want any interference because we thought it could have been detrimental. I think it was probably a bit of an overreaction on our part, but we wanted to do our thing. We said to Andy 'We don't want any guidance unless we ask for it.' He asked us and paid us to do a job, and that's what we aimed to do on our own. As highly visible as he was, he respected that."

Mario's first test in the 1,000-horsepower Lotus-Ford ended early with a broken driveshaft and left him wondering if he'd made the right move. "That car was terrible," Mario says. "It didn't do anything right. It was flat spooky to drive. We made a list of about 100 items that needed fixing." They returned the car to the factory for more work and started the season with a much-modified version of the previous year's Hawk.

"We got rid of the seat tanks and put fuel in outboard fuel tanks for aerodynamic reasons," McGee says. "We were able to get a little more ground effects with the wider bottom on the tub."

Adds Mario: "The oil coolers were in the sidepods, which didn't work very well. But the sidepods gave us more downforce. This was strictly our design. We were the aerodynamicists and the engineers."

After dropping out of the last NASCAR race of his career at Riverside, on February 1, Mario's racing season started in earnest with the opening round of the F1 World Championship at Kyalami, South Africa, on March 1. He drove well and took positions away from Denis Hulme and Jo Siffert to challenge Lotus teammate Graham Hill for second before his gearbox failed.

Three weeks later Mario was at Sebring, co-driving Ferrari's brand-new 312P sports racer with Amon. They started from the pole and took control of the race after the factory Porsches fell out with broken suspensions. At one point, Mario and Amon enjoyed a three-lap lead, but then the engine started overheating. A long pitstop followed, and with their pace reduced to a crawl, they were caught and passed just before the finish by the John Wyer Ford GT40 driven by Jacky Ickx and Jackie Oliver.

Above: Driving this Ferrari 312P sports car with Chris Amon, Mario dominated the 1969 Sebring 12 Hours. Amon put the car on the pole, and the pair led by three laps at one stage before encountering engine trouble and limping home second. (Dave Friedman) **Opposite:** Mario drove the last midget race of his career at the Houston Astrodome in March. He was teamed with midget great Mel Kenyon (at right) in a pair of Thermo-King cars. Kenyon's car features an early roll cage, while Mario's has only the traditional roll hoop. Kenyon's left hand had been terribly damaged in an earlier accident. To assist in turning, the glove on his left hand was fitted with a post that fit into the steering wheel. (Ken Coles)

Above: Chris Amon and Mario also ran the Ferrari 312P (No. 1) in the Monza 1000Ks at the end of April, where Mario took the pole and led again before another engine failure. Here he runs third behind teammate Pedro Rodriguez (No. 2) and the winning Porsche 908 driven by Jo Siffert and Brian Redman. (Studio Falletti)

Opposite: Mario drove this Holman-Moody Ford in the Motor Trend 500 at Riverside on February 1, 1969. The race was delayed by rain and took place one week later than scheduled. Mario qualified seventh but his engine blew two-thirds of the way through the 500-mile road race. This turned out to be the last of fourteen NASCAR races Mario ran in his career. (Bob Tronolone)

120

The USAC Championship season opened at Phoenix the following weekend, on March 30, but a broken clutch stopped Mario during his first pit stop. The next scheduled event was a 200-mile race at the Hanford, California, oval.

A month earlier a Firestone tire test at the track had yielded surprising results. On one set of test tires Mario turned some quick laps despite the car feeling loose and requiring constant steering corrections on the straights. Measuring the tires revealed that there was an inch difference, or "stagger," between the circumference of the left-and right-side tires. "I knew stagger, of course, from my midget days," Mario says, "but we never thought about running stagger in a Champ car. We did it by accident in that tire test."

"So we decided to make a set of control tires [the control tire is the baseline tire at any tire test], with different circumferences, and man I was quick! I said to the Firestone guys, 'That's got to stay with me for one race.' " The Firestone engineers agreed to Mario's request.

Mario carried the advantage to Hanford, but race day was marred by tragedy that began when Art Pollard's car caught fire during refueling. Pollard's crewmen, Grant King and Red Stainton, were engulfed in flames and in trying to avoid the fire Stainton stepped back into the path of Mario's car as he approached his pit. Mario braked hard, but his left front wheel struck Stainton and hurled him into the air. Stainton's skull was fractured when he hit the pavement. The race was red-flagged while Stainton was rushed to a hospital because of burns and a severe head injury. He died the next day.

"I did everything I could to avoid hitting him, but there was nothing I could do," Mario says. "I hit him so hard the whole car shook. That was the worst thing that's ever happened to me in a race car."

After the race was restarted, Mario beat Lloyd Ruby by more than a lap. It was the first USAC Champ car win for Granatelli in 23 years of trying, but nobody celebrated.

Mario flew home from the California race, then went to Italy the next weekend for the Monza 1000Ks, where he teamed again with Amon in a Ferrari 312P sports car. As they had at Sebring, Mario and Amon battled for the lead, but this time their engine blew.

Next on Mario's schedule was the month of May and Indianapolis, where the considerably modified Lotus had arrived a few days before the factory cars for

Graham Hill and Jochen Rindt. Chapman had attended to all the problems Mario and his team had identified in the preseason test. Brawner and McGee took a few days to complete the final details on the Lotus, and when Mario took to the track, he was even more convinced of the car's potential.

"It was a gorgeous car," Mario recalls. "There was no afterthought on the aero pieces. You could tell there was some engineering behind it even though nobody used a wind tunnel in those days. Looking at the wings and the body and the flow of it, I could tell some good minds had worked on that car."

Right away, Mario was on the pace and soon established himself as the man to beat, becoming the first driver to lap the track at 170 mph that year. Entering the first weekend of qualifying, Mario and the 4WD Lotus were quickest at 171.789 mph, followed by A.J. Foyt at 170.908, and Foyt's teammate, Roger McCluskey, at 170.783 mph. Nobody else was in the 170 mph bracket.

The first qualifying weekend was rained out, so Mario began working on his race set-up. The turbo Ford's fuel efficiency was extremely poor, and Mario learned he would have to reduce his pace by four or five mph to make the necessary mileage. He also grew worried about the overall fragility of the Lotus, particularly its unconventional transmission, which was located immediately behind the cockpit rather than at the tail of the car and was mounted back to front to drive the 4WD system.

"I'd do three or four laps at a time in practice and come into the pits, and the gearbox would be so hot!" Mario recalls. "There was no oil cooler for the 'box, and there were no answers from Colin or the Lotus engineers as to how they were going to cool it. Everything seemed so nice, but fragile. There were just too many inherent problems, and I wasn't seeing any big push from Lotus to try to fix them."

Disaster struck in the middle of the next week, when the Lotus's right rear hub failed in the Speedway's fourth turn just as Mario was laying into the throttle for a hot lap. The car spun backwards into the wall and disintegrated, catching fire as it slid along the wall.

Covering his face with one hand, Mario unbuckled his harness and scrambled out as the wreckage came to a stop. Pollard and McCluskey had been following him

"It was a big thing to win for Andy as well. If anyone deserved to win that race at the time, it was him, with all the effort he'd put into it. He created a lot of excitement, first with the Novi, then with the turbines. I liked the dynamics of being involved with him and his personality. Because Andy was so visible, it was good for me, too, because I knew we were going to get worldwide publicity in the aftermath."

But for Dee Ann, Mario's Indy win and the stardom that followed it carried a steep price. "That was the most difficult time that I remember over his whole career because we just got inundated with requests for interviews and appearances," she says. "That was when I finally realized that I didn't have a husband anymore. He belonged to the public. That hurt, and it took a lot for me to accept it. But eventually, if you're going to stay with the marriage, you have to accept it."

At Milwaukee the next weekend Mario qualified on pole and led the race until his turbocharger lost pressure. He kept going, falling back steadily, only to run out of fuel near the finish. After coasting into the pits, the Hawk was refueled, but Mario couldn't restart his engine and was classified in seventh place.

The following week Mario learned that his friend Lucien Bianchi had been killed while practicing for Le Mans, yet another grim confirmation of racing's inherent danger.

Mario carried on and was on the pole again at Langhorne that weekend, on June 15. He led most of the rain-delayed race before his right rear tire began to lose air. He hung on to finish sixth.

Next came Pike's Peak on June 29. It was Mario's third and last time on the Colorado mountain, where he won easily in a Chevy-powered Grant King dirt car. That was the only time Mario drove a purpose-built car at Pike's Peak. But Mario's luck deserted him the next weekend at the Castle Rock, Colorado, road course. Af-

ter an oil leak forced him into the pits, he was disqualified when USAC officials caught Brawner and McGee violating the rules by adding oil to the engine.

From Colorado, he flew home to Nazareth for Mario Andretti Week, a celebration of his Indy 500 victory. Included were go-kart races, a congratulatory dinner, and a parade through Nazareth. Also, Market Street, where the Andretti family lived, was renamed Victory Lane, and the week concluded with a USAC Championship dirt-car race on Saturday night at Nazareth Speedway.

Following Saturday's parade, a very pregnant Dee Ann was rushed to the hospital. Meanwhile, Mario qualified second and capped a memorable week with a dominant victory. He joined Dee Ann just in time for the birth of their daughter, Barbra Dee.

His great season continued at nearby Trenton the next weekend, on July 19, when he scored his fifth win of the year. He won again the following month on the dirt at Springfield, Illinois, and wrapped up his third USAC championship by winning the year's second Champ car race at Trenton near the end of September.

There were also two more F1 races, both in an experimental 4WD Lotus 63, a smaller, less powerful version of the type 64 Indy car. At the Nurburgring in August, Mario lost a wheel on the opening lap. He also drove the fragile Lotus 63 at Watkins Glen in October, the car again failing him. That was an emotional day for Lotus boss Chapman as Rindt scored his first Grand Prix win, driving an older 49B model, while Hill's legs were broken in an accident in his 49B.

Mario's eighth Champ car victory on the Kent, Washington, road circuit in October and ninth USAC win on the Riverside road course in December helped him set a USAC record of 5,025 points and made his third national championship that much more emphatic. The Unser brothers were a distant second and third, Al accumulating 2,630 points, and Bobby 2,585. "We had a banner year. I won on the dirt, I won on a superspeedway, and on a road course. I even won Pike's Peak that year. That was a wonderful year for STP and for us." Looking ahead to a brand new decade, anything seemed possible.

Above: During the Pike's Peak weekend Mario signs autographs for admiring young fans. Evidence of the burns he received in the crash of the Lotus at Indianapolis six weeks earlier can still be seen on his upper lip and cheeks. (Joe Farkas)
Opposite: Mario pitches in with the Holman-Moody crew during a test session with "The 429'er" McLaren Can-Am car. Although the name suggested that the displacement of the all-aluminum Ford engine was 429 cubic inches, it was in fact a very potent 494 cubic inches, and produced more than 700 horsepower. "In the race at Texas the right rear tire started blistering on the banking," says Mario. "Those road race tires were not up to the job." (Joe Farkas)

Chapter 10

Rising and Falling Fortunes

The 1969 season, it turned out, was the end of the very successful partnership between Mario, Clint Brawner, and Jim McGee. Together for five-and-a-half years, they had won thirty races and three championships, but neither Brawner nor McGee was happy working for Granatelli. There was increasing friction as Granatelli wanted his brother, Joe, and son, Vince, to be more involved, and Brawner and McGee decided to go to work for Jim

Opposite: When the fuel pump in Mario's Ferrari 312B failed during the only dry qualifying session for the Monaco Grand Prix, Mario was forced to try to make the field in the rain. His time was off by the narrowest of margins, and he did not qualify for the race. (Jutta Fausel) **Above:** Mario celebrates his March 1971 Questor GP victory at the Ontario Motor Speedway with the trophy queen in black and Dee Ann in yellow. A smiling Aldo is behind them. (Richard George)

Hayhoe in 1970, building cars for Roger McCluskey.

"It was disappointing to me that they left," Mario says. "I always tried to be as influential as possible in getting the best deal for the mechanics, to make sure Clint and Jimmy were compensated properly and had the best deal, and I think I was successful. When they left, that hurt me, because I was totally in the hands of the Granatelli group, and things went sideways. Granatelli reached too far outside the box by doing the deal with McNamara."

The ever ambitious Granatelli announced plans to build his own cars in Germany in partnership with Francis McNamara, a former Green Beret who had served in Vietnam before settling in Lenggries, West Germany. McNamara had built Formula Vee, F3, and F2 cars, but had no experience in any major racing categories. "The project wasn't planned or coordinated very well, which supports the decision we made originally in 1969 to keep the Granatellis out of it," Mario says. "I take my fair side of the blame because I was always reaching as well. I could have resisted all that, and I didn't. I went along with it, but those years cost me in time and frustration."

Granatelli told Mario that STP would sponsor the new March Formula One team and offered him a third factory March beside regular drivers Chris Amon and Jo Siffert in races that didn't conflict with USAC events. As attractive as the F1 opportunity was, Mario was wary enough about Granatelli's plans to talk with Parnelli Jones and his partner, Vel Miletich, about driving for their team, paired with Al Unser.

Ultimately Mario decided that as his team's only driver, he would be best served with Granatelli. But as the McNamara project began to unfold, he had more misgivings. McNamara's designer was a former Lola junior engineer, Jo Karasek, who brought a briefcase full of Lola drawings with him. The more Mario worked with Karasek, the less he trusted his ability.

"Karasek was an engineer, but he was more of a musician than anything else," Mario recalls. "He didn't have a really good feeling for race-car design. He came out with a very short wheelbase car, and the suspension was a take-off from Lola. I remember us drawing swing-arm lengths and trying to figure out the geometry."

Granatelli's plan was to build four McNamaras, one specifically for Indianapolis, another tailor-made for the new Ontario Motor Speedway, a third for one-mile ovals, and a fourth for road circuits. One of these was actually a mildly fettled version of the previous year's Hawk, and as the winter wore on it became increasingly apparent to Mario that he would start the season in the reliable old Hawk because the McNamaras were behind schedule.

Sports-car races for Ferrari and the opening F1 races of the season provided Mario with some distraction from the McNamara problems. Ferrari had built a fleet of new 512S sports racers with 5-liter V-12s to compete against Porsche's latest 5-liter 917s. The new Ferraris and Porsches made their debut at the end of January in the Daytona 24 Hours, and Mario put his Ferrari on the pole.

Five Ferraris started the race, but Mario's car, also driven by teammates Jacky Ickx and Arturo Merzario, was the only one to finish. This car also was bedeviled by problems. Neither the chassis nor the suspension was up to the job, and in the last six hours Mario and his partners lost more than an hour in the pits while broken pieces were re-welded. The final insult came in the closing minutes, when the Siffert/Redman 917 stole second place from Mario's crippled car for a one-two finish for Porsche.

Next came the first F1 race of the year in South Africa and the debut of the new March 701. There were five new Marches in the field, and although they ran competitively, Jackie Stewart's Tyrrell-owned 701 was the only one to finish, in third place. Mario dropped out a third of the way into the race because of a broken water radiator.

Two weeks later Mario was back behind the wheel of a Ferrari 512S for the Sebring 12 Hours. He qualified on the pole, and after an early battle with the other leading Ferraris and Porsche 917s, Mario and co-driver Merzario took control of the race. After eleven hours they enjoyed a massive thirteen-lap lead only to have their gearbox fail.

Mario returned to the pits to retire from the race. He was tired and disappointed when Ferrari team manager Mauro Forghieri asked him to take over the remaining 512S, a closed coupe driven by Nino Vaccarella and Ignazio Giunti that was now following the two leading Porsches.

"The car was running third, and I knew I wasn't going to fit it. I was ready to get the hell out of there. But this guy on the P.A. system was going on and on about McQueen and how he was going to win the race. I said, 'To hell with it. I'm going to get in this thing.' "

Steve McQueen had starred in the movie "Le Mans" the previous year and was a very competent amateur racer who was co-driving a 3-liter Porsche 908 that weekend with Peter Revson. Because McQueen had suffered a broken foot in a motorcycle accident the previous weekend, he was on crutches and wearing a cast, so Revson did most of the driving.

"The only reason I went into the other Ferrari was because I was tired of

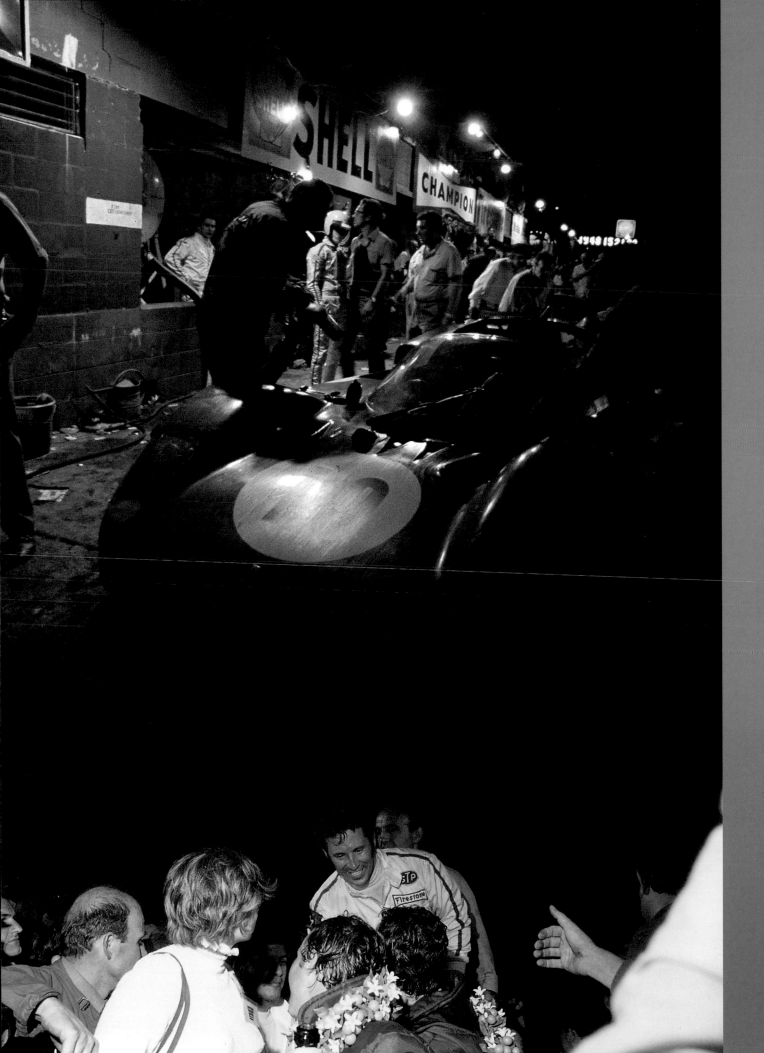

Above: Mario drove the STP dirt car powered by a Keith Black Dodge engine in the five USAC championship races. His best finish was second at Sedalia. "That car was never right," he explains. "Look at all the coolers strapped on all over the place! It overheated all the time. I think I crashed in that race, blew the engine lapping somebody and backed it into the guardrail. It was the only time I ever crashed a dirt car." (Bob Tronolone)

Top left: Mario's car sits broken in the pits, while in the background Ferrari team manager Mauro Forghieri tries to persuade him to take over the third-place 512S coupe driven by Nino Vaccarella and Ignazio Giunti. Ultimately, it was the P. A. announcer's preoccupation with second-place driver Steve McQueen that motivated Mario to get into the other Ferrari and drive to an epic win. (Barry Tenin)

Left: The victory lane celebrations begin at Sebring. Mario's satisfaction is obvious as he shakes the hands of Vaccarella and Giunti. Mario often refers to this win as the most satisfying of his career. (Barry Tenin)

Opposite: For most of the Sebring 12 Hours, Mario and co-driver Arturo Merzario were running away with the race in their Ferrari 512S. But the Ferrari's gearbox failed on the 227th lap, ending its run. (Barry Tenin)

hearing the guy on the P.A. system talking about Steve McQueen," Mario says. "It's still ringing in my ears. Poor Peter Revson drove his tail off, and even at his best McQueen was well off Revson's pace, but Revson wasn't even mentioned."

Vaccarella brought the third-placed Ferrari in for fuel with more than an hour to go, and Mario climbed in, intent on catching and beating the second-placed Revson/McQueen Porsche, if not the Rodriguez/Kinnunen 917, which now led by a lap.

"We could never have beaten the Porsche that Pedro was driving, but I knew I had a shot at catching Revson, and I went for it. I got in there, and I was driving like a man possessed. I was on a mission; I really was. I was lapping five or six seconds quicker than Vaccarella, and I was doing the kink past the pits flat out, which I had never done with my Spyder.

"The coupe felt heavier, but it also felt more stable. I couldn't reach the pedals very well, and I didn't have the proper support in the seat for braking, so I was sliding forward, but I said, 'I can deal with this.' I was poised for it, and I hunted him down and passed him and got the lead."

Just after he passed the Revson/McQueen 908, Rodriguez's leading 917 suddenly ground to a halt with a failed wheel hub, and Mario clinched a victory he often refers to as the most satisfying of his career.

The USAC season began in Phoenix at the end of March. Mario qualified his Hawk on the pole only to suffer engine trouble in the race and fail to finish. At the Sears Point, California, road course the following week, he drove without a clutch to a second-place finish behind Dan Gurney, and at Trenton three weeks later battled it out with Al Unser and Lloyd Ruby, eventually finishing second to Ruby.

Between Sears Point and Trenton, Mario flew to Spain for the second race of the F1 series on April 19. It turned into an arduous weekend because of a pinched nerve in his back and a fever. "I was seeing elephants. I was delirious, sweating and shivering, and Dee Ann wrapped me up in the bedspread. It was an awful night."

Despite his condition, Mario ran the entire race and finished a lap down in third place behind Jackie Stewart and Bruce McLaren. "Looking back, it's funny because that was the best race I had with Andy in F1!"

In May at Indianapolis the first McNamara arrived late, and right away there were problems. The first day a U-joint broke, and Mario crashed in the fourth turn,

just as he had with the Lotus the previous year. There was no fire this time, but the car was damaged seriously and Granatelli's team, run by his son, Vince, worked tirelessly to rebuild the car in time for qualifying.

Mario was disappointed to qualify eighth, the first time he wasn't on the first two rows for the 500. The race turned into a real struggle when something went wrong with the rear suspension. "The car was OK for the first few laps," Mario recalls. "Then I was like an accident waiting to happen. I thought about coming in about ten times because I was dangerous out there."

With less than thirty laps to go, Mario was forced to drive across the infield grass to avoid a multi-car accident. "I heard something snap, and I thought I broke something. Then, when the green came on, it was a whole new race car. I couldn't believe it.

"What happened was a spring had gotten hung up on the spring perch. When they jacked up the car during the pit stop, the spring didn't settle down properly on the hat that holds it in place. Later we tried to simulate it, and it jacked about 250 pounds of crossweight. So I had actually been running most of the race to that point on three wheels!"

During the final fifteen laps he was able to run laps three or four mph quicker and gained a few places, finishing sixth.

At Milwaukee the next weekend, Mario took the pole but finished fifth. Three weeks later, at the Castle Rock, Colorado, road course, he scored a dominant win, but it would be his only USAC victory of the year. The remainder of the Champ car season was lost to numerous mechanical failures.

Mario came close to winning the inaugural California 500 at the brand-new Ontario Motor Speedway in September, but the McNamara's gearbox broke while he was leading with just six laps to go. His best result in the second half of the USAC season was second to Al Unser in a dirt-car race at Sedalia, Missouri, two weeks after the California 500. As Mario's year waned, Unser's came to life. Unser won eight of nine races run from July through October and took his first USAC title, breaking Mario's record from the previous year by 105 points.

Nor was there much joy for Mario from the year's remaining sports-car and F1 races. His third and final race of the season in a Ferrari 512S was the Watkins

GERMAN-AMERICAN BEAUTY--STP-McNamara poses for first photo at STP-West Coast racing shops. Combined talents of German-U. S. builders developed radical new Championship racer with novel engineering ideas.

Glen Six Hours in July when he and co-driver Giunti fought fuel vaporization and brake troubles to finish third, three laps behind a pair of factory Porsche 917s.

Mario also raced the 512S in the following day's Can-Am race, finishing fifth after the car's fuel injection system was clogged by dust kicked up by Jackie Stewart's Chaparral 2H "sucker car." The season also included a string of failures in the British, German, and Austrian Grands Prix in July and August, driving the STP March 701.

In the middle of the summer, after he had brought Ferrari its only sports-car victory of the year at Sebring, Mario was asked by Enzo Ferrari to drive full-time for the Italian team in 1971 in both F1 and sports cars.

"I pursued Ferrari. I was always in touch with him, and somehow he liked me. I felt this was my opportunity to do Formula One. I couldn't go back to Lotus because Colin [Chapman] was upset that I had gone with Andy and the March deal."

Mario visited the Ferrari factory in Maranello and was deeply impressed. "The Old Man took me around and said to me, 'Mario, all of this is working for you.' I'll never forget that. In those days, Clint Brawner had a garage behind a bank in Phoenix, and A. J. Watson used to work out of a small garage. And I went to Ferrari, and there's this huge place. There was a chassis shop, a body shop, and an entire engine department. It was daunting."

But despite all the advantages, Mario had to turn Ferrari down because his ties with Firestone were too lucrative. As part of Firestone's investment in the Andretti name, Mario and brother Aldo had bought Rodger Ward's Firestone tire store in Indianapolis in the spring of 1970, and Firestone wanted Mario to focus on the USAC Championship schedule. The decision made, Ferrari left the door open for Mario to do a handful of F1 and sports-car races that didn't conflict with his USAC commitments.

Persuaded by Mario, McGee rejoined Granatelli's team in an attempt to improve the McNamaras. But even McGee's hard work, knowledge, and ability couldn't help the McNamara project or Granatelli's team. The new McNamara was better than the 1970 car, but it couldn't match the new cars from Eagle, McLaren, and George Bignotti's Colt/Lolas.

The new cars weren't ready for the first race of the 1971 season, a two-part event on a new oval in Rafaela, Argentina, at the end of February. Behind from the start, Mario and Granatelli's team never caught up. USAC had decided to abandon its growing experiment with road racing and to cast out all dirt tracks from the championship series. For 1971 there were just fourteen Champ car races, all on paved ovals.

"In my opinion, this will not add to the importance of the National Championship," Mario wrote at the time in his regular column in the *Indianapolis Star*. "This variety of events gave the USAC Championship a rare prestige, which even the Europeans appreciated since they fully accepted the USAC national titleist for the first time as the American driving champion."

USAC's trend was pushing Mario more than ever toward Formula One. He had driven more than 1,000 miles testing the new Ferrari 312B F1 car in Italy in December and was excited about his prospects.

On the first weekend in March he qualified fourth in South Africa, immediately behind teammate Clay Regazzoni and ahead of a third Ferrari driven by Ickx. As the race started Mario almost ran into Stewart and Amon, who were directly ahead of him on the grid. He had to brake hard, and fell to seventh at the end of the opening lap, then steadily worked his way toward the front. By the race's final stages Mario was up to second place and closing on leader Denny Hulme. He turned the race's fastest lap and was a little more than two seconds behind with four laps to go when a bolt fell out of Hulme's suspension. Hulme's car wobbled and slowed, and Mario swept through to score his first F1 victory.

"South Africa was the type of race where I was not outstanding, but I was up front. I was ahead of all the other Ferraris. I was challenging Hulme, but pretty much couldn't catch him. I don't think I would have beaten him, but it was a good victory nevertheless. It was big to score my first Formula One win, and to do it for Ferrari made it very special."

Two weeks later at Sebring, Mario put in another good show for Ferrari. He qualified the first of Ferrari's new 3-liter 312PB sports cars second to Mark Donohue's Penske Ferrari 512M, and in the race he and co-driver Ickx dominated. After five hours they held a four-lap lead when the transmission suddenly failed while Ickx was at the wheel.

The following weekend saw the second race of the USAC Championship series at Phoenix on Saturday, then the non-championship Questor GP on the Ontario Motor Speedway road circuit on Sunday. The Questor was a two-race contest

Above: The start of the Watkins Glen 6 Hours in 1970. Mario started on the front row in the No. 92 Ferrari 512S he shared with Ignazio Giunti. Jo Siffert in the No. 1 Porsche 917 was on pole. Mario and Giunti finished third after suffering brake and fuel system problems. Mario raced the car again in the following day's Can-Am event, finishing fifth. (Daytona Racing Archives) **Opposite:** The caption attached to this publicity photo of the new McNamara USAC car reflected the team's optimism at the beginning of the season. But the car proved fraught with problems, requiring constant refinement as designer Karasek struggled to understand it. Mario endured a very difficult year. (Andretti collection)

Before the start of the Grand Prix season Mario tests the new Ferrari 312B F1 car. "That was a perfect car, " he says. "The twelve-cylinder Boxer engine had a low center of gravity that helped its handling. It was well balanced. Even then it was an old-looking car, but it worked." (Jean Minassian/Andretti collection)

between F1 and Formula 5000 cars. Mario flew back and forth between Phoenix and Ontario and had trouble in both places. The new McNamara was fraught with problems and, in mid-week practice at Ontario, Mario crashed his Ferrari while trying to pass Lothar Motschenbacher's Formula 5000 car.

Mario made it home a non-competitive ninth in the race at Phoenix and was able to reach Ontario late on Saturday afternoon in time to run a handful of qualifying laps that were good enough for twelfth fastest.

"Jacky Ickx shook the Ferrari down for me after it had been repaired, and I was able to get in a few qualifying laps. That was a beautiful car. It was really well balanced, and that Boxer engine was great. It had good power and low center of gravity, and I went through the field and passed Stewart to win. To beat Stewart was really big for me because, at that time, he was the yardstick.

"I felt great about that one because I really earned it. In the second heat I started on pole and, while my tires came in, Stewart took the lead for a little while, but I stalked him and passed him and won the second race as well." He won the second race despite losing a cylinder in the closing laps.

Mario was less lucky at the Spanish GP in Barcelona the following month when his fuel pump quit. Back in the United States at Trenton the next weekend, Mario began to figure out the McNamara. Thirty laps into the race he took the lead from Al Unser and started pulling away only to drop out when the turbo broke.

As the month of May began, rumors and newspaper stories appeared about a possible split between Mario and Granatelli. Mario did his best to downplay the speculation as he got down to work at Indianapolis. Though the latest McNamara was a definite improvement on the previous year's car, most other builders had made even more progress, and Mario was unable to match their pace. He qualified ninth, his 172 mph average some six mph slower than Revson's pole performance in one of the spectacular new McLarens.

The Monaco GP took place on the second weekend of qualifying at Indianapolis, and Mario flew over for his first race in the glamorous principality, considered the crown jewel of Grand Prix racing. But it rained most of the weekend, and his Ferrari's fuel pump failed during the only dry session. While everyone else qualified at that time, Mario had to qualify in the wet final session and narrowly missed the field.

Mario returned to Indianapolis for an even more disappointing Indy 500. On the twelfth lap, STP teammate Steve Krisoloff's engine blew, throwing oil on the track and triggering a multi-car accident. Mario was hit by Gordon Johncock's car, ending his race. Meanwhile, rumors persisted about trouble between him and Granatelli. The *Indianapolis Star* reported that Texas oilman and sometime team owner John Mecom was going to buy the team, and then it was learned that McNamara had sued

Below left: Mario scored his first F1 victory in the 1971 season-opening South African Grand Prix driving a Ferrari 312B. Mario took the lead with just four laps to go after Denny Hulme's leading McLaren broke. He beat the pole winner, Jackie Stewart, by twenty seconds. (Dave Friedman) Below middle: To improve performance on oval tracks, the stance of the McNamara was offset with the goal of making more downforce on the left side. But Mario says the design didn't really work: "It had a lot more body on the left side for aerodynamic offset. Only the body was offset, not the chassis. It was not a good car." (Bob Tronolone) Below right: Mario drove this 7-liter Ferrari 712S in the Can-Am race at Watkins Glen, finishing fourth behind Peter Revson and Denny Hulme in the factory McLarens and Jackie Stewart's Haas Lola. The 712S was a fantastically powerful car, but it was never seriously developed, and ran only a few other races with Chris Amon driving. (Dave Friedman)

Granatelli, claiming the STP boss owed him $30,000. The team continued to unravel.

"Vince Granatelli and his guys weren't used to running the whole season," Mario says. "They were basically Indy specialists. They just weren't up for the job, and we struggled, not to mention the problems with the McNamara. I was so frustrated. I was upset at myself because I was wasting my career at a critical stage."

The rest of Mario's USAC season was equally bleak. Changes were made to the brakes, body work, wings, and cooling system in an attempt to make the McNamara more competitive, but reliability problems plagued the team all year.

Mario continued to run F1 and sports-car races for Ferrari as his schedule permitted. At Watkins Glen in July, he and Ickx failed to finish the six-hour race when their 312PB's engine wouldn't restart during a pit stop. The following day Mario gave the monster 7-liter Ferrari 712P a rare run in the Glen's Can-Am race, finishing fourth behind the McLarens driven by Revson and Hulme and Jackie Stewart's Lola.

One of Mario's most satisfying races of 1971 was the German GP at the mighty Nurburgring. It was his third start at the classic fourteen-mile track, and he finished fourth behind Stewart, François Cevert, and Ferrari teammate Clay Regazzoni.

"I was beginning to get the hang of the Nurburgring, and I began to love that track and anticipate all the right corners. I was doing Adenau really right, and the Foxhole, and the Flugplatz, and I was a terror going into the Karrusell.

"Ickx taught me how to do the Karrusell. If you trusted where you were, once you dumped yourself into the banking, you could really punch it and squirt out of there. Ickx told me to line myself up with the peaks of two pine trees when you came up the hill, and he was so right. You'd line yourself up on the trees, come over the blind brow, and—boom—there it was. It's funny how a little thing like that can help. I wouldn't have found that in a hundred years."

In USAC, Mario's only good result in the second half of the year was a second-place finish to Bobby Unser (albeit two laps behind) at the second Trenton Champ car race in October. He finished the year ninth in points, his worst year on record.

In October, before the season was over, Granatelli announced that Mario and he were parting ways. In addition to his misgivings about the Granatellis' abilities to sustain a winning effort, Mario was fed up with their car designers. "McNamara and his people did not have the experience, and we were paying dearly

for it. I was a guinea pig, and that was not fun."

A few days after the announcement of Mario's split with Granatelli, another announcement was made. Mario would drive for Vel's Parnelli Jones in USAC in 1972, teamed with Al Unser and Joe Leonard, and would continue to drive for Ferrari in non-conflicting F1 and sports-car races. There was even talk of Ferrari building a V-12 Indy-car engine for Mario to run in a VPJ Indy car.

"I had been thinking about it for some time but was determined to finish out the season. I didn't want to change horses in midstream, but there was no question in my mind that the move to Vel's Parnelli Jones was the best thing for me."

Mario flew to South Africa in November for a non-championship, nine-hour sports-car race at Kyalami. Ickx and Mario were there to race test the latest version of Ferrari's 312PB sports car in preparation for a full assault on the 1972 World Sports Car Championship.

Mario qualified on the pole and led from the start only to get stranded on the track when the fuel pump broke. He had to fashion his own repairs to get back to the pits, then lost more time with a flat battery. Mario and Ickx lost twenty-three laps because of these problems, but they stormed back through the field to finish second to teammates Regazzoni and Brian Redman.

"As soon as we got the car fixed, we were going like it was a Grand Prix. That was the most fun I ever had because we just went hell-bent. We drove like there was no tomorrow. I don't know how many little cars we must have clipped coming through the field, and at the end of the race the car was seriously bruised. It was amazing that it stayed together.

"The next day the car was on display at an Italian garage where Ferrari used to work in downtown Johannesburg, and it looked like it had been in a figure-eight race! I felt so good about that. It was the best second place I ever had."

Above: In an all-too-rare moment at home, Mario displays his culinary skills with eighteen month-old daughter Barbie, whose good looks are already in evidence. (Andretti collection) Opposite: At the Nurburgring in August, Mario qualified third and finished fourth. Teammate Ickx gave Mario a tip that helped him master the challenging Karrussel and improve his understanding of the fourteen-mile circuit. To the right in the white shirt is Firestone engineer Nigel Bennett. (Jutta Fausel)

Chapter 11

The Super Team

Mario was attracted to Vel's Parnelli Jones Racing by the team's impressive record and by Parnelli himself. Based in Torrance, California, the team won the 1970 and '71 Indy 500s and 1970 USAC championship with Al Unser and the 1971 USAC championship with Joe Leonard. For 1972, the team expanded to three cars, adding a third for Mario.

Jones was one of the greatest drivers of the 1960s. He won the Indy 500 in 1963 and rivaled A. J. Foyt

Opposite: Joe Leonard, Al Unser, Parnelli Jones, and Mario pose at the introduction of the new dihedral-wing Parnelli VPJ1 at Ontario in 1972. The day would demonstrate that there were serious problems to overcome with the Maurice Phillippe-designed car. (Richard George) **Above:** Viewed from the rear, the new Parnelli was a mess. "Phillippe never finished that car from the cockpit on back," Mario says. "It wasn't too bad looking from the front, but the back was just forgotten. Everything was open, completely unclothed. It was so untidy. We asked Phillippe why and he had no answer." (Richard George)

and Dan Gurney as an all-rounder, winning races in sports cars and Trans-Am cars as well as Champ cars. Many of those who raced against Jones say he had no equal on high-speed paved tracks, Indianapolis in particular. After he retired from open-wheel racing in 1967, Jones set up his own Indy-car team in partnership with car dealer Vel Miletich and they called it Vel's Parnelli Jones Racing.

There was also an important commercial fit with VPJ because Parnelli, like Mario, was a Firestone tire dealer, and his team enjoyed a lucrative contract to race on Firestones.

Two years earlier, Mario had turned down the idea of joining Al Unser in a two-car VPJ operation, but now he was happy to be part of a three-car team with Unser and Leonard. He felt that of all the team openings it was his best option, and the team's other key personnel appealed to him. George Bignotti was a renowned master mechanic and the most successful crew chief of his time. His cars had won fifty-eight USAC Championship races and five Indy 500s when he started at VPJ. "Driving for Bignotti was almost a sure ticket, just like driving for Colin Chapman," Mario says. "Bignotti created champions like no other chief mechanic in those days. He made champions out of Foyt, Al Unser, and Joe Leonard."

Jim McGee followed Mario from Granatelli to VPJ to work as Mario's chief mechanic with Bignotti overseeing all three cars. Mario and Unser's cars were sponsored by Viceroy cigarettes with Leonard's car sponsored by Samsonite. The star-studded group was dubbed the "Super Team."

Before the USAC season got under way, Mario's schedule included a number of sports-car and F1 races for Ferrari. In January, he raced twice in Argentina, in a 1000K sports-car race on January 9 and the season-opening Argentine GP two weeks later.

Ferrari had produced a new 312PB sports car that was lower and lighter than the previous year's car. Mario drove with Jacky Ickx, and they led the 1000K through the first hour and a half before electrical problems slowed them to a tenth-place finish. At the F1 race, Mario qualified ninth, directly behind teammate Ickx, but a misfiring engine brought his day to an early end.

Two weeks later, on February 6, Mario was in Daytona for the year's second World Sports Car Championship race. That year the traditional twenty-four-hour race was shortened to six hours by an FIA edict that reduced all long-distance races, save Le Mans, to either six hours in duration or 1000 kilometers in length.

Mario qualified on the pole, but his car lost a cylinder in the early going, and he and Ickx began to fade. But problems afflicted the other front-runners, as well, and Mario and Ickx came through to win, taking the lead from teammates Tim Schenken and Ronnie Peterson after Schenken pitted to replace a punctured tire with just fifteen minutes to go.

Next came the South African GP on March 4. Mario qualified sixth, half a second slower than Jackie Stewart's pole lap, and finished fourth, well ahead of Ferrari teammates Ickx and Clay Regazzoni. All three men were unhappy with their Ferraris' handling, which was inconsistent and unpredictable for reasons that were not immediately known.

From South Africa, Mario flew to California for the unveiling of VPJ's new Indy car. Mario had persuaded Jones and Miletich to hire Maurice Phillippe from Lotus to design an all-new car for the team. It was a move he would soon regret.

"I had a relationship with Lotus, and I really liked Maurice Phillippe, and I brought him over," Mario says. "I gave him credit because I think he helped me in '68 to win the pole at the Glen just by working with me in that car. I thought he understood a lot more than subsequently proved to be the case.

"Phillippe had a lot of weird ideas. He was very good at detail work. A lot of things like the suspension and uprights and welding was very neat, but as far as understanding the working of a race car, I don't think he was there."

Phillippe's new car, built in California and called a Parnelli, bristled with technical innovations. It featured torsion bars rather than coil springs as well as dihedral wings that projected at a forty-five degree angle from the sides of the car. Phillippe also designed a pair of camber compensators. These were long, tubular links that connected left- and right-side suspension to put positive camber into the outside

Opposite: When the Daytona 24 Hours was reduced to a 6-hour race in 1972, Mario and co-driver Jacky Ickx scored the first of three straight World Championship for Makes victories with the Ferrari 312P sports cars. Mario was on the pole at Daytona with Clay Regazzoni beside him. Tim Schenken was on the inside of the second row in the third factory Ferrari. (ISC Archives) Above: The Daytona 6 Hours victory was the Ferrari team's second of the year, following Ronnie Peterson and Tim Schenken's early January win in the Buenos Aires 1000Ks. Mario and Jacky Ickx would win four races that year, with Ickx adding two more wins co-driving with Regazzoni and Brian Redman. Ferrari dominated the World Championship for Makes in 1972, winning nine of ten races. (Hal Crocker)

Above right: Maurice Phillippe looks on as Jim McGee applies a pair of metal shears to a wing trim tab. The laborious process of sorting out the car has begun. Bignotti had specified a conventional rear wing to provide better grip to the back end. This was just one of many moves away from Phillippe's unorthodox technology in favor of proven race-car components. (Richard George) **Below right:** In this view of the Parnelli's rear suspension the camber compensators can be seen. These are the vertical links attached to the lower wishbones and connected to the opposite side of the car by horizontal cross links. Mario was baffled by the concept of two camber compensators, which essentially stopped the car's body from rolling at all. (Richard George) **Above:** A monocoque chassis under construction at the VPJ workshop in Torrance. The team didn't lack resources. VPJ employed some of the finest fabricators in the business and its cars were beautifully constructed. Parnelli's operation also took full advantage of California's booming aerospace industry to produce components for its cars. (Richard George) **Opposite:** Master mechanic George Bignotti discusses the situation with Unser and Parnelli's partner, Vel Miletich. Bignotti was one of the most successful crew chiefs in the sport's history and would be the key man in sorting out the pointlessly avant-garde Parnelli. (Richard George)

rear wheel when the car rolled. "I think we should have kept our feet on the ground, but we were always looking for that elusive, unfair advantage," Mario says.

McLaren had used a single camber compensator on its successful 1971 Champ car, and Phillippe apparently decided that two of these devices would do the job even better. "When the car rolled, it would keep the left rear from picking up negative camber," Mario says, "a good thing if you have excessive roll. But putting two on made no sense. That would stop the car from rolling altogether."

The first Parnelli Champ car made its debut to the press at the Ontario Motor Speedway. At that point the car hadn't yet turned a wheel. "Al Unser and I were there to drive the car," Mario recalls. "Al took the first ride, and Phillippe was there in his double-breasted blazer. He looked like the Duke of Windsor, proud as a peacock as the car rolled out."

Expectations were high that the Super Team's new machine immediately would challenge the 195-plus mph test laps produced by Bobby Unser and Jerry Grant, who were driving new Eagles. "Al went out, and he's warming up and warming up; then he comes in and says, 'Hey, Wop. You drive it.' I asked, 'It's that bad?'"

Mario got in and quickly discovered Unser was right. "In the short chute between turns three and four, I punched it and almost lost it. I thought, 'What's going on?' The car wouldn't even go down the straightaway!

"I pulled in and drove straight into the garage. I said, 'Use whatever excuse you want, but get rid of everybody. I don't want to talk to anybody because we've got a huge problem. This car is not going out again today.'"

The first thing they did was disconnect the camber compensators. "We started going the next day without them," Mario recalls, "but all we could do was 160 to 170 mph, and we were scaring ourselves."

Mario and Al Unser charged George Bignotti with turning Phillippe's experimental car into a practical, driveable machine. "We said, 'George, you Bignotti-ize this car. Do whatever you need to do,'" Mario recalls. "We kept the dihedral wings for a little bit, but realized they were useless. We had to scrap them and go back to regular rear and front wings. That's when I started really doubting Maurice Phillippe. And when you lose confidence in your designer, forget it.

"We took the torsion bars off the back end and put conventional coil springs and shocks on. We left the torsion bars on the front, but the only ones that would work were the stiffest bars that were made for the rear! We got the car starting to handle, but it was never really finished."

Teammate Al Unser minces no words in assessing Phillippe's work. "He built

shitboxes, and if he was alive today I'd tell him that to his face," Unser says. "He just didn't appreciate the stresses and load levels on our cars compared to Formula One cars. The front end on those dihedral wing cars flexed so bad. If you looked at how he put those things together, you wouldn't believe it. It was way underbuilt."

Jones offers another perspective on Phillippe: "His problem, in my opinion, was he didn't care. His attitude was this is what he built and the mechanics have got to do their best to make it work. He didn't work with them as well as he could have. I think that was his downfall, but he was a brilliant man."

The USAC season opened at Phoenix on March 18 and, while the Parnelli was revamped, Mario, Unser, and Leonard raced modified versions of the previous year's VPJ Colts. Mario had a good run, finishing second to Bobby Unser, who qualified on the pole and dominated the race in All-American Racers' impressive new Eagle-Offy.

The next week Mario was in Florida for the Sebring 12 Hours. Once more, he put his Ferrari 312PB on the pole and led the opening laps only to run into a series of problems. Mario and co-driver Ickx lost time with a cut tire, a broken battery cable, and an oil leak, but were able to come back in style, beating teammates Schenken and Peterson once again. This was Mario's third win at Sebring.

"I really enjoyed those races with Ickx," Mario says. "Jacky was one of the best teammates I ever had. He would let me qualify, which I loved to do, and physically, we were about the same size. His arms were longer than mine. I used to set up the car to suit me, and he would never change a thing." Mario and Ickx won again in the 1000K race at Brands Hatch, England, on April 16. Peterson and Schenken finished second, making it four one-twos in a row for Ferrari.

At Trenton the next weekend the new Parnelli finally was ready to race. Unser and Leonard had been able to do some useful testing with the car, but because of his F1 and sports-car commitments Mario had run only a handful of laps in the revamped Parnelli. He qualified fourth at Trenton and ran well in the race until a series of problems stopped him. Despite this Mario was happy with the car and believed he would be competitive at Indianapolis.

Mario, alone with his thoughts in Ferrari's 312B2. In contrast to the 312P sports car, the new Ferrari F1 car was a disaster. Mario ran five F1 races in 1972 and his best result was fourth in South Africa, where he had won the year before. "That car was awful. The chassis would twist badly. It had no grip at all. It was easy to get it sideways, and then the chassis would spring back. It was impossible." (Hal Crocker)

The following weekend Mario was in Spain for the third race of the F1 World Championship. He qualified his Ferrari fifth and passed Denny Hulme early in the race for fourth place before his engine blew. By that point it was clear the chassis of the latest Ferrari F1 car was torsionally weak, causing serious handling problems.

Ferrari team manager Mauro Forgheiri was also chief engineer and implored Mario not to tell Enzo Ferrari the truth about the car. "Forgheiri only told the Old Man what he wanted to hear," Mario says. "He used to tell stories, blaming the tires, blaming everything but the car itself. I remember we were playing tennis, and he knew I had the Old Man's ear. He said to me, 'Tell the Old Man there's nothing wrong with the car,' which would imply that it was the drivers' fault. And I said, 'So that means we can't drive. Is that right?'

"I said, 'I'm sorry; the car is a piece of junk. I don't recognize what's happening with this car, and neither does anyone else.' I told him I didn't think anybody could drive the car. 'You've got to face it,' I said, and he didn't like my response. That car was a disaster, and they never really got it any better."

At Indianapolis there was plenty of work to be done on the Parnelli for the month of May. Giant wings and unlimited turbocharging had resulted in a huge performance leap during the winter, and although the new Parnelli was a good deal faster than the previous year's car, it was no match for the latest Eagles and McLarens.

The performance gap was as much about horsepower as it was handling and aerodynamics. VPJ's turbo Offies were inferior to those built by All-American Racers in particular. Bobby Unser qualified the factory AAR Eagle on the pole eight mph faster than Mario and broke Peter Revson's 1971 track record by no less than seventeen mph.

"After we qualified at Indianapolis, I told Parnelli the cars won't finish," Bignotti recalls. "They said, 'What can we do?' I said 'You've got to fly your metal men back here, and we'll reconstruct some stuff.' We had to fix the shocks, and we needed bigger radiators and oil coolers to run 500 miles. They said, 'OK,' and we put Maurice in a room with a drafting board. He drew it all up, and it worked fine, except the front never did come in right because all the pressure in the shocks was put on the centerline, and it gave it a chance to rock a little."

Bignotti was unhappy when the team took away his engine-building responsibilities and Miletich created his own engine-building company, R & D Service, with veteran engine man Dick Jones. Bignotti recalls: "They shortened the stroke on the engines, and I said, 'You're going to lose horsepower.' And they said, 'Oh, you don't know.' So we ended up with short-stroke engines, and they lost about thirty horsepower."

In the race, Mario's engine performed poorly, delivering too little boost pressure and using too much fuel so that he had to contend with the worst of both worlds—no power and bad fuel consumption. He was running fifth with four laps to go when his car ran out of fuel. Mario finished eighth while teammates Unser and Leonard made it home in second and third, well behind Mark Donohue's winning Penske/McLaren, which raced with a regular, long-stroke VPJ Offy.

"Penske blew up six engines or something like that," Jones recalls, "and at the last minute we sold them one of our engines, and they beat us. So our engines ran one-two-three."

Tires were another part of VPJ's struggles. "We were getting beat because Firestone didn't have a very good tire," Jones declares. "You can't badmouth the hand that's feeding you, so we just had to live with that. The day that Firestone got out of racing we put on Goodyear tires and went three or four mph quicker. That's a big, big difference. Publicly, you're blaming your cars, blaming your drivers, blaming everything else. We knew what the facts were, but we just couldn't say anything."

At Milwaukee the week after Indy, Bobby Unser ran untroubled all the way, beating Donohue and Bettenhausen while Mario finished eighth. At Michigan in July, Mario stalked Unser's AAR Eagle until Unser's engine blew. Mario took the lead and stayed in front until his transmission broke with fifteen laps to go. Meanwhile, Leonard made the finish, and took the first checkered flag for the Super Team.

The next weekend Mario ran his last sports-car race of the year for Ferrari, co-driving with Ickx at Watkins Glen. The pair took their fourth win of the year and beat teammates Peterson and Schenken by fourteen seconds. The rest of the field was fourteen or more laps behind.

Back in a Parnelli Champ car for the Pocono 500, Mario qualified third behind Bobby Unser's Eagle and Gordon Johncock's McLaren. After Unser, Johncock, and Gary Bettenhausen encountered mechanical trouble, Mario inherited the lead and led most of the race's second half. But after running out of fuel on the way in for his last pit stop with 35 laps to go, his gearbox failed. The team had to jack the car up and force it into third gear. Mario almost destroyed the clutch leaving the pits and eventually finished seventh, twelve laps behind.

Incredibly, Leonard survived to win again at Pocono, then scored his third win in a row at Milwaukee two weeks later. Mario qualified on the pole for the year's second race at Milwaukee and led from the start, pulling away steadily through lap 109. Then he had more trouble in the pits.

"Mario came flying in, and some sand had been thrown on the track because

somebody had spilled some oil, and Mario hit that and skidded like crazy." Bignotti says. "He knocked the fuel nozzle off the tank and caught my best guy, Jimmy Dilamarter, on fire. We had a hell of a time, but we got him out and going. It wasn't all his fault. He was such a racer. He didn't waste any time anywhere."

At the California 500, Jerry Grant and Bobby Unser became the first drivers to qualify for a motor race at 200 mph or better. Unser, Grant, and Johncock all had beaten the 200 mph mark in testing. Mario qualified on the second row and ran well in the race, leading Unser, the fastest qualifier, until his engine blew after some 125 miles. Roger McCluskey went on to score his first win in four years aboard Lindsey Hopkins's McLaren-Offy from road racer Mike Hiss. Leonard was among the non-finishers but still managed to wrap up a lackluster championship with two of ten races still to run.

Mario's season had been disappointing, and Bignotti felt some responsibility. "As a fellow Italian, I always felt bad that I didn't really do a great job for Mario," Bignotti says. "I would set up all three cars, then give Mario and McGee their car and let them do what they wanted. I would take care of the other two, and McGee and Mario did their own thing.

"At Ontario, Mario came over to me after qualifying and said, 'Hey, I can't drive this car.' I said, 'Well, the other two are fine. You want me to fix it?' He said yes, so I put Al and Joe's cars on the scales and checked them over, and they were identical. Then I put Mario's on the scales and made it identical to the other two cars, and when the flag dropped Mario just started coming up through the pack. Then the engine went. So he never really had the luck he should have had. Maybe if I had just one car with Mario we probably would have done a lot better together, because I knew what to do and he knew how to drive it."

It was at Ontario that Bignotti decided he wasn't going to continue with Vel and Parnelli. "Pat Patrick said he'd like me to join his team," Bignotti says. "He said Goodyear wanted me to be on his team. He told me he could get $800,000 from Goodyear if I would work for him. Parnelli and Vel were great guys, but I didn't like the fact that they took the engines away from me and were telling me that I was old fashioned. I think I showed over the years that followed that I'm not that old fashioned."

The year's last two races were both won by Bobby Unser. Bobby beat Donohue at Trenton for his third win of the year and scored his fourth win at Phoenix with Mario third behind Mike Mosley.

By the end of 1972 Mario had gone two-and-a-half years without winning a USAC race. Mario credits Leonard's chief mechanic, Johnny Capels, as the critical difference in Leonard winning the 1972 USAC title. "Stuff was falling off my car, and Joe's car ran the distance, race after race. That's when Parnelli Jones told me, 'You could break an anvil with a rubber hammer.' He told the press as well. I mean, of all people! In his driving days Parnelli wasn't exactly the easiest on equipment."

Jones still stands by those words today, although he rates Mario highly. "I think over any driver I know Mario could maximize a car and get the most out of it for one lap," Jones says. "If you line them up and put the drivers in the same car, Mario would turn the quickest time.

"Al Unser, on the other hand, knew how to be there at the end better than any driver I've ever seen in my life. I think we had two of the best at totally different ends. Al was a perfect car owner's driver. He wasn't the most colorful or outspoken guy like Mario, but he was easy on equipment. The first year in '70, when we won Indianapolis with Al, you could have lined that car up and run another 500 miles, and he led 191 of the 200 laps. And of course, Mario, if he didn't fall out, he'd probably win."

Jones says proof that Mario was tougher on his equipment than Al Sr. was evident in the wear and tear on the parts from his car. "As the mechanics went through the cars after each race, Mario's gears would be a little rougher than Al's, that sort of thing."

All in all, 1972 had been a bad year for Mario in both USAC and F1, though he was pleased with his sports-car races with Ickx. Nevertheless, it was the last of four straight years Mario raced sports cars for Ferrari because he wanted nothing more to do with Forghieri's evil-handling Grand Prix cars.

"Ferrari went through a bit of a crisis period then," Mario says. "They were going in different directions trying to find themselves, until Niki Lauda got them back on track in '74. I was glad I didn't sign up at the end of '71. We were talking about a three-year deal, and it would probably have destroyed my career. Those were probably the worst three years in Ferrari's history. Had I been there, I would have been squarely to blame, and I would have lost my confidence. In retrospect, I dodged a bullet there."

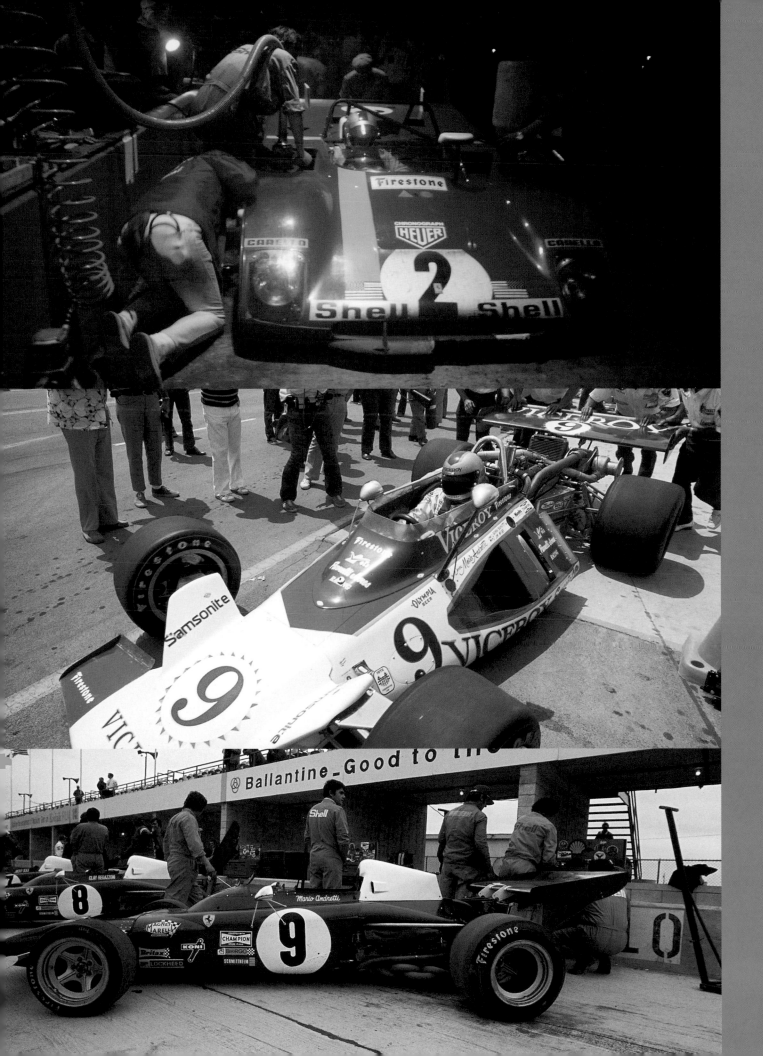

Top left: Mario won the Sebring 12 Hours for the third time in 1972, with Jacky Ickx. Mario and Ickx were the dominant forces in long-distance racing that year in the small, lithe Ferrari 312P sports car. "Jacky was an excellent teammate. He was as quick, or quicker, than anybody when he needed to be, and he was reliable. We got along so well." (Barry Tenin)

Middle left: The VPJ team was beginning to make sense of their car by September's California 500 at Ontario. Mario qualified fourth, and with George Bignotti's help produced a car that was quick enough to lead some of the race until its engine blew. (Dave Friedman)

Bottom left: Mario's Ferrari 312B2 waits in the pits at Watkins Glen before the 1972 U. S. Grand Prix. Mario and Jacky Ickx would finish sixth and fifth respectively in the problematic car. (Dave Friedman)

Opposite: Parnelli commissioned a new and much more conventional car from Phillippe for 1973. Here Unser, Mario, and Parnelli fool around at the new car's debut in December 1972. The car is painted half in Viceroy colors and half in Samsonite livery. (Richard George)

Chapter 12

The Price of Loyalty

Although George Bignotti had left to work for Pat Patrick's operation, hopes were high at VPJ entering 1973. Phillippe had produced an all-new, boxier-looking Champ car with completely different aerodynamics, weight distribution, centralized fuel tanks, and a lower center of gravity. Mario went into the new season having done more testing than ever before. The VPJ team also had discovered what AAR's Bobby Unser and Dan Gurney had been doing

Above: At Mosport in June, Mario jokes with old friend and fellow USAC star Bobby Unser (middle) and F5000 champion Brian Redman as they lean on Unser's AAR Eagle F5000 car. Mario scored the first of four 1975 F5000 victories at this event. (Nate Korn) **Opposite:** At the inaugural Long Beach GP in September, 1975, Mario drove an F5000 Lola featuring a taller, more oval-shaped airbox and a delta wing. "There was Maurice Phillippe influence in that wing," Mario says. "We used that wing on the Formula One car as well." (Bob Tronolone)

Above: Mario drove the Agapiou Brothers' McLaren M20-Chevy twin-turbo Can-Am car at Laguna Seca and Riverside in September, 1973. "That car had more power than God!" he marvels. "But it had tremendous throttle lag. You had to go flat on the throttle fifty yards before the corner so you had boost pressure to come off the corner. But down the straightaway, man, that thing flew! That car was actually scary to drive. It could lift the front wheels in any gear." (Dale Von Trebra) Right: Hanging it out on his way to victory at DuQuoin, Illinois, in September 1973 aboard one of VPJ's fearsome four-cam Ford-powered Championship dirt cars. Mario won two of three dirt car races he ran in 1973, but was beaten to the now-separate dirt car championship by teammate Al Unser. (Ken Coles) Opposite: Mario waits in the qualifying line at Indianapolis with the 1973 version of the Parnelli. He set two world closed-course speed records with the Parnelli in 1973, going more than 211 mph in April at Texas World Speedway, and then over 214 mph in October. "The car was all enclosed with a proper engine cover and bodywork for the record run at Texas," Mario says. "That car ran well at Ontario and other similar tracks." (Dave Friedman)

with their engines to produce so much power for qualifying in 1972.

"AirResearch accidentally sent us one of AAR's blowers, or maybe they did it on purpose," Parnelli Jones says. "We put it on the dyno, and there was 100 horsepower difference! Then we knew why they were outqualifying us so bad."

Until 1974, there was no boost limit or in-car boost gauges, and the top teams would pump up the turbocharger to explosive levels for qualifying. In an early test, Mario had lapped the Ontario Motor Speedway at 197 mph and was faster than 201 mph in his second test. Before the season started he set an unofficial world closed-course record of 211.765 mph at the high-banked Texas World Speedway while testing tires. Later in the season he pushed the record above 214 mph in official qualifying for the year's second-to-last USAC race, although Bobby Unser subsequently went even faster.

"What I used to love about qualifying in those days was you never experienced the power until you qualified," Mario says, grinning. "You didn't dare pump the engine up in practice because it would destroy it. Coming off the corners the thing had so much power it would vibrate. We had 1,200 horsepower. The turbo was pushing three-and-a-half atmospheres, probably 120 to 130 inches of pressure, and that Offy would live for a couple of laps."

As fast as the Parnelli was, it was dismally unreliable, its engines in particular, for all three of VPJ's superstar drivers. After the Phoenix season opener was twice rained out, the year got under way at Texas in April. Mario's engine blew at the start of practice. Then he later pulled in with a broken suspension upright and had to qualify with limited practice and an upright scavenged from teammate Al Unser's car. Then, in the race, an oil pump drive pin broke on the second lap.

"Imagine testing your new car for a couple of thousand miles and being super pleased that you now had the best oval racer of your career," an exasperated Mario wrote in his *Allentown Morning-Call* column. "Then in a matter of hours encountering more mechanical problems than you've had in three months of rugged testing."

Despite Mario's problems, teammate Al Unser survived and won in Texas. The next weekend featured a pair of 150-mile races at Trenton. A. J. Foyt won the first race with Mario fourth, but Mario won the second race after changing the turbocharger, springs, and wing angles. He outran Foyt and Billy Vukovich to score his

first USAC win in almost three years.

Indianapolis followed the next month. Mario and his teammates knew they now had the speed to match the fastest Eagles and McLarens. Johnny Rutherford in one of the factory McLarens beat Bobby Unser to the pole with Mario qualifying sixth, three mph slower than Rutherford and Unser. That year's 500 took three days to run, delayed by rain and accidents, starting with Art Pollard's fatal crash during practice early in the month.

The first attempt at starting the race ended in a multi-car accident in the first turn. Eleven cars were involved, and Salt Walther was badly burned. The race was stopped; then rain settled in before it could be restarted. More rain the next day meant the race took place on Wednesday after a morning shower. For Mario it was all very anticlimactic as he coasted into the pits after just four laps with a burned piston. Later in the day, Swede Savage was burned grievously in an accident, and one of his teammate's crewmen, Armando Teran, was struck and killed by a fire truck in the pit lane. Savage died two months later.

After that deeply tragic May, new rules were introduced for the rest of the season. Wing sizes were cut in an attempt to reduce downforce, fuel tank capacity was slashed from 75 to 40 gallons, and all of the fuel was required to be carried on the left side of the chassis. The new restrictions on fuel capacity and location played havoc with the latest Parnelli's handling.

"It threw our cars out of balance more than the others," Mario says. "Our car was designed very wide and low for an even placement of 75 gallons. Then, all of a sudden, things changed. Things that worked for us in testing in February started working against us."

The rest of the year was deeply frustrating as Mario's only good results were second-place finishes in the Pocono 500 and again at Michigan in September. At the end of the season the team continued to unravel as Jim McGee left to join Bob Fletcher's team for 1974. "Mario wanted to go over to Formula One," McGee says, "and I could see that VPJ wasn't going anywhere. Bignotti had left the year before, and I decided the time was ripe for me to leave as well."

Then, in 1973 and '74, I was winning with the dirt car, and in 1974 and '75 I was winning with the Formula 5000 car. I was running everything and just hoping that the Indy car was going to get straightened out."

In retrospect, Mario believes he probably should have left Vel and Parnelli's team. "If I ever learned something in my career, it was that I was a little bit too loyal. I often felt that loyalty didn't always pay off for me, but you've got to do what feels right. And, at the time, there really weren't any good options." All-American Racers was the only serious rival for VPJ then, while Roger Penske was still concentrating on the Can-Am and Trans-Am series, and ran just three USAC events.

Mario's primary interest in 1974 was the burgeoning Formula 5000 series. In the winter of 1973-74, VPJ decided to buy a Lola T332 for Mario to drive and hired crew chief Jim Chapman away from Carl Haas's F5000 team and driver Brian Redman to run the operation. USAC had recognized the engine problems that were descending on its primary series and started talking to its archrival, the Sports Car Club of America (SCCA), about co-sanctioning the F5000 series and possibly adopting the F5000 stock-block formula in 1975 or '76.

VPJ's F5000 team tested frequently and was reckoned to be the most serious in the category's short history. Mario qualified fastest in all but one of that year's seven races but was plagued by a series of engine failures. He won at Watkins Glen; Elkhart Lake, Wisconsin; and Riverside, worked from the back of the grid to finish second on the Ontario road course, and finished third at Laguna Seca, California, after a flat tire. But those problems allowed the fast and steady Redman to beat Mario to the championship.

"Many times in Formula 5000 something happened that lost me the championship," Mario says. "At Laguna Seca the valve stem wasn't in, and the tire deflated. Another time a toe link fell off on the last lap because it wasn't properly tightened,

The next few years were tough times for USAC as the old club struggled to deal with rapidly escalating speeds, technology, and costs. The new forty-gallon fuel limit substantially changed the strategical nature of the races with twice as many pitstops, which Mario thoroughly disliked. USAC also introduced an 80-inch turbo boost pressure limit for qualifying, enforced by a "pop-off" valve, which released the pressure if it exceeded 80 inches.

The forty-year-old Offy four-cylinder used by most teams had been stretched beyond its limits in big boost turbo form. Drake Engineering, manufacturers of the Offenhauser, no longer could deliver a consistent product, and blown engines were all too common. But there was no alternative because Foyt owned the rights to Ford's four-cam turbo V8.

For 1974, VPJ built its own copy of an AAR Eagle, then bought and raced Eagles starting at Indianapolis. Mario drove the Phillippe Eagle copy just once at Trenton in April and didn't like the way it handled.

The 1974 season started badly when Joe Leonard's legs were broken in a crash at Ontario, effectively ending his career. Mario's USAC season was miserable. He fell out of race after race. At Indianapolis he qualified fifth but lasted only two laps before burning a piston. His best finish was third in the last race of the season at Phoenix.

"We certainly struggled through that period," Mario says of his haphazard experience with the cars at VPJ. "The only thing that kept me going was the fact that I was able to win in other disciplines. In 1971 and '72 I was winning in sports cars.

Above: Co-driving an Alfa Romeo P33 sports car with Arturo Merzario, Mario won the Monza 1000Ks in April and failed to finish at Watkins Glen in July. "It wasn't a great car," he says. "It was very clumsy, but we had power at Monza that day. I got a new engine and I was turning big revs and put it on the pole. We had been two-and-a-half seconds slower than the Matras in practice, then all of a sudden we were right there. In Monza they do certain things for the Italians." (LAT Photographic)

Above: After they finally gave up on the recalcitrant Parnellis, Mario and teammate Al Unser drove Eagles in most 1974 USAC races. In fact, the team produced its own copy of an Eagle, which Mario ran in some events. He is shown here in the Eagle copy at the Pocono 500, where he qualified third and finished seventh. (Barry Tenin)

Top left: Mario holds off arch-rival Brian Redman, both driving Formula 5000 Lola T332-Chevies. Mario raced F5000 in 1974 and '75, as USAC combined with the SCCA to sanction the series with the idea of adopting the F5000 stock-block formula for USAC. Mario won three of seven F5000 races in 1974. (Pete Biro) **Bottom left:** Mario took USAC's 1974 dirt car championship by winning at Sedalia, Missouri, and Springfield, and finishing second to Al Unser at Syracuse. "The days of the Offy were gone forever because of the surface preparation of the racetracks," he explains. "The Offy was fantastic in the warm-up, early in the morning when the track was heavy, but by race time the tracks used to get really hard and slick, and that's when the Ford came into its own." (Andretti collection)

and I had no steering. Another time a mechanic forgot to put a nut on the bolt that holds the shifter to the linkage, so I lost my gears. All these cost me the race I was leading, and any one of them would have meant the difference in the championship."

VPJ approached racing in Formula 5000 as preparation for entering Formula One, and later that year the team rolled out its new Phillippe-designed F1 car. Despite the fact that the VPJ1 Indy car had been a near disaster, the team believed Phillippe would produce a competitive car. "We thought F1 would be his forte," Mario says of the former Lotus Grand Prix engineer. "But he built a car that was out of date. He built a 1972-style car in 1974. It had all the qualities of the Lotus 72, which was obsolete by then. It took John Barnard to bring that car to a competitive level."

The plan was to run the 1974 season-closing Canadian and United States GPs to get ready for a serious assault on the F1 World Championship in 1975. At Mosport for the Canadian GP, Mario qualified sixteenth and drove a great race, battling hard with Denny Hulme for sixth place and finishing seventh, just a quarter of a second behind Hulme.

Two weeks later at Watkins Glen, Mario shocked the F1 regulars by qualifying fastest on the opening day only to crash on the second day of practice. The car was repaired in time to run a few laps late on Saturday, but by then Carlos Reutemann and James Hunt had pushed Mario to the second row in final qualifying.

There was more bad luck on race day when an electric fuel pump failure meant the Parnelli couldn't get off the line. The VPJ mechanics leaped over the guardrail, pushed the car to the side of the track, and changed the faulty pump. But after he joined the race, Mario was black-flagged for receiving illegal outside assistance. He was sidelined after just four laps, but driver, team, and car had shown considerable potential.

Mario's up-and-down season ended by winning USAC's dirt-car title. Teammate Al Unser and he dominated this stepchild of a series driving Grant King dirt cars powered by four-cam Ford engines. Unser had won the championship in 1973, and Mario took the title in 1974, winning three of that year's five dirt-track races. "The power band of the overhead-cam Ford delivered good, progressive power, especially on the slicker race tracks," Mario says.

This was the only season Mario drove a dirt car fitted with a protective roll cage.

Though he approved of the increased safety, he lamented the loss of purity. "All of a sudden people did not respect the car. You had some guys doing crazy things that they would not have done before, but now they knew they had a safety blanket. It took a lot of the finesse out of driving those cars."

In 1975 Mario had a busy schedule. He planned to contest the full F1 schedule, all nine SCCA/USAC F5000 races in a two-car team with Al Unser, but only three or four USAC Championship races. All-American Racers also cut back its USAC program because of the skyrocketing costs of poor engine reliability. Many racers hoped USAC would adopt F5000's stock-block rules.

Barnard would prove instrumental in turning the Parnelli F1 car into a competitive machine. Barnard would go on to design the ground-breaking Chaparral 2K Indy car and McLaren MP4/1 Formula One car. "The Parnelli F1 car had promise, but only after John Barnard joined the group," Mario says. "He was a junior designer for Lola, and we brought him to the States. Vel and Parnelli gave his wife a job at the dealership as a controller, and he began his career as a full-fledged designer with the team."

"What Barnard brought was a lot of common sense and a practical approach," says Mario, who relates a story about testing the Parnelli F1 car at Riverside just before going to South Africa for the start of the 1975 season. "I was a couple of seconds off my Formula 5000 times, and that was when panic set in. Barnard put the car on the pad and strapped it down and jacked it up. As the car was rolling we were losing stiffness. We had a decreasing spring rate instead of an increasing rate, and he just threw all that away."

Barnard also scrapped the exquisitely machined, $2,000 torsion bars specified by Phillippe. "The ones Phillippe made for the front were no good. They were way

Above: At Laguna Seca in October, Mario duels with Redman. James Hunt trails in third place in one of AAR's Eagle F5000 cars. Though Mario qualified on the pole and led most of the race, a flat tire caused by an improperly installed valve stem would cause him to fall behind Redman and Hunt in the closing laps. (Jutta Fausel) Opposite: Mario first raced the Parnelli F1 car at the Canadian GP at Mosport at the end of September, and then at the United States GP at Watkins Glen two weeks later. He was a rousing seventh at Mosport, then shocked the F1 regulars by qualifying second at the Glen, only to be excluded from the race for receiving outside assistance. Designer Phillippe crouches beside him. (Dale Von Trebra)

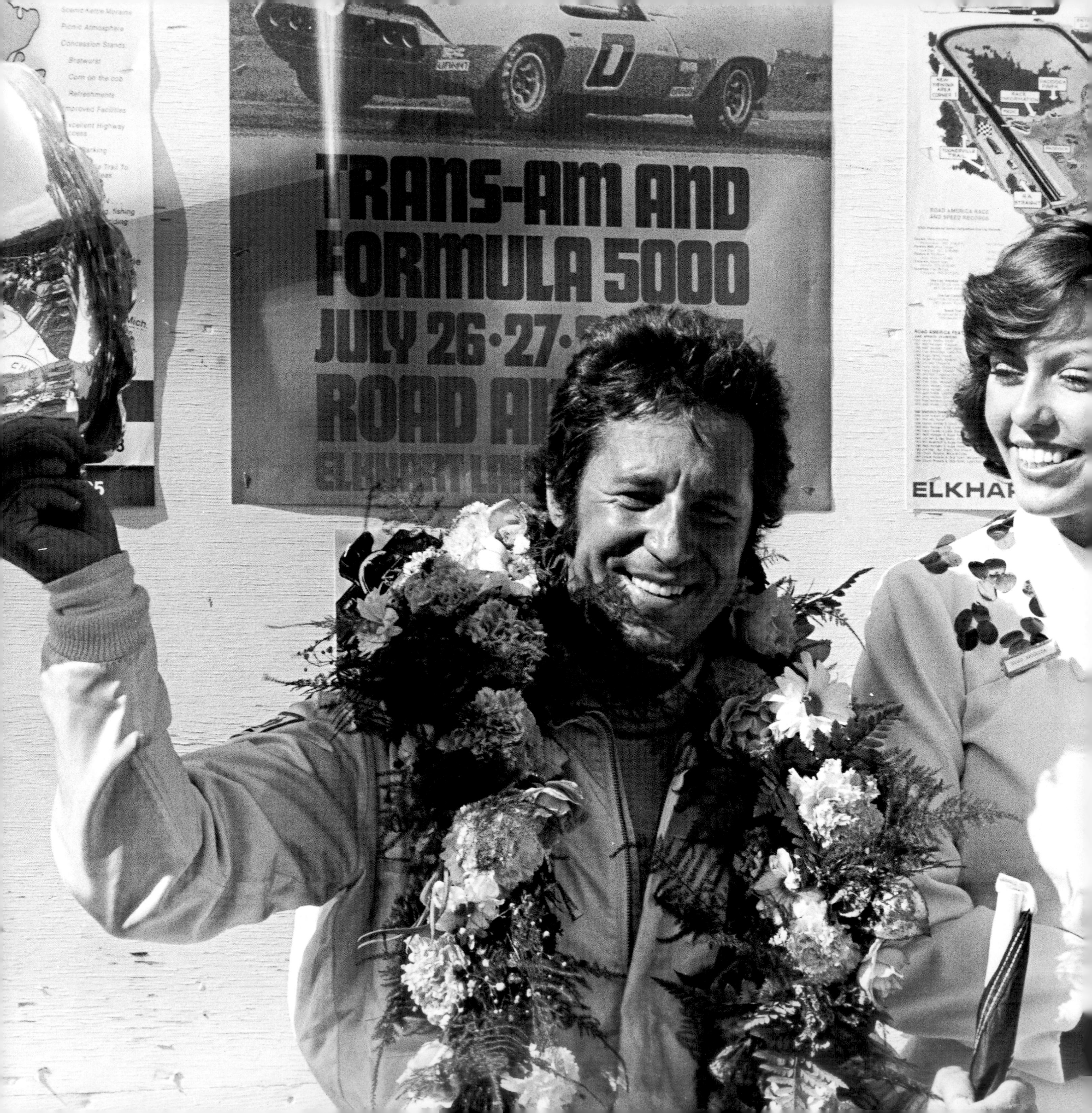
TRANS-AM AND
FORMULA 5000
JULY 26·27·

too light, so we used the rear bars on the front. We went to a normal damper and spring combination in the rear, and right away I started matching my Formula 5000 times.

"Then we went to South Africa, and I was running seventh near the end of the race when a driveshaft broke. But the car was so loose. At the first turn—the right-hander at the end of the straightaway—I was totally sideways every lap."

As it had everywhere, VPJ ran Firestone tires in South Africa, but during the last year it had become clear that Goodyear's tires were superior by seconds a lap at some tracks. As its tires became increasingly non-competitive, Firestone decided to pull out of racing early in 1975, which left the team without a sponsor. The company made a financial settlement with Jones and Vel Miletich worth approximately $1.5 million.

Mario, of course, had had a long personal sponsorship with Firestone and was now in an awkward position. "I had my tail between my legs," Mario recalls. "I thought I was totally out with Goodyear. The season had already started, and we were in Brazil. I figured I might as well face the issue, so I went to Leo Mehl's hotel room [Mehl was Goodyear's worldwide director of racing operations], and I said, 'Leo, I'm on my knees. I've got to be one of you now.' He said, 'You don't have to be on your knees. You can be one of our top testers.' I always appreciated that. It was so professional. Goodyear never held anything against me. They felt it had been fair competition and that competition was healthy between the two companies."

Mario's best F1 race of the year came in the non-championship Daily Express Trophy Race at Silverstone, England, in the spring. He finished third, about half a minute behind Niki Lauda's Ferrari and Emerson Fittipaldi's McLaren. At Barcelona for that year's Spanish GP, Mario qualified third and led the race for ten laps before the rear suspension broke, a consequence of being hit in the tail at the start by Vittorio Brambilla.

"We could have won in Barcelona," Mario says. "I was able to drive that car

sideways. It was really working. I caught Hunt and passed him, and I was truly gone. But there was quite a bit of vibration in the rear tires under acceleration and finally the upright just snapped."

Later in the year Mario finished fourth in the Swedish GP after starting fifteenth. He was fifth in France, but failed to finish the year's last three F1 races. Once again, he was at his best in F5000 in which he won four races: at Mosport, Elkhart Lake, Laguna Seca, and Riverside to equal Brian Redman's victory total, although Redman beat Mario to the championship again through better consistency.

"It must've driven him 'round the bend," Redman says with a chuckle. "That was a very strong effort of theirs. They took our chief mechanic, of course."

Redman has a particularly strong memory of chasing Mario at Mosport in 1975. "The fast qualifying time was half a second slower than the Formula One record," Redman recalls. "Just before the race I noticed Mario had lowered his rear wing, and I said to Jim Hall, 'Look, he's dropped his rear wing.' And he said, 'What do you think?' I said, 'Well, I'm happy with the car. We haven't tried it with the wing lower, so I'll stay as I am.'

"Well, Mario was incredibly quick up the straight. I could get back with him by the pit turn, which was only the second turn after the straight, but I couldn't pass him! There was no real good place to pass, no real feasible chance. We finished just like that. I was a car's length behind him. It was a tremendous, fierce race."

Toward the end of the 1975 season, USAC announced that it had decided against adopting the F5000 stock-block formula for Champ cars and made a five-year commitment to the existing turbo engine rules. VPJ therefore started developing a USAC version of the F1 car that Mario and Al Unser had tested briefly at Indianapolis during May. The car was powered by a turbocharged Cosworth engine, and Al Unser drove it in the last Champ car race of 1975.

For 1976 the F5000 program was cut back to a single car for Unser while Mario focused solely on the F1 program, which was clearly in jeopardy. VPJ had lost Viceroy sponsorship, so the cars were turned out in blue and white with Parnelli's wheel company, American Racing Wheels, as the putative sponsor. In fact, while VPJ was sorting out its F1 future, Mario drove a factory Lotus on a one-off basis in the season-opener in Brazil, then reverted to the Parnelli for the South African GP and

Opposite: Mario celebrates his second F5000 victory of the year at Elkhart Lake in July. As Mario's USAC fortunes waned, most of his success in 1975 came in F5000 road races and to a lesser degree in F1 with the Parnelli. (Pete Luongo)
Above: Mario and Al Unser tested the prototype Parnelli Cosworth DFX Indy car for the first time at Indianapolis in May 1975. The F1-based car would revolutionize Indy car racing with a smaller overall shape and profile, and a turbo version of the Cosworth DFV F1 engine. (Pete Biro)

Long Beach, but he felt he was on his own.

"There was no interest from anyone at VPJ in doing a lot of testing," Mario grumbles. "Quite honestly, I was the only guy who wanted the F1 program to happen. Vel and Parnelli were never behind it. Neither of them had any feel for Formula One, and they soon found an excuse to get out. It was unfortunate, but that's why it didn't go anywhere. We went through the '75 season, but in '76 they made up their minds that they wanted out."

Jones says a lack of sponsorship was the deciding factor. "When we went to Long Beach next year for the first race," Jones says, "we figured if we didn't have some sponsorship by then we'd have to pull the plug. And that's basically what we did." But they neglected to tell Mario.

"I found out in the cockpit at the start of the race at Long Beach," Mario says. "Chris Economaki put a microphone in front of my face and said, 'Mario, how's it feel to be in your last Formula One race?' I said, 'What do you think? That I'm going to kill myself or something?' He said, 'Vel Miletich just announced this is his last race.' Vel hadn't said anything to me."

Jones insists that in their hearts Miletich and he wanted the F1 program to continue. "I know Mario was upset, but we had spent everything we had gotten from Firestone and more," Jones says. "We didn't put anything in our pocket. You couldn't blame Mario for being upset because he wanted an American team to go over there and do it, and we'd have loved to. We worked like heck to try to get sponsorship, but Formula One in this country at that time didn't seem to carry the prestige that it does today."

The morning after that year's Long Beach GP, Mario bumped into Colin Chapman at breakfast. "I was really down," Mario says. "I had this mindset of doing Formula One. I didn't want to do anything else. I felt this was the time in my career. If I missed this opportunity, I would have been too old for another. I was 35 years old, and it was already a little late.

"So I'm asking myself, 'What do I do?' And here again, as fate would have it, Colin

had the worst race weekend he ever had and we're having breakfast in the Queensway Hilton, both of us alone. I told him, 'I want to do Formula One.' Colin said, 'Right. You come on as number one.' I wasn't all that excited because his cars were junk. They hadn't done anything in a few years. He was involved in his new car company and a boat company. The car company went public, and he made a pile of money. That's where his interests were at the time."

The 1975 season had been the Lotus team's worst since entering F1 in 1958. Between 1963-73 Lotus had won six F1 Constructors Championships, but in 1975 the team failed to win a race and by Long Beach in '76 top drivers Ronnie Peterson and Jacky Ickx had left the team.

"I said the only way this will work is if you come back full-time to racing," Mario continues. "Forget about your car company and the boat company, and come racing, and he agreed. I felt like the horizon had just opened because there was so much potential there."

Mario made the decision to leave VPJ. "I had a three-year deal with Vel, and I quit. I said, 'Sue me.' I was so pissed that they got out of F1 without talking to me about it. As soon as I hung up from Vel, I called Roger Penske and asked him if he was interested in me running some USAC races, and he said he was."

After four years and a few months, Mario's intriguing episode with the Super Team was over. Ahead was a new venture with Chapman, who had given Mario his first opportunity in Formula One. It would be a revolutionary pairing of talents.

Above left: Mario finished fifth in the 1975 French GP at Paul Ricard. Here he leads Carlos Reutemann's Brabham and Ronnie Peterson's Lotus. This was one of only three trouble-free races Mario enjoyed that year with the Parnelli. The F1 car was sorted out by young engineer John Barnard, who replaced Maurice Phillippe as VPJ's chief designer. (Jutta Fausel) Above right: At Phoenix in November 1975 for the year's last USAC Championship race, Mario drove Jerry O'Connell's Sugaripe Prune Eagle. He qualified and finished third. Here he leads Johnny Rutherford's factory Gatorade McLaren and Wally Dallenbach aboard one of Pat Patrick's Wildcats, all three cars powered by turbo Offies. (ISC Archives) Opposite: Mario failed to finish at Monaco, but he enjoyed a number of good races in 1975 with the Parnelli F1 car. At the Spanish GP he led until his suspension broke. "This car was a couple of years too late," he says. "It was basically a Lotus 72, which was a viable car in 1972 and '73, but not in '75." (Jutta Fausel)

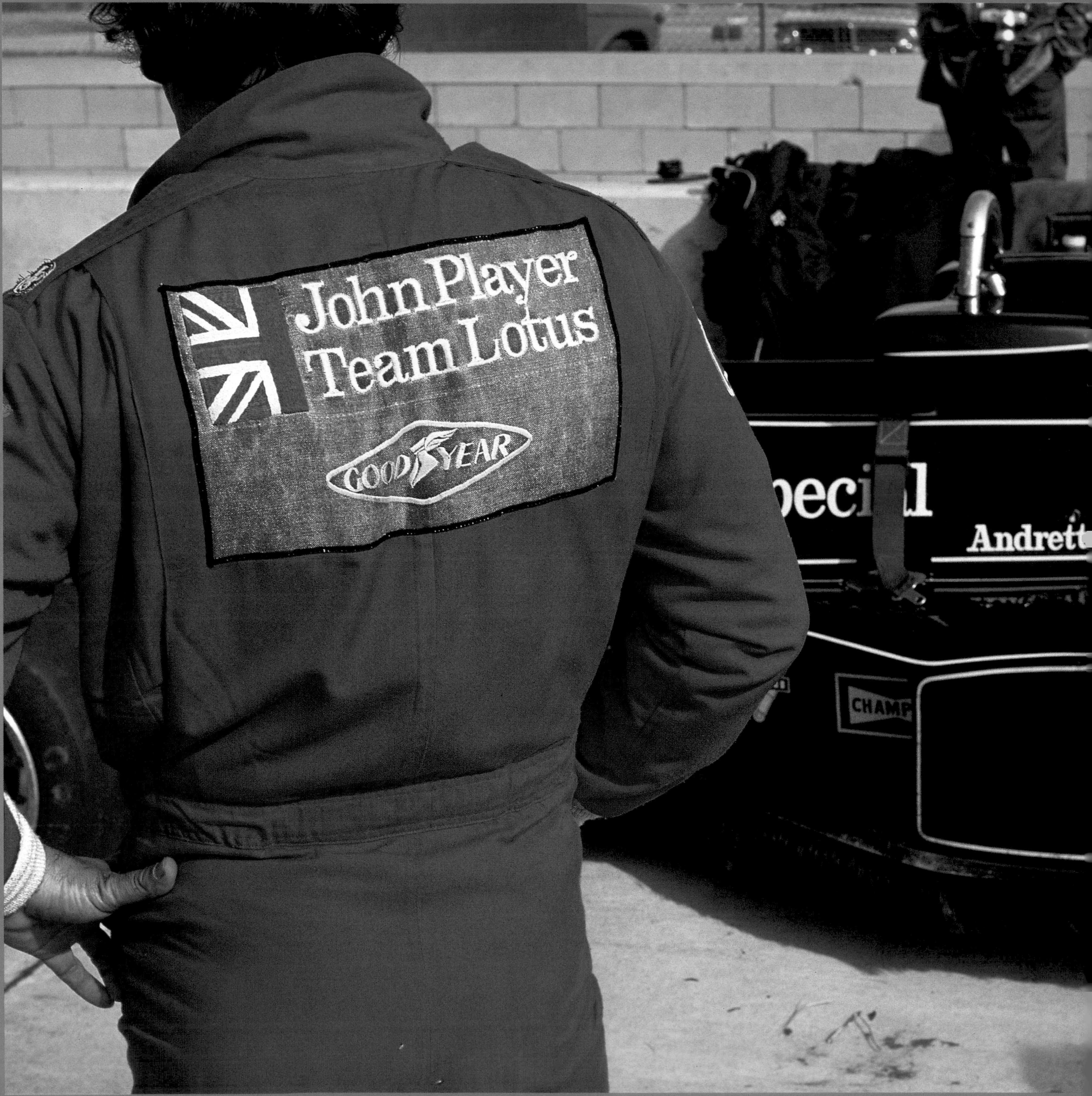
John Player
Team Lotus
GOODYEAR
pecial
Andrett
CHAMP

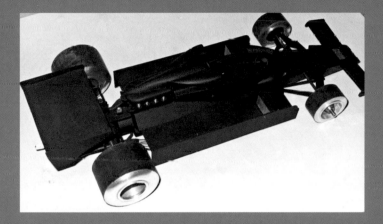

Chapter 13

The Dawn of Ground Effect

Mario's arrival energized Team Lotus, which quickly began a vigorous program of testing and developing the type 77. "The 77 was called the 'fully adjustable' car," Jabby Crombac says. Crombac was the editor and founder of France's *Sport-Auto* magazine. He is the eminence gris of the F1 press corps and was very close to Colin Chapman and Team Lotus during the sixties and seventies. "Colin had lost his way. He didn't know where to go on

Above: The wind tunnel model for the Lotus 78 shows how the side pods were developed to seal the gap between the bottom of the car and the track. That seal generated the road-sucking aerodynamics known as ground effect. (Tony Matthews)
Opposite: Mario returned to Team Lotus and Colin Chapman after the demise of the VPJ F1 effort. By the end of the 1976 season, Mario and the team had transformed the woefully uncompetitive Lotus 77 into a winner. (Gary Gold)

wheelbase, track, and weight distribution, so he built an infinitely adjustable car," Crombac adds.

Making sense of such a Rubik's cube of set-up possibilities was precisely the sort of challenge Mario relished. "I said to Colin, 'We're going to test and test and we're going to win a race before the season is out,'" Mario says. "There wasn't time to build a new car, so we just kept making it better and better."

Crombac recalls how Chapman, in signing Mario, at once motivated his driver and managed his cash flow: "Colin couldn't afford Mario, but he had the brilliant idea of paying him on results. He offered a lot of money provided Mario would win a lot of races, and it worked for both of them."

Mario was paid $10,000 per point, which meant he could earn $90,000 for winning a race. "I wanted some prize money," Mario says. "Colin never knew how to deal with that because of the way they got paid by [Formula One Constructors Association head Bernie] Ecclestone. So instead Colin said, 'I'll pay you so much per point' and I threw that number at him."

At the F1 race following Long Beach, the Spanish Grand Prix at Jarama, Mario's presence had immediate effect. Teammate Gunnar Nilsson qualified seventh with Mario ninth. A third of the way into the race they were up to fourth and fifth before Mario pulled in with a broken gear selector. Nilsson went on to finish a rousing third behind that year's world championship leaders, James Hunt and Niki Lauda.

At the Swedish GP in June, Mario shocked everyone by qualifying on the front row beside Jody Scheckter's six-wheel Tyrrell. Favorites Lauda and Hunt were back on the third and fourth rows of the grid. Mario leaped away at the start, beat Scheckter into the first turn, and pulled steadily away until his engine started to sour. By the time it finally blew, he had led more than half the race.

During the rest of the season, the experimental and constantly developing Lotus 77 showed equal parts promise and unreliability. Mario finished fifth in the French GP, then qualified third at Brands Hatch in England only to have an engine blow early in the race. In Austria he came from a midfield starting position to finish fifth, then drove a great race to finish third at Zandvoort, just two seconds behind the win-

ner, Hunt. For the Canadian GP at Mosport, Mario enjoyed one of his best races of the year, finishing third behind Hunt and Patrick Depailler's Tyrrell.

The final race of 1976 was the inaugural Japanese Grand Prix. Mario put the 77 on the pole—his first F1 pole since his debut with Lotus at the Glen in 1968. The team's development efforts were paying off.

That evening heavy rain settled in and continued into race day. After a number of spins and accidents in the morning warmup, there was talk of delaying the start of the race until conditions improved. But the Japanese officials would have none of it. The race began on time, in a deluge. The conditions were so bad that four drivers—Emerson Fittipaldi, Carlos Pace, Larry Perkins, and championship contender Lauda—quit after only a few laps.

Halfway through the first lap, Brambilla and Hans Stuck blew by Mario, but their banzai run was short lived. They both went off on that lap, almost simultaneously. Meanwhile, Mario regained the lead, followed closely by Hunt. The heavy rain stopped just past the mid-race point, and the track began drying slowly. With about a quarter distance to go, Hunt's only hope of passing Mario was to pit for slicks. The gamble nearly paid off. Hunt won the championship by racing his way back to third in the closing laps. Mario won the race by nursing his tires to the finish, searching for puddles that would cool them and help them last. Both leftside tires were down to the canvas carcass. The left front showed an unbroken band an inch wide all the way around. Mario estimated he had less than a lap left in the tires.

"I was determined not to do anything stupid today," Mario told *Autosport*'s Pete Lyons. "I've lost races in the past just the way James did today. I lost an F5000 race at Atlanta last year when I had a big lead and used my tires up, so this time I was going to be patient if it was the last thing I did. I could see the weather was going to clear

Above: The Lotus 78 shown under construction in November 1976. The substantial width and depth of the sidepods is evident. Note the brushes along the bottom edge that were the interim solution to sealing the gap between the car and the road while the team experimented with skirt designs. (Tony Matthews) Opposite: Chapman ponders his notes while Mario prepares for another practice run. Chapman and Mario worked wonders with the fully adjustable Lotus 77, steadily developing it over the course of the season. The working relationship Mario enjoyed with Chapman over the next few years was exactly what he had always imagined from the ideal team owner. (Jutta Fausel)

In the final Grand Prix of 1976 at Mt. Fuji, Japan, Mario scored a superb victory in the rain. He qualified the Lotus 77 on the pole and then drove a canny race, judging tire wear perfectly as the rain eased off to beat the field by a lap after James Hunt was forced to pit for new tires. (Joe Honda/Andretti collection)

up, and the way I figured it, the race wasn't going to start until the halfway mark.

"Winning Japan was a good thing because it really launched us into the following season with a lot of resolve."

Outside of Formula One, the only races Mario had run in 1976 were four USAC events in one of Roger Penske's McLaren M16C/Ds teamed with Tom Sneva. Although Mario had been the fastest qualifier at Indianapolis, he started back in the field because he qualified on the second weekend after missing pole day, which had conflicted with the Spanish GP. In the race Mario had climbed to eighth when the event was called just beyond the halfway point because of rain. A month later he led much of the Pocono 500 but lost the engine near the end and was classified fifth. Mario was fourth in Texas and third in the season-ending race at Phoenix in his only other USAC starts.

By this time the next generation of Andretti drivers was beginning to make its mark. Michael was thirteen and brother Jeff was twelve, and both were competitive go-kart racers. With Mario rarely at home, the boys had teamed with a neighbor, W. L. Gregory, whose son, John, was a friend of Michael's and also raced. The Andretti boys showed characteristic talent.

"I think Michael had one thing in mind," Mario says. "He was going to be up front no matter what, so there were a lot of kids with tire marks on their helmets! It was amazing. The kid had an uncanny way of working through traffic.

"Jeff was a little more intimidated when he started. If he was at the front, he could go. But if he was in the back, he didn't have the aggressiveness of Michael. Jeff and his cousin John used to pair up together. John was a little ahead of Jeff in years and had done a little more, but he helped Jeff quite a lot."

Meanwhile, Team Lotus had carefully set the stage for the 1977 Formula One season. While the race team made the most of the type 77, Lotus engineers Peter Wright and Ralph Bellamy were working on an all-new car. The result of these efforts was the Lotus 78, which would revolutionize motorsports as the first "ground effect" F1 car. Ground effect, in simple terms, is the management of air flow underneath the car to generate downforce, aerodynamically sucking the car toward the road and increasing its grip, allowing for higher cornering speeds.

Wright worked for Lotus from 1973-1994 as an engineer on road cars, racing cars, boats, and airplanes. Wright is now the FIA's technical advisor with worldwide responsibility for racing and passenger car safety, and in the late sixties he designed a wing-shaped BRM F1 car that was never built. He later suggested to designer Robin Herd that he try the airfoil-shaped sidepods that were used on the

March 701 F1 car that Mario raced in 1970.

"Out of the BRM work came the March," Wright says, "and out of the March really nothing more happened until we started the program with Ralph Bellamy on the type 78. Ralph was the designer, and I was told to run the wind tunnel with Ralph in my spare time."

Wright did his wind tunnel work at London's Imperial College, where an early rolling road had been installed. The rolling road was critical because it replicated the aerodynamic environment of a car traveling at speed in extremely close proximity to the road surface. "We heard that when the type 78 came out Ferrari built an equivalent version and tested it in a tunnel in Italy without a rolling road. They said, 'Ah, it doesn't work.' But if you don't have a rolling road, you will definitely get the wrong airflow conditions underneath the car."

One day in the wind tunnel Wright suddenly discovered the aerodynamic chimera he had been chasing. "We started getting very inconsistent results, and I noticed that the sidepods were sagging. We did some back-to-back tests. We wired up the sidepods and got them to work properly so that they didn't move, and then we got consistent results again. Thinking about it, we said it must have been the gap between the sidepod and the road. So we filled in the gap with pieces of card paper and—eureka!"

Mario recalls an engineering meeting in which he discussed his experience seven years earlier with the March 701 F1 car. He had tested the March with and without sidepods and was convinced that the pods moved the aerodynamic center of pressure too far forward. This lesson was absorbed by the Lotus engineers, who moved the airfoil sections further back in designing the Lotus 78.

"But until we actually closed the pods with skirts, they didn't know this was ground effect," Mario says. "In the wind tunnel they realized it was more than just a wing making downforce. It was creating suction. That's how the Lotus 78 was born. It all happened totally by accident. It was very exciting because it was one big discovery after another."

It was at an early test of the then-secret type 78 that Mario and the team learned the importance of completely sealing the gap between the sidepod and road. "We were testing at Hockenheim, and Colin put brushes on to try to go as close to the ground as possible. We had some photos taken, and it showed that the brushes were blown out going down the straightaway. We were losing all the air."

As an experimental fix, chief mechanic Bob Dance replaced the brushes with solid strips made from heavy plastic sheets he had bought at a nearby hardware store. "After we put solid plastic on there," Mario relates, "I'd go out and for a lap or two, and I was just flying. I was almost taking the chicane flat, but then the plastic would wear out and we would lose speed. That's when we came up with the idea of skirts."

Wright and Bellamy spent a year developing skirts and skirt systems. "We had a Renault 4 van, which we used to mount skirts on the back and rush around with me hanging out the back watching them, which was very instructive," Wright says. "It was all about making skirts that didn't wear out and that worked. Part of it was coming up with a ceramic rubbing strip for the skirts and then building ones that

sucked *down* instead of sucked *up*. That was worth seconds a lap."

It would take a few years for anyone to realize that much stiffer spring rates were required to fully exploit the ground-effect capabilities of the car. "The 78 worked well mechanically because we were really quick in slow corners where you don't have much aerodynamic effect at all," Mario says. "But even then we weren't taking full advantage of the aerodynamics because the suspension was too soft."

Another drawback to the 78 was that it had considerably more aerodynamic drag than its competition. "We were paying the penalty on the straightaway," Mario says. "The car was a slug. Overall, it was not as superior as many people thought."

Nonetheless, with the 78, Mario became a serious contender for the 1977 world championship. He had a memorable win at Long Beach, outbraking Jody Scheckter for the lead with four laps to go and holding off a late attack from Niki Lauda.

In Spain the following month, Mario qualified on the pole and led all the way for a crushing victory. Six more poles followed during the season, but engine failures meant there were only two more wins. Teammate Nilsson scored his only Grand Prix win at the Belgian GP at Zolder in June, driving a great race on a half-wet track. He beat Lauda by fourteen seconds despite two spins and a slow pit stop to change tires. Mario was on the pole in Belgium but crashed after colliding with John Watson in the first turn.

At Monza Mario beat Lauda by sixteen seconds after taking the lead from Scheckter early in the race. It was a dominant and emotional victory made even more complicated by a sudden offer to rejoin Ferrari in 1978. Lauda had announced he was leaving the team following a series of arguments with Enzo Ferrari and the firing of his chief mechanic Ermanno Cuoghi. Ferrari hired the young French Canadian phenom Gilles Villeneuve to replace Lauda for the year's last two races, but wanted Mario for 1978.

Mario decided to meet with Ferrari. "I won the race, and that made my visit even stronger. I was coming from a position of strength anyway, but having won Monza made it even better."

Suddenly, Mario had a tough decision to make. Should he stay with Lotus or go to Ferrari? "Believe me, it was a dilemma," Mario says, shaking his head. "It was like asking a child to choose between your mother or your father."

Involved negotiations took place during the next few weeks. "I was a bit disgruntled at Lotus because we had Cosworth's development engines, which was the wrong thing to have. We did not need the extra five or ten horsepower. We needed a reliable engine. I would have won the championship, but I dropped out of so

Top left: In a one-off drive, Mario finished seventh in a Wolf-Williams F1 car at Silverstone's non-championship race in April, 1977. Lotus had elected not to run at the event. (Andretti collection)

Middle left: In the Long Beach victory celebration, Mario stands with Chapman (in yellow shirt) after his superb win. Long Beach promoter Chris Pook has always said Mario's win that day saved the race from financial ruin. Not only did ticket sales begin to climb, but so did the level of American interest in Formula One overall. (Pete Biro)

Bottom left: Mario ran eight USAC races for Penske in 1977. He first drove a McLaren M24 turbo-Cosworth, then a Penske PC5-Cosworth, which was the first Indy car built by Penske Cars. Mario's best USAC race that year was the Pocono 500 at the end of June, where teammate Tom Sneva led him across the line in a Penske one-two. (Andretti collection)

Opposite: Mario leads Niki Lauda to score his first win with the Lotus 78 at Long Beach in 1977. "The Lotus 78 was better on a street course like Long Beach than on a fast track," he says. "It had some good qualities, but the straightaway speed was awful. It was like a brick aerodynamically." (Dave Friedman)

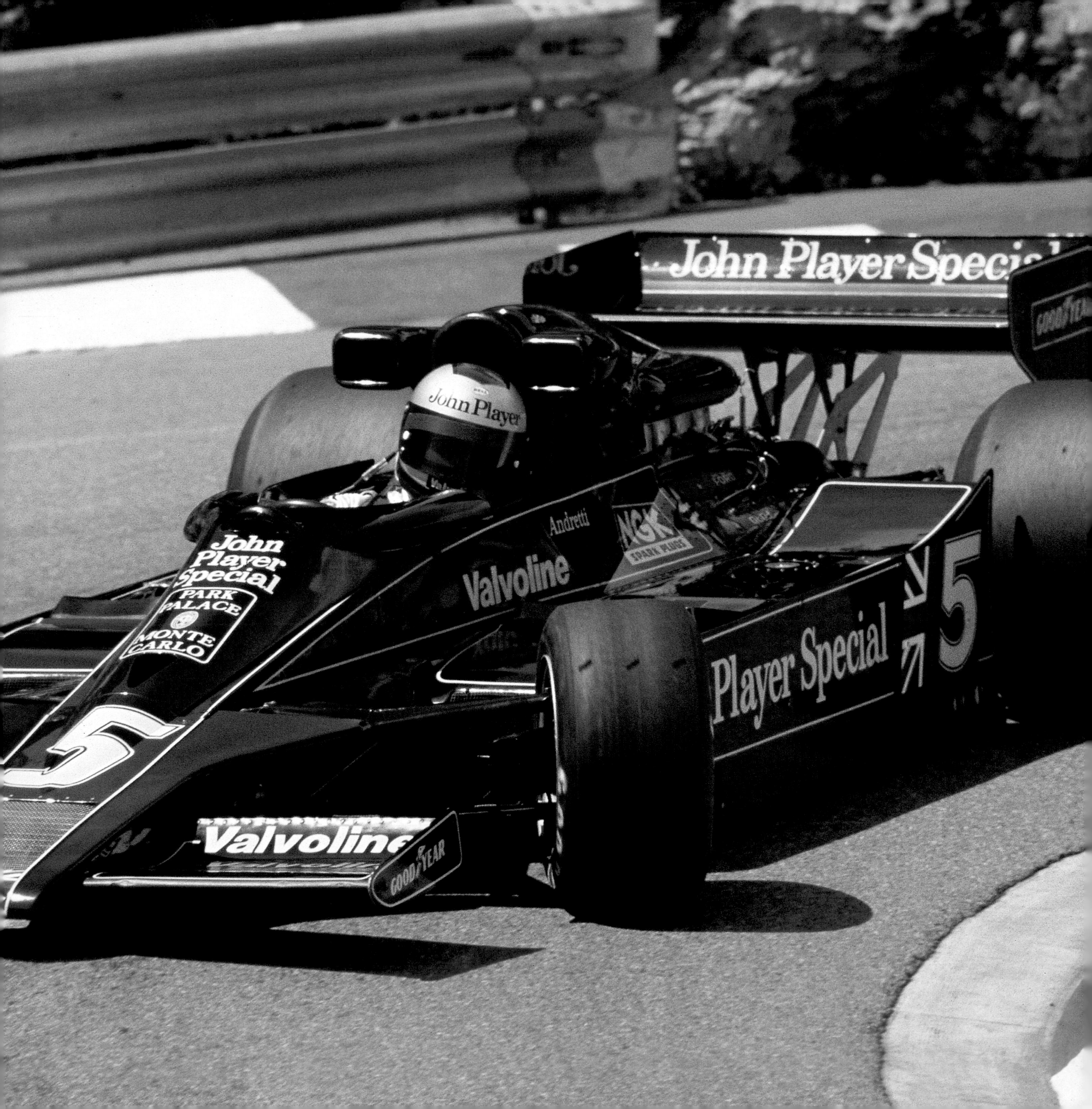
John Player Special
John Player
John Player Special
PARK PALACE
MONTE CARLO
Andretti
Valvoline
NGK
SPARK PLUGS
5
Player Special
5
Valvoline
GOODYEAR

many races that I was leading, while the Ferraris used to run like trains. I could blow them off, but they would run to the finish. So I was thinking, 'What have I got to do to win the championship with a car that was so good?' I'm looking at Lauda, and he's going his merry way and finishing races, so Ferrari was very appealing to me."

Chapman implored Mario not to go and said he would not release him from his contract. "I said, 'I know we have a deal. We shook hands, but I must go.' So it came down to what Ferrari was going to pay me. That's always a difficult thing to discuss with the Italians, especially with him. I said, 'What are you willing to pay me provided I can get out of my agreement?' I'll never forget what he said. 'I cannot put a price on your talent. You have to tell me.' That was smart. He put the ball right back in my court."

Chapman had offered Mario $350,000 for 1978. "That was the going rate," Mario says. "Nobody else was getting any more. So I shot Ferrari a big figure, knowing, really, that I couldn't go with him because I had a deal with Colin. I said $700,000, and he said OK. He never thought about it. I was just flabbergasted. I said, 'I can't promise you because I have a deal with Colin.' He said, 'If you want to do it, we will. That's what lawyers are for. We can handle it.' "

Mario flew home to Nazareth, and it wasn't long before a phone call came from Chapman. "He said he'd talked to Ferrari and told him, 'No way,' " Mario recalls. "So I called Colin's bluff. I said, 'I'm going.' I wanted to hear his reaction. He said, 'You're not going.' I said, 'Colin, you can't afford me at this point. I'm not going to drive for the money we agreed because I was offered twice as much, and I'm not going to turn my back on that. You don't want an unhappy driver on your team. I don't drive strictly for the money, but every time your car breaks and a Ferrari finishes ahead of me and I'm getting paid half as much, well, it's not going to be a

pleasant situation.' "

Chapman hung up, then called back two hours later to offer Mario the same retainer as Ferrari. "The money came from Courage Beer, who owned Players. So at that point I had to call Mr. Ferrari and tell him I just couldn't do it. And he said, 'I understand.' So thanks to him, I got a big raise. But if Colin had not been as aggressive and determined to keep me, I would have gone."

Mario finished second to Hunt in the rain at Watkins Glen the following month, then qualified fastest and dominated most of the Canadian GP at Mosport, lapping the field after Hunt crashed while trying to lap teammate Jochen Mass. But three laps from home, Mario's engine blew. He was on the pole again in Japan for the season finale, but crashed on the second lap after colliding with Jacques Laffite's Ligier.

Mario finished third in the championship chase behind Lauda and Scheckter while Lotus beat McLaren to second place in the constructor's championship behind Ferrari. Mario and Team Lotus were back, but teammate Nilsson's career came to an abrupt and unhappy end when he was diagnosed with cancer at the end of the season.

"I really liked Gunnar," Mario says. "I spent time with him in Sweden at his place. He was a pal of Danny Sullivan, and we had some fun together. I remember one time we came back to his apartment in London about three in the morning. The main entrance to the building was locked, and he didn't have the keys so we looked up and could see his bathroom window was halfway open. So we tossed a coin to see who would go up, and I lost the toss.

"I climbed up an outside sewer pipe, and as I was halfway up, twenty feet in the air, somebody flushed the toilet. All of a sudden the temperature of the pipe changed. It was leaking a little, and I almost let go! I was totally grossed out. I remember vividly what a feeling that was and those guys standing down below laughing their heads off."

Before going to that year's Japanese GP, Nilsson visited the Andrettis in Pennsylvania. "He was hurting, so we went to my doctor," Mario recalls. "We didn't know what was wrong with him, but that was the beginning of the awareness of his problem, and the whole weekend in Japan he was very subdued."

Nilsson spent the winter in a London hospital. His replacement would be another Swede, Ronnie Peterson, who had driven for Lotus from 1973-75. Peterson was renowned as a spectacular and extremely fast driver—qualities not entirely to Mario's liking. Nigel Roebuck, *Autosport*'s Grand Prix editor, recalls that Mario was very unhappy at the prospect of having Peterson as his teammate.

"Ronnie's career at the time was in the doldrums," Roebuck says. "He came back to Lotus because his longtime mentor, Count Zanon, was paying for it, and Mario was immensely pissed off that Ronnie was coming to Lotus. I remember him growling, 'Tell me where it's written we need two stars in this team?' More than any other driver, Mario got Lotus back to the top. Everybody knew how quick Ronnie was, and the question was: Would this guy come in and steal it, and capitalize on all Mario's hard work?"

Despite being engrossed in Formula One for most of 1977, Mario also drove in six USAC races for Penske in a McLaren M24 and Penske PC5, both Cosworth-powered. His best result came in the Pocono 500, in which he finished second to teammate Tom Sneva, who went on to win that year's USAC title.

Nick Goozee, who is now managing director of Penske Cars in Poole, England, was one of Mario's Penske mechanics from 1976-80. He reflects upon working with Mario during that period.

"The friendship and rapport that Mario built with the crew became very close," Goozee says. "Mario was very considerate of his mechanics. He was always courteous and very defensive of us."

Goozee recalls Mario admonishing an overzealous USAC official at Indy in 1977. "I remember being manhandled off the grid at the first Indy 500 I attended, and Mario clutched hold of the official and said to him very clearly, 'You've got to say, 'Please,' and 'Thank you.' Never forget it.' Those words have always stuck with me."

During this time Mario was bringing his American oval set-up skills to F1, tuning his car's handling, using tire stagger, and crossweight, which is adjusting the suspension to alter the amount of weight borne by each corner of the car. "In those days," Mario says, "they never crossweighted the car, but Chapman told me, 'Go ahead.' I didn't know how to explain it, and as an engineer he couldn't even suggest it because I had to go strictly by feel."

Mario's tuning approach was governed by the predominate direction—left or right—of the turns on a track. "If the track favored right-hand corners, I would find a bigger left rear tire, but then the car would be very unbalanced. So I would balance it by using cross-weight the other way. I was throwing away one or two corners at some of the tracks by really concentrating on the most important corners. That's where stagger truly worked for me.

"A good tire guy in those days was worth his weight in gold because the variable in cross-ply tire sizes was incredible." A savvy tire engineer would catalog bias-ply tires based on their circumference, then, through testing, would select the optimum sizes for each corner and create matched sets. This is no longer the art that it was because modern radial tires are much more consistent in size and dimension, and stagger is accounted for in the manufacturing.

Mario's use of tire stagger and cross-weight was considered black magic by most people in F1. While Mario may have introduced the importance of measuring tires in Formula One, he disguised its true purpose. "I remember one time we were at Paul Ricard testing in winter, and we had the tapes out," Mario says. "We were next to Ken Tyrrell, and he asked, 'What's all this tire measuring?' We said, 'Oh, we just want to see how big they are. We're just seeing what works with the gear ratios.' Someone from McLaren asked us what we were doing and we said, 'Oh, we're just playing with differentials.'"

For his part, Chapman couldn't make logical engineering sense out of Mario's procedures, but based on the results he allowed his driver to do what he wanted. "I'd come in, make two or three adjustments, and go out and set a time. And Colin would be shaking his head. 'What did you do?' he'd ask. And I'd say, 'It works.' I had that up my sleeve."

Above: Despite the intense competition on the track, relations between F1 drivers were usually friendly and relaxed. Here Mario enjoys a poolside game of backgammon with fellow drivers John Watson (left) and Ronnie Peterson (far right) as well as Swiss journalist Roger Benoit. (LAT Photographic) **Opposite:** Mario stands on the pit wall at Watkins Glen, with teammate Nilsson to the left and Chapman to the right. Already in considerable pain from what would soon be diagnosed as cancer, Nilsson had visited Mario's doctor before going to Japan for the Japanese Grand Prix. (Gary Gold)

Triumph and Tragedy

If the Lotus 78 had set everyone in racing to thinking about a different approach to the single-seat,
open-wheel race car, the new type 79 was the semi-
nal machine that established new parameters of
race car design for the rest of the twentieth century.
Peter Wright says much of the design of the Lotus
79 was sacrificed to aerodynamics. "We got the
aerodynamics a whole heap better, but it wasn't a
very nice car. The structure of the car was a bit

Above: Rated one of the most naturally talented drivers of his day, Ronnie Peterson
put additional pressure on Mario when he joined Team Lotus for 1978. Despite this,
Mario and Peterson quickly became close friends. (LAT Photographic) **Opposite:**
While waiting for the restart, Dee Ann and Mario get the word that Peterson's inju-
ries are serious though apparently not life-threatening. But the championship that
Mario would win at Monza that day would be overshadowed by the news of
Peterson's death the following morning. (LAT Photographic)

Above: Two weeks after the Belgian GP, Mario and Peterson finished one-two again in Spain, with Peterson also driving a type 79. They had qualified together on the front row, and Mario easily took first place ahead of Peterson and Frenchman Jacques Laffite's Ligier JS9. Here, Peterson, Mario, and Laffite share the victory podium. (Bernard Cahier/Andretti collection)
Opposite left: Mario leads Bobby Unser and the rest of the field on his way to an IROC victory at Daytona in February of 1978. This was his first IROC win, enabling him to finish second to Al Unser in the combined 1977/78 IROC championship. (ISC Archives) **Opposite middle:** Shown under construction, this view of the engine and rear bodywork of the Lotus 79 helps explain why the car had such serious problems with its exhaust headers overheating and breaking. With so little space for cooling air it's not surprising that the body occasionally caught fire, as well. (Tony Matthews) **Opposite right:** In 1978 Mario competed in eight USAC events driving a Penske PC6. He had little luck and rarely enjoyed a trouble-free race, although he scored his first USAC victory in more than five years at Trenton in September. (Bob Tronolone)

flaky, but it had something that other people didn't have." The 79 pioneered the modern racing car designed around the ground-effect concept and a single, central fuel tank, as well as an increased level of downforce.

The car's weakest links were its exhaust system, which was enclosed in the sidepods and would often overheat and fall off, and inboard brakes with magnesium brake calipers that leaked and put air into the brake circuit. Former Firestone tire engineer Nigel Bennett was a race engineer for Team Lotus in those days, then went on to design championship-winning CART Champ cars for Lola and Roger Penske. He recalls the 79's other flaws. "Aerodynamically, the 79 was still pretty dirty and crude around the rear suspension. I don't think we fully realized how neat all that ought to be."

The 500-525-pound springs were also much too soft for optimum clearance for ground effect. "We were running the cars very high with soft suspension that made it doubly difficult for the skirts to follow the ground," Bennett notes. "The following year, when we really started working it out, we were running 2,000-pound springs! We were nosing around in the dark, really."

During the next two years the effectiveness of the set-up subtleties Mario had brought to F1 vanished in a rush of downforce. "Once serious downforce arrived, all that became immaterial," Mario says. "It took a lot of the feel I had for the chassis out of the equation."

Team Lotus ran the previous year's 78 through the Monaco GP in May. Mario won the first race of the season in Argentina and Peterson took the South African GP. Mario practiced, but didn't race, the first 79 at Monaco. The new car made its debut in the Belgian GP at Zolder two weeks later, when Mario qualified on the

pole and ran away with the race while Peterson finished second in a 78.

A second 79 was ready for Peterson at the next race in Spain. Mario and Peterson scored the first of three one-two sweeps with the new car, with the others coming in France and Holland. By mid-season, Mario had established himself in command of the championship and the team, outqualifying and outpacing Peterson in eight of the first nine races. At the British GP at Brands Hatch in July, Peterson outqualified Mario for only the second time that year.

"If you look at the results, the first half of the year Ronnie rarely got near Mario." Roebuck says. "As much as anything that was because Ronnie was an absolutely useless test driver, and Mario was brilliant. The car was pretty good out of the box, but it got better and better almost entirely because of Mario."

By winning the pole at Brands Hatch, Peterson earned the choice of starting from the inside or outside of the front row. He chose the outside because the normal pole position had a disadvantage. The road sloped to the right, making it almost impossible for the pole-sitter to avoid wheelspin when he released the clutch. As the second-fastest qualifier, Mario now faced this problem.

"I lined up with my car pointed at Ronnie's," Mario says. "That way, my rear wheels were properly cambered, and when I got the wheelspin I went forward rather than sliding to the right. He got away cleanly, but I got a hell of a start. I just launched, and off I went. I got in front and he never got close enough to make a move."

Unfortunately, neither Lotus ran to the finish. Mario's engine blew and Peterson's car developed a fuel leak. After the race, Niki Lauda came up to Mario. "You're a ballsy bastard," Lauda said with a grin, referring to Mario's start. "That was a good lesson. I'll remember it."

Top right: On the opening lap of the Italian GP, the accident that would claim Peterson's life begins to happen as the leaders dive into Monza's first chicane. Mario and Gilles Villeneuve took off from the front row, but waving yellow flags and then a red flag would bring the entire field to a stop at the end of the first lap. (LAT Photographic) **Bottom right:** Mario collects his thoughts as he surveys the wreckage in the distance. Ten cars were involved in the accident after James Hunt and Peterson collided. The remaining cars came to a stop on the grid after the first lap. Mario's former Ferrari and Alfa Romeo sports-car teammate, Arturo Merzario, is at left in the background. (LAT Photographic)
Opposite: At the Dutch GP Mario started from the pole and won the race. He rates the Lotus type 79 as his best car ever: "I've had a lot of favorites along the way, like the Lola T332 F5000 car and the Ferrari 312P sports car," he says. "But they were not the outstanding favorite like the Lotus 79." (Jutta Fausel)

and he just said out of the blue, 'I'm going to McLaren.' I was stunned by that," Roebuck recalls. "It hadn't leaked out into the press room at all."

Mario and Peterson qualified and finished one-two at Zandvoort, running nose to tail all the way. Mario's engine sounded ratty in the closing laps, and his car's rear bodywork was on fire at the finish after his exhaust system came apart. "At Zandvoort the sidepods on my car were overheating, and I was losing downforce," Mario says. "My car was all over the place in the fast corner leading onto the front straight. I was really hanging it out, driving the wheels off that thing to keep my speed up, because Ronnie's car was strong, and he was able to take a smooth, consistent line. But he never got close enough to make a move." Niki Lauda finished third in a Brabham-Alfa, moving into third place in the championship standings, but by then Peterson was the only man who had a mathematical chance of beating Mario for the world title.

Next came the Italian GP at Monza. Nigel Roebuck and Mario had agreed that Roebuck would write a book about the year so Roebuck spent a lot of time in the Lotus motorhome. "At Monza there was sort of a subdued atmosphere," Roebuck says. "It wasn't as if they'd fallen out. But it was quiet, tense, if you like, because it really was coming down to the wire, and either of the two of them was going to win the championship."

Mario qualified on the pole for the seventh time that year, edging Ferrari's Gilles Villeneuve, while Peterson had a series of mechanical problems and qualified on the third row. Peterson had to spend one of Friday's practice sessions in the team's only spare car, a Lotus 78, then had to revert again to the 78 for the race after crashing his 79 in the morning warmup when the rear brakes failed. Peterson wasn't too perturbed, saying the 78 had felt good in practice, but a ragged start to the race saw Hunt nudge Peterson's car, which slewed sideways and plowed into the guardrail.

The front of Peterson's car was torn off, and it erupted in flames. Hunt and Clay Regazzoni scrambled out of their cars and ran to Peterson's destroyed machine, pulling the injured Swede from the wreckage. Ten cars were involved in the accident, and Vittorio Brambilla also was injured, suffering a severe concussion. Both drivers were taken to a hospital.

Meanwhile, the much-delayed race took place over a shortened distance. Villeneuve made a flier of a start, beating Mario off the line, and they quickly motored away from the field. Villeneuve led most of the way, with Mario struggling a little with fading brakes. Despite that, he was able to outbrake Villeneuve with six laps to go and pull away to win by two seconds.

There was no joy however, not only because of Peterson's accident, but also because Mario and Villeneuve were penalized one minute for jumping the start. As a result they were moved back to sixth and seventh respectively, with Lauda taking the official victory. Nevertheless, with Peterson sidelined for the remaining two races and Lauda still twenty points behind, Mario had won the world championship. The lifelong quest that had begun in 1954 as a spectator at Monza was now complete.

"On Sunday evening," recalls Roebuck, "we were in the motorhome, and Mario knew he was world champion. We were mainly talking about Brambilla because he was the guy who seemed to be in trouble. He had a bang on the head and had been unconscious for a long time. We knew Ronnie had bad leg injuries, but in that era leg injuries were quite commonplace.

"Mario was sitting there, and there was a magnum of champagne on the table. He was completely drained. He was immensely pissed off because he'd won the race on the road, and he and Gilles had been given a minute penalty. But regardless, he knew he was world champion. But because of Ronnie he felt he couldn't celebrate.

"Then Professor [Sid] Watkins [F1's medical director] rang the motorhome from the hospital, and Mario came off the phone just elated. He said, 'Sid said he's got bad leg fractures, but all the vital signs are good, and he's going to be fine.' The only point of issue was whether he'd be fit enough for the following season. And then Mario opened the champagne, and we all drank it, and the atmosphere was totally different."

But Mario's joy at finally winning the title would be short-lived. "I got up Monday morning with Dee Ann, and we drove to the hospital," Mario recalls. "I took the Autostrada, and as I was getting off at the tollbooth, the guy said, 'Are you going to the hospital?' And I said, 'Yes.' And the guy said, 'Ronnie just died.' I said, 'No!' And the guy said, 'Yeah, I just heard it on the radio.' I was totally devastated. It was like the guy had hit me over the head with a sledgehammer. I couldn't believe it. Dee Ann and I had just been talking about his rehabilitation."

Overnight, Peterson's condition had taken a sudden turn for the worse. Bone marrow from his leg fractures made its way into his bloodstream, creating a blood clot that resulted in a fatal stroke for the thirty-four-year-old driver.

When Mario arrived at the hospital, Emerson Fittipaldi was there with veteran

"Formula One had meaning because that was the essence of my dream in motorsports. Anything else was on the road to that dream."

Italian writer Pino Allievi of *La Gazzetta Dello Sport* and Swedish journalist Fred Peterson. "Somebody, Pino I think it was, said, 'Don't go in there. It's a mess. It's too late.' And I turned around and left. I couldn't believe it because I didn't think his injuries were life-threatening. I thought he was going to be hobbling around for several months. I knew his legs were destroyed, but I thought it was just broken bones. I thought, 'Surely they can put that together.' But they made a mess of it."

The only comfort for Mario was that Dee Ann was with him. "It was good she was there that weekend because she helped me get through it. It would have been very difficult without her. She loved to go to Italy, and most of the time I raced in Monza she came with me."

In the wake of Peterson's death, the rest of the season, which should have been a time for Mario to savor his victory, proved nothing short of miserable. Mario qualified on the pole at Watkins Glen, a full second quicker than anyone else, but he crashed in the race day morning warmup when a stub axle broke. He took over temporary teammate Jean-Pierre Jarier's car, but the car didn't handle well and also started to lose its brakes. Before the race reached half-distance, the engine blew.

"He so desperately wanted to win at the Glen," Roebuck says. "Somebody had painted on the track, 'Mario, Win this One for Ronnie.' And Mario's very susceptible to things like that. It was just a shame that the season ended as an anti-climax in every respect. Ronnie was gone and then two bad races."

The season-ending race in Montreal the next weekend was no better. Mario couldn't get his car balanced for the first Canadian GP at a new circuit built on Ile Notre Dame and qualified ninth. He passed three cars on the opening lap, but tried too hard a few laps later to outbrake Watson. The cars collided, with both spinning. Mario stalled and rejoined after a push start to finish a lap down in tenth while Villeneuve went on to score the first F1 win of his career in front of an adoring hometown crowd. Finally, two weeks later, Mario's year of triumph and tragedy ended with the news that his previous teammate, the cancer-stricken Gunnar Nilsson, had passed away in a London hospital.

And despite winning the championship without once needing the benefit of the team orders he had chosen to reveal, Mario failed to receive the full measure of plaudits he deserved from some in the racing press. The conventional wisdom, repeated many places in print, was that Mario won the championship because of team orders. Many wrote that Peterson would have beaten him to the title had he been allowed to do so.

"In *Motor Sport*, Rob Walker [who had been a gentleman privateer team owner in F1 and wrote for several racing publications] gave me a nine instead of a ten and

awarded Lauda a higher mark because he said, 'Team orders overshadowed Mario's performance.' That was grossly unfair to me," Mario says. "He was totally misinformed, and he should have been better informed to pronounce something like that.

"Ronnie was a master of car control and was a force to be reckoned with, but I had his match. I didn't win eighteen poles in F1 and the most poles in Champ car racing by being a slouch. I was quick, too. Not as spectacular, but I wasn't wasting as much time. Ronnie looked spectacular hanging it out, but that was not always the quickest way around. I learned on slick dirt tracks that quick times come from keeping the car going forward, not getting it sideways. Ronnie only out-qualified me twice, and on the occasions that he did I still beat him to the first corner."

Mario was deeply fulfilled by finally winning the world championship. "In an international arena, there was more responsibility," he says, "but also there was much more value to my bringing home a result because I was representing my country. If you're the winner in Formula One, your national anthem is the first one they play. It's like the Olympics. It has a totally different feel, which is so valuable. That's what Formula One meant to me.

"To be with Lotus and beat Ferrari had different meaning as well, because these were all my idols. Formula One had meaning because that was the essence of my dream in motorsports. Anything else was on the road to that dream. The real dream and real purpose of my becoming a professional racing driver was Formula One."

In the foreword to Roebuck's book about Mario's championship season, *Mario Andretti: World Champion*, Chapman paid Mario high praise. "His only fault as a driver," Chapman wrote, "is his tendency to trust other drivers too much in the first two or three laps of a race. I believe this stems from his experience on the dirt in Championship racing, where you need to trust other drivers more. Otherwise, I can't fault him. My relationship with him both professionally and personally is far and away the best I've had with a driver since the days of Jimmy Clark.

"Some people have said it was the car's superiority which allowed Mario to take the title, but that is a view which I don't share. If he hadn't been with us Team Lotus would not have been anything like as competitive. Of that I'm quite certain. His personal contribution to the Lotus 79 was absolutely immense. Without him it would have been a different car. In terms of sheer ability, I think that as a mature, truly professional Grand Prix driver he is simply brilliant, quite brilliant."

Roebuck observes that this, coming from Chapman, was the ultimate accolade. "You know what 'Chunky' was like. He did not throw compliments around."

After crashing in the morning warm-up at Watkins Glen, Mario jumped into temporary teammate Jean-Pierre Jarier's car for the race. Here he is surrounded on the grid by photographers as well as Chapman and legendary trophy queen Linda Vaughn. Son Michael stands immediately behind Chapman, just four days short of his sixteenth birthday. (Gary Gold)

183

Chapter 15

Team Lotus Falters

As world champion, Mario's hopes for the 1979 season were as high as ever. He had a new car and a new teammate in Argentinian Carlos Reutemann, who had moved from Ferrari to Lotus. Colin Chapman unveiled the new super ground-effect Lotus 80 for the 1979 season, in the livery of new primary sponsor Martini & Rossi. The car was designed without front wings and featured skirts along the nose as well as the sidepods.

Above: Mario left the struggling Team Lotus at the end of the 1980 season to drive the Alfa Romeo 179C, shown here at Long Beach. "There were two versions of that car," he notes. "The older one had a fatter nose. We weren't very competitive only because we weren't using the hydraulic system for lowering the car that most other teams were using." (Dave Friedman) **Opposite:** Mario discusses the shortcomings of the Lotus 80 with Chapman. "We got to the point where we had the downforce, but the 80 used the same basic tub as the 79, which just wasn't stiff enough," Mario explains. "It was a Band-Aid here and a Band-Aid there. Colin understood the idea of downforce, but he never followed up on the mechanical end." (Jutta Fausel)

"In the wind tunnel the 80 was vastly superior to the 79," says Nigel Bennett. "When it did work, it had tremendous downforce. We could never get the curved skirts to work properly. The work that was done on them was unbelievable. There were teams of people working 'round the clock."

As great a leap forward as the 80 was in theory, it quickly proved a disaster in reality. Early testing immediately revealed a myriad of problems, and a pair of Lotus 79s was pressed into service to start the new season. It quickly proved to be a desultory time for Mario.

Things went reasonably well with the 79s in the first few races. Reutemann finished second and third in the opening two races of the championship season, and was second again in the Spanish GP at the end of April. Mario also collected points in three of the first four races and then finished an encouraging third with the new type 80, just six seconds behind Reutemann in the car's debut in Spain. But Mario raced the troublesome 80 only two more times before reverting to the 79. Reutemann never raced the 80.

"I think Colin had the right idea, but he got lost," says Mario. The problem was that the increased downforce placed an extraordinary strain on the car and its suspension, and Chapman hadn't reinforced the construction to bear the loads. "Finally, Colin put a collar around the cockpit to strengthen it, but then the suspension's pick-up points began popping the rivets. Now something else was being overloaded.

"To deal with the downforce you really had to increase your spring rates tremendously to hold the car up. But also there was a lot of pressure and load being transferred through the chassis, and the car was twisting under the strain. You'd jump a curb, and the car would pick up crossweight. From one corner to the next you didn't know what the balance of the car would be, in Spain especially, where you used more curbs than race track."

Above: The start of the Spanish GP, which was Mario's first and best race with the Lotus 80. Qualifying on the second row behind the Ligiers driven by Jacques Laffite and Patrick Depailler, Mario finished third, about thirty seconds behind winner Depailler, and six seconds behind his new teammate Reutemann, who took second in his type 79. (Jutta Fausel)
Opposite: Mario celebrates his IROC championship with Linda Vaughn (right) and a Union 76 race queen at Atlanta in March, 1979. He finished second in the race and won the championship after winning at Riverside the previous October. Mario ran the IROC series six times between 1975 and 1987, and was second to A. J. Foyt in 1976 and Al Unser in 1978 before winning the title in 1979. (Hal Crocker)

Peter Wright agrees with Mario. "The rocker suspension design and aluminum monocoques really weren't up to it anymore. When we took the cars apart at the end of the year, the cracking inside the chassis was horrific."

The type 80 and modified 79 were completely eclipsed by other cars, particularly by the new Ligier JS11, driven by Jacques Laffite and Patrick Depailler, which won three of the first five races, and the Williams FW07, which made its debut at the Spanish GP and quickly proved to be the car to beat. Clay Regazzoni scored the FW07's first win at the British GP while teammate Alan Jones won four races, including three in a row, in the season's second half.

"Williams were the first to really understand how stiff the chassis and the underbody and sidepods had to be," Mario says. "Chapman seriously underestimated it with the Lotus 79 and the 80. Nigel Bennett and I went to look at the Williams with the body off in Spain that year, and we said, 'That's the way our car should be.' You could see all the coachwork was very strong and solid, and ours wasn't."

Says Nigel Roebuck: "It was sad, poignant in a way, that after having an incredible year in 1978 everything went wrong in '79." The season went from bad to worse as Mario finished only two of the last ten races, and Reutemann dropped out of five of the final six races. Reutemann was sixth in the championship while Mario finished tenth.

"I think the Lotus 80 could have been an even better car than the 79 if Colin had listened and really tried to understand what we were saying about stiffening the chassis and springs," Mario says. "He blew his top because he didn't want a driver telling him what to do technically. Colin got frustrated, and as soon as Williams and Patrick Head built a proper ground-effect car he lost interest. Without him

"I should have won Indy that year," Mario says. "The car was really working, and we got an electrical short. It was a stupid thing. That was one of my biggest disappointments. Of all of the races, I thought I had that one."

being there as the driving force, it didn't work. You had to be riding the crest with Colin; otherwise it would be pure hell. He'd lose his patience, and the ugly side of him would come out, and that was not good."

Outside F1, Mario ran only one other race in 1979, the California 500. This was the year Champ car team owners broke away from USAC and formed Championship Auto Racing Teams (CART). Mario drove one of Roger Penske's new PC7s in the year's last 500-mile race, and the team scored a resounding one-two-three sweep with Bobby Unser winning from Rick Mears and Mario.

As the 1980 season began, Mario had one more year on his Lotus contract, but Reutemann jumped to the rapidly emerging Williams Grand Prix team, replacing Regazzoni beside Alan Jones. Twenty-one-year-old Italian Elio de Angelis joined Lotus after one year in F1 with the Shadow team. Chapman produced a new, more conventional car, the type 81, and Essex Petroleum took over as the team's sponsor. Essex also sponsored Mario's Penske Champ car in CART.

The Lotus 81 was plagued with reliability problems, and Mario finished only five races, earning just a single point with a sixth-place result in the final race of the season at Watkins Glen. De Angelis fared slightly better, accumulating thirteen points during the year, but well before the end of the season, Mario was seeking work elsewhere for 1981.

Mario enjoyed much more success in the four Champ car races he drove for Penske in 1980 aboard the latest PC9. At Indianapolis Mario qualified in the middle of the front row ahead of teammate Bobby Unser. Johnny Rutherford was on the pole with the Chaparral 2K and won the race, but Mario and Unser offered Rutherford a serious challenge until both Penskes ran into ignition problems.

"I should have won Indy that year," Mario says. "The car was really working, and we got an electrical short. It was a stupid thing. That was one of my biggest disappointments. Of all of the races, I thought I had that one. I could almost play with the rest of them."

"Mario was in complete control, and he was bitterly disappointed," Nick Goozee says. "When it became obvious we couldn't fix the problem, he sat in the car for a little while. He just counted his thoughts and got out, shook his head, took his helmet off, and shook our hands. He said, 'We had that. We had that.'"

The Pocono 500 came a month after Indy, and Mario again ran at the front until his gearbox broke. His third race with a PC9 was at Michigan in September, where his car was turned out in the brown and beige of Penske's new sponsor, A. B. Dick. Mario qualified on the pole and scored a very satisfying victory after a ferocious battle with Rutherford and teammates Unser and Mears. Rutherford fell back in the closing stages, and Mario beat Bobby Unser by less than a second with Mears another six seconds behind in third.

Goozee remembers that win with Mario above all others. "After the race when we were back in the garage, he displayed an emotion that I'd never seen before," Goozee recalls. "He just quietly whooped and raised his arms up as if it really meant a great deal to him because this was a very competitive race, and he beat his two teammates in similar equipment."

In what would be his last race for Penske at the end of the year at Phoenix, Mario again qualified on the pole. A broken valve spring left him struggling through the race's second half, although he hung on to finish second and his engine finally expired as he crossed the line.

Mario left the struggling Lotus team to join Alfa Romeo in F1. He also departed Penske for Patrick Racing in CART. Penske's new sponsor, A. B. Dick, wanted to run the full CART schedule in 1981, which conflicted with Mario's F1 commitment. Another reason to join Patrick was old friend Jim McGee, who had quit Penske near the end of 1980 to run Pat Patrick's team.

Mario had F1 offers for 1981 from Alfa and McLaren, both teams sponsored by Marlboro. "I talked to Teddy Mayer at McLaren, and Marlboro was prepared to pay me the same money wherever I went. But I was influenced by [Bruno] Giacomelli's performance in an Alfa at the Glen at the end of 1980, when he led all but ten laps. His performance there is what convinced me to go with Alfa Romeo," Mario says.

"I thought now is the time Alfa Romeo is going to get their licks in. But it turned out that was a big career mistake for me, of course, because I chose from the heart, being Italian and having some friends there like [engineer] Gianni Marelli and

Top left: The brainchild of FIA president-to-be Max Mosley, the BMW Procar series was designed to promote BMW's spectacular M1 road car. The series ran primarily as a support race to many European Formula One races, with a regular group of wealthy amateurs and semi-pros competing against the top five qualifiers in the accompanying F1 race. Here Mario practices his BMW Procar during the Belgian GP weekend in 1979. (Jutta Fausel)

Middle left: In his only Indy car race of 1979 Mario finished third behind teammates Bobby Unser and Rick Mears in a Penske sweep of the California 500. Mario provided direction in improving the Penske PC7's aerodynamics. "The shape of the tunnel would change under pressure, sucking down as the car built up speed, so it was losing a lot of downforce," he notes "They made a fundamental mistake not realizing how much vacuum it was creating. The tunnels really needed to be stiff." (Bob Tronolone) **Bottom left:** As defending IROC champion, Mario won the 1979-1980 IROC season opener at Riverside, and was third in a second round the following day in one of Jay Signore's Chevrolet Camaro stock cars. "I enjoyed the IROC, especially when there were still some road races," he says. "I liked the diversity." (Bob Tronolone)

Opposite: With the Lotus 80 underperforming, Mario reverted to a Lotus 79 for the last seven races of 1979. Seen here practicing in Canada, he runs between the Ferraris of Gilles Villeneuve (No. 12), and Jody Scheckter (No. 11). Scheckter and Villeneuve finished first and second in that year's championship, each winning three races. (Nate Korn)

[chief mechanic Ermanno] Cuoghi. Ultimately, that choice is what drove me out of Formula One."

While McLaren began to climb back to the top of the F1 mountain, Alfa was in decline. McLaren had been taken over by Ron Dennis, who hired John Barnard to design an all-new car called the MP4/1 built around a revolutionary carbon-fiber chassis. The new McLaren went from strength to strength, scoring its first win in Watson's hands at that summer's British GP while Mario and teammate Giacomelli struggled at Alfa Romeo. After an encouraging start to the season with a fourth-place finish at Long Beach, Mario didn't earn another point in 1981.

Sliding skirts were banned that year, and a minimum gap was specified of six centimeters between the sidepod and road. Because that gap could be measured only in the pitlane, most teams, led by Brabham, soon adopted a system to lower their cars when they were on the track. Mario argued unsuccessfully with Alfa's veteran racing boss, Carlo Chiti, about building a Brabham-like hydraulic jack.

"We were testing at Paul Ricard, and the Brabhams were going well with Nelson Piquet," Mario recalls. "I said 'Let's just simulate it and bring the car down as if we had a hydraulic system like they had,' which we did, and we were right on the pace. But Chiti wouldn't let us use it in the race. 'Oh, it's illegal,' he said. Then I said, 'If it's illegal, why does everyone else have it?' Things didn't get any better over the rest of the season.

"Chiti and I had some other run-ins," he adds. "We were in Zolder, and I wanted to try some much softer springs in Sunday morning warm-up, and he wouldn't let us. After the warm-up we were still not going anywhere, and he said, 'Now you can change the springs for the race if you want.' That really infuriated me. I was ready to walk! I could never get along with him."

Mario and teammate Giacomelli failed to finish half the races because of engine failures. "He was paid a huge amount of money for the time," says Roebuck. "But as he said, the problem was he let emotion make his decision. In his innocence he was thinking it was going to be like Ferrari, but he had so many retirements that year. I don't know how many engines they blew up, and the reason given for retirement was always an oil leak.

"I remember after one race I walked past Cuoghi and said, 'Oil leak?' He said, 'Si, oil leak, like always. Come here, I show you. See? This is the oil leak, leaking out of this hole in the engine!' It was a sad finale. That was Mario's last full season in F1, and it was just sad to see."

At the Dutch GP in August, both Mario and teammate Giacomelli crashed hard in the race as a result of identical suspension failures.

"The upper right rear titanium wishbone broke," Mario says. "I crashed in almost the exact same spot about five feet away from Bruno. I went backwards into the dirt bank and had a sudden stop, and I still have a lump on my spine from the impact. I was never able to determine if I had any damage there. All I know is I had a pain there for at least five years. But I endured that, and I didn't know what to do because in those days you didn't have a trainer with you. So I just endured."

Mario's right knee was also injured in the Zandvoort accident, and as he was passing through London's Heathrow airport on the way home he suddenly found himself unable to move. "I had to limp to the emergency phone and ask for some help. So they sent a cart over, and I was hoping that nobody would see me. I was really worried. I thought, 'Damn, I've broken something here.' My knee hurt more than my back at the time. Chiti said, 'Are you all right? Are you sure you don't want to go to a doctor?' And I said, 'No, no.' I just refused to get it examined.

Above: Mario credits his win at the September, 1980 Michigan 150 to his invention of a "listening tube" attached to the pop-off valve: "I ran a rubber hose from the bottom of the valve to my ear. It would start to make a little whistling noise and you could back off the throttle and keep the valve closed. You not only knew you were maxed-out, but you could go beyond the boost limit by as much as a full inch." (Nick Goozee collection) Opposite: The Lotus 81 looked good in its Essex colors, but it was desperately unreliable. Mario failed to finish nine of that year's fourteen races and earned just one miserable point with the car by finishing a distant sixth place at Watkins Glen. Thus ended a five-year partnership with Lotus. (Bob Tronolone)

"Those are the stupid things you do. You say, 'I cannot afford to be sidelined. So I'll just work through it.' You downplay it and grit your teeth. I had a big bump on my knee. It was black and blue with a big lump on it, but I managed."

In CART, Mario ran eight races for Patrick in 1981. He didn't win, but finished second at Indianapolis to Bobby Unser, and was second at Atlanta in June and Michigan in September, both times behind Rick Mears. He also took a pair of thirds at Milwaukee and in the first of the twin 125s at Atlanta, all in June.

Mario had started that year's Indy 500 from the back of the field because his car was qualified for him by Wally Dallenbach while he was busy racing for Alfa Romeo in Formula One.

"I was competitive all day, not outstanding but competitive," Mario says. "Bobby was quicker, no question, but toward the end of the race we were right there. I was actually gaining on him. I remember clearly when we were going out of the pits. He was in front of me, and I was second. It was during a caution period, and the pack was right alongside us."

Unser passed nine cars under the yellow flag while leaving the pits. "Bobby motored right to the front," Mario continues. "I was going to go behind A. J. Foyt, but he let me in front of him. In fact, he waved me in front of him, but there were ten cars between Bobby and me."

Unser went on to beat Mario by five seconds. "After the race we didn't even think about protesting," Mario says. "There was scuttlebutt about it, but the next morning at seven o'clock Jim McGee called and said, 'Mario, you won the race. The official posting says Bobby's penalized a lap for passing under the yellow, and you won the race.' So I had to get up and go for the victory photos. Then we went to the banquet, and they gave us the check and took all the photos with the Borg-Warner trophy."

Roebuck went to the Indy 500 for the first time that year. "On my flight to New York from Indianapolis the next day," Roebuck recalls, "the pilot announced that USAC had penalized Bobby and given the race to Mario and the entire aircraft erupted into applause.

"I went to Monte Carlo the next weekend, and on Thursday morning in Monaco I was walking with Mario from the paddock up to the pit lane, and Gilles [Villeneuve] was coming the other way. His face was lit up with an enormous grin, and he just grabbed Mario's hand and was slapping him on the back. Gilles was so happy for him and had so much respect for him. I remember wishing somebody was there to photograph it because it was just a lovely moment between these two wonderful blokes."

But Unser and Penske appealed USAC's decision, bringing in a Philadelphia lawyer to plead their case. The matter dragged on all summer and finally was resolved in October, when Unser was reinstated as the winner and fined $40,000—the cost of USAC's legal fees.

"The way the whole thing was handled politically left me with a sour taste," Mario says. "Both Pancho Carter and Jerry Grant were penalized from second place in different years for doing something less than what Bobby had done, which was to screw up on the yellow. The rule stipulated clearly that the driver had to be penalized enough so that he loses at least one position. In those days it was the standard thing to penalize you a lap. There was no question about the validity of Bobby's penalty.

"After that, I wasn't surprised anymore by anything USAC did. I don't blame Penske or Bobby for fighting. They did what they had to do. If I had been in their position, I probably would have done the same thing.

"The thing that really took the cake was the following year at the drivers' meeting when [chief steward Tom] Binford said, 'If any of that repeats itself, there won't be any $40,000 fines. This time we're really going to hit you. This time it's really going to get serious.'

"I said sarcastically, 'Thanks, Tom.' But, in fact, he had acted properly because he did penalize Bobby. It was up to USAC after that to uphold what he did and back him. Binford did his job."

Opposite: Mario moved to Pat Patrick's team for the 1981 CART season and ran eight races in a Wildcat Mk 8, starting at Phoenix. "We got those cars going pretty well, but we should have won more races," he says. "Aerodynamically it was a very critical car. By that time you couldn't have moveable skirts, so the ride height and seal became critical for creating downforce." (Bob Tronolone) **Above:** Home of the United States GP for twenty years, Watkins Glen lost the race in 1981 because it could no longer afford the prize money demanded by F1 czar Bernie Ecclestone. The Glen held a pair of unsuccessful CART races in 1980 and 1981. Mario waits for the rain to stop with his Wildcat and some Patrick team members in this photo from 1981. (William Green)

Chapter 16

Monza Electrified

After his miserable 1981 season with Alfa Romeo, Mario's F1 career had come to an end. His plan for the '82 season was to focus on CART with Pat Patrick's team.

"I look back on my time in Formula One with a lot of pleasure," Mario says. "I won twelve Grands Prix, and being world champion was the pinnacle of my career, the thing I'd always wanted most. But it was always clear to me that I wouldn't stay in F1 indefinitely.

Above: In 1982 Monza was again the venue for a momentous event in Mario's life. He had been asked by Enzo Ferrari to drive the final two races of the season, and at Monza he won the pole in dramatic fashion and created a level of excitement among the fans that had not been seen for years. (Andretti collection)
Opposite: In the cockpit of the Ferrari 126C2 Mario gathers his thoughts before the Italian GP. Mario had not driven a Ferrari Grand-Prix car in ten years, and he was fêted wherever he went in the week before the race. For Monza's ardent *tifosi* it was like the return of a native son. (Studio Falletti)

I was 36 before I gave it my best shot and really concentrated on it. I probably should have done it five years before I did. But I knew that, all being well, I could eventually go back to full-time Indy-car racing. My roots were in it, and it's a form of racing I love.

"In some ways it was easier for me to leave F1 than I expected. I had a bad experience with Alfa and there weren't any good opportunities anywhere else. And by 1981 the cars were getting absurd, really crude with no suspension movement whatsoever. Stab and steer was the way you drove. There was no delicacy, no need for throttle control. It seemed like experience in set up was not as important as it used to be. I think it reached a point where technology took over too much to the detriment of the human element and the driver's contribution and finesse."

In April of 1982 Mario was invited by Frank Williams to drive at Long Beach in place of Carlos Reutemann, who suddenly had decided to retire. He tested the car immediately before the race at Willow Springs. "I ran pretty quick. Nigel Mansell was there with the Lotus and got upside down, as a matter of fact. But he ran very quickly. I think I was two-tenths of a second off his time, and I felt fine."

At Long Beach Mario qualified fourteenth, nine-tenths of a second slower than Williams team leader Keke Rosberg, who went on to win that year's world championship.

"Long Beach is not really an important downforce track," Mario says of the bumpy street course. But he discovered the Williams team had set up his car to optimize downforce at the expense of suspension compliance.

"The shocks were packed solid with bump rubbers. I said, 'That's never going to work around here.' And they disagreed. 'That's the way we run it,' they said. Keke took his packers out after the first day, but they never told me. Nobody said a word. The car was like a pogo stick. It was awful. In the race I was sliding all over the place, and I hit a wall." Mario had moved up four positions, but his race ended with broken suspension.

Mario ran the full CART schedule for Patrick in 1982 driving a new Wildcat Mk 8B, but again, he didn't win a race. He finished second to Mears in the Phoenix season-opener and qualified fourth at Indianapolis.

"I worked pretty hard that month. Never before had I gone through so many tires to choose my race set-up. I went through the whole pile, and it was set twenty-three that we determined would be my last set for the race."

Ride height was critical to the Wildcat, and it generated considerably more downforce when the sidepods were as close to the ground as possible. "I wanted to find one set of tires that had a little bit smaller circumference so that at the end of the race with a smaller set of tires I'd pick up downforce."

Mario never had a chance to put his exhaustive preparation to work because at the start of the race Kevin Cogan lost control of his car and took Mario with him. Mario was uninjured but enormously frustrated, so he went to the garage to collect his thoughts. Meanwhile, Mario's teammate, Gordon Johncock, was out of contention. Johncock was renowned as an extremely brave driver, but one with little or no set-up ability. "Johncock was understeering so badly that after a while I went out to the pits and told McGee to give Johncock my set number twenty-three. But they put that set on too early. They put them on a couple of stops from the end, and he came right into contention. He started going like stink. Then he didn't want to take those tires off!"

After the final series of pit stops, Johncock was leading Rick Mears. But in one of the 500's most memorable finishes, Mears caught and nearly passed Johncock in the closing laps. Johncock hung on to beat Mears by sixteen-thousandths of a second. "At the end of the race the tires were almost gone, and Gordy almost lost," Mario says, "but without my tires he would never have won."

The rest of the CART season brought plenty of good results. Mario finished second to first-time winner Bobby Rahal at Cleveland, second to Johncock in the Michigan 500, third at Milwaukee in August, second to Rahal in the Michigan 150 in September, and third behind Tom Sneva and Mears in the Phoenix season-closer. Although Mario didn't win a race, he was third in the CART championship standings behind Mears and Rahal and had his best season in Indy cars since he won his third USAC title in 1969.

At the end of that year Mario was invited by Enzo Ferrari to drive one of Ferrari's turbocharged cars in the last two F1 races of 1982 at Monza and Las Vegas in place of Didier Pironi, who had been badly injured in an accident at the German GP.

It was a tragic time for Ferrari because Mario's friend Gilles Villeneuve had been killed in qualifying for the Belgian GP in May. Patrick Tambay replaced Villeneuve, and Mario was brought in to replace the sidelined Pironi for the last two races. There was a huge welcoming crowd for Mario's arrival at the Milan airport, which went delirious with joy when he emerged from the plane wearing a red Ferrari cap.

Top left: At Long Beach in 1982, Mario substituted in the Williams team for Carlos Reutemann, who had suddenly decided to retire. The team had insisted that he run with a stiff suspension set-up, which Mario believed would not work on the bumpy street circuit. In the race his suspension broke. (Dave Friedman) **Middle left:** Mario tested Harley Cluxton's Mirage M12-Ford DFL at Riverside in 1982 in preparation for the Le Mans 24 Hours with son Michael. At Le Mans officials would not let Mario take the start, citing a rules infraction concerning the placement of the car's oil cooler. "I was strapped in, and five minutes before the start they just pushed the car off the grid. I couldn't believe it," Mario says. "Jabby Crombac wrote an exposé in *Sport-Auto* with before-and-after photos that documented how we got screwed." (Bob Tronolone) **Bottom left:** Mario drove a Ferrari 126C2 turbo at Monza in September 1982, qualifying on the pole in spectacular style. "That was a fine weekend," Mario says. "Monza has always meant a lot to me. It's a great place to race with tremendous history, a lot of atmosphere, and of course the fans are unbelievable." (Studio Falletti) **Opposite:** The racing Andrettis pose for a group photo with Mario's Wildcat, Michael's Ralt Super Vee, and Jeff's kart at Phoenix in 1982. Michael turned twenty that year and won the Super Vee championship while eighteen-year-old Jeff was in his last year in karts. (Bob Tronolone)

A slew of photographers and Ferrari mechanics surround the 126C before the start. "I loved to drive that car," says Mario. "It was very powerful. I had been out of Formula One for a year and I had never driven a turbocharged F1 car. I went out there and—boom—right away, I was competitive. It was a great feeling; immensely satisfying." (Studio Falletti)

"There were three key points in Mario's life at Monza: When he saw Ascari at the Italian GP in 1954, when he won the championship in 1978, and when he qualified on the pole in the Ferrari in 1982."—Pino Allievi

"It was the normal thing, really," Mario says, grinning. "You drive for Ferrari, and you're like the Pope. You don't pay for anything. You go down the autostrada, and you never pay any tolls. It's amazing. You pull up to pay your toll, and the fellow leans out of the booth and says, 'No! No! Mr. Andretti, go on through!'"

Pino Allievi recalls Mario's arrival. "Ferrari sent a car with a chauffeur to the airport, and Mario arrived in Maranello about ten o'clock in the morning. He spoke with the Old Man, and then they went to eat something. The Old Man asked him what he wanted to eat, and Mario said he wanted to eat tagliatelle and tortellini. So they went to Ferrari's private dining room in the back of the Ristorante Cavallino.

"After a relaxing luncheon Ferrari said to him, 'When do you want to practice the car at Fiorano? Tomorrow?' 'No, no,' Mario said, 'Now!' And he went to Fiorano, and after one hour he had the lap record!"

Mario relished his experience with the turbo Ferrari. "I did almost ninety laps at Fiorano—Bang! Bang! Bang! There's no straightaway at Fiorano. You're always turning. I wanted to really get the feel for the car, and I set a record and felt good about it. Then they brought in a different underbody for me to try. I said, 'I'm not here to test for you guys. I'm here to race. Leave it the way it is. I'm fine.' The next day it was in the paper that I was going to be testing at Monza, and I decided not to test. I told the mechanics to take the day off."

Instead, Mario called his friend, the eponymous car maker and Moto Guzzi factory owner Alessandro de Tomaso, to ask for a motorcycle so that he and Dee Ann could take a ride into the mountains of Tuscany. "He sent a brand-new Moto Guzzi Le Mans to the hotel, and Dee Ann and I took off for a nice wild ride up through the Abetone Pass. The Mille Miglia used to run through there. It's a great stretch of road. On the way out we rode past the track, and there were thousands of people waiting for me to go out to test. We rode by, and I said to Dee Ann, 'If they only knew. . .'"

On the first day of official practice and qualifying at Monza, Mario was sixth fastest, but in Saturday's final qualifying he took the pole. The place erupted in utter pandemonium.

"It was absolutely fairy tale stuff," Nigel Roebuck recalls. "I was in the Ferrari pit for the whole of that session, and it was one of those rare times that you're very aware that you were present at something historic that was never going to be forgotten.

"Those were the days when they used to pour water on the tires to cool them, and they took the wastegate off and the boost was off the clock. And, of course, it was right at the end of qualifying when he took the pole. I can remember afterwards going into the motorhome, and Tambay was just laughing. 'Jesus Christ!' he said. 'Can you believe that? Right at the end. Beaten by the old man.' But there wasn't an ounce of anger in him. Patrick was as thrilled as anyone, which says something about Mario."

"The biggest enthusiasm I ever saw in the Italian public was Mario's qualifying lap at Monza in 1982," Allievi says. "Today, Monza probably has more fans because there are a lot more grandstands, but you no longer have the kind of enthusiasm, admiration, and love for a driver like all the Italians had for Mario Andretti on that day. It was the first time that I saw [team manager Mauro] Forghieri very emotional, close to crying. I remember even Mario was very close to crying.

"Mario had a lot of pressure on him, but the pressure was pushing him. He was not scared. He was enthusiastic about it, and when he got the pole position it was fantastic! The fans were racing with Mario on that qualifying lap. No one today has the capability to create the same bond with the fans. That day with Ferrari, Mario did something special that all the Italians remember. Everyone remembers Mario's pole position, and nobody remembers who won the race. Everybody in Italy was happy to see the last big performance of Mario in Formula One.

"There were three key points in Mario's life at Monza: When he saw Ascari at the Italian GP in 1954, when he won the championship in 1978, and when he qualified on the pole in the Ferrari in 1982," Allievi adds.

At the race's start Mario smoked his tires a little too aggressively and fell to fourth, then ran into trouble with a sticking throttle and faulty turbocharger. He eventually finished third behind Rene Arnoux's Renault turbo and teammate Tambay.

The last F1 race of Mario's career came two weeks later at the unlikely Caesar's Palace parking lot track in Las Vegas. The Ferrari was less suited to the tight track, but he still qualified sixth ahead of Tambay. He was running fifth at one-third distance when the car's rear suspension failed.

"I never touched a thing, and the suspension broke, the right rear. I don't know why. Maybe it was a vibration or something because I used to get a lot of wheelspin there."

Nigel Roebuck recalls talking with Mario and Dee Ann at the Las Vegas airport the following morning. "He just said, 'Can you believe it? That was my last Grand Prix and the first time I can ever remember a Ferrari breaking its suspension.' But he was in a very reflective mood because he knew he'd raced a Formula One car for the last time."

Chapter 17

Building A New Team

Near the end of 1982 Mario entered into a partnership with Chicago-based Lola distributor Carl Haas
and movie star Paul Newman, who had built a successful second career as a racer and a team owner.

Unlikely as this alliance may have seemed at first,
it would prove to be the most enduring professional
relationship of Mario's career.

Newman and Haas had been competitors in the
SCCA's CanAm series. Haas's team won the series

Above: The creation of a new team—Newman/Haas—brought with it yet another
new car for Mario to develop, the Lola T700, shown here at Laguna Seca in October 1983. "That car had a flexible chassis and [designer Eric] Broadley didn't really
understand ground effect," Mario says. "To give him credit, as the season went on,
the car got better and better and we won two races. But Eric aged me fifteen
years." (Bob Tronolone) **Opposite:** A Newman/Haas strategy session in 1984 with
crewman John Tzounakis, engineer Tony Cicale, and Lola's chief designer Nigel
Bennett. Both Cicale and Bennett were Mario's personal selections for their respec-
tive jobs. Mario had worked with Bennett at Lotus in the seventies and earlier at
Ferrari when Bennett was a Firestone tire engineer. (Pete Biro)

aluminum angle iron just bent on his *out lap*. At maybe fifty mph, it collapsed."

Cicale says Broadley's solution did not inspire confidence. "He said, 'Oh, it's no problem. We can fix this very easily.' He asked one of the mechanics to cut off a quarter-inch thick piece of angle iron from their truck's ramp and bolt it to the right rear suspension to support this vertical spring/shock unit!

"I said, 'Don't you think we should do the other side?' And he said, 'No. That's not necessary because that side is *very* lightly loaded, even less than this side.' We were truly amazed."

Mario went out again, only to have the left rear suspension immediately collapse. "And we cut the other ramp off and bolted it on!" Cicale says, laughing. "The year was just filled with stuff like that. Eric was just absolutely unbelievable. That car was so bad. It had no torsional stiffness. We measured it one time, and it had something like 500 foot pounds torsional stiffness, less than a quarter of what it should have been."

The car gave Mario more gray hairs than even the dihedral wing Parnelli from 1972. "Broadley had no idea," Mario says. "He kept coming up with all kinds of new suspension geometries. But he was barking up the wrong tree. The real problem all along was the aerodynamics. I wanted to be cooperative so I put a zillion miles on the thing with all these different pieces. The car was scary to drive. I didn't enjoy it at all."

After four or five months of trying to work with Broadley, Mario had a frank conversation with the veteran designer. "What we've been doing is like putting a Band-Aid on a leper," Mario told him.

"Mario very clearly pulled that project in six months from something that was an embarrassment to something that was fairly respectable," Cicale says. "I think if

you had any other driver it would have taken six years to get to that same level, if it ever got that far. He kept pushing Carl and pushing Eric and pushing everybody, convincing them how horrible the car was, that it wasn't even close."

The first version of the T700 wasn't pleasant to drive in general, let alone on a superspeedway, but Mario persevered through the early part of the season and the long month of May at Indianapolis. He qualified eleventh for the 500, eight mph off the pace set by pole winner Teo Fabi's factory Forsythe March. It was Mario's worst Indy 500 qualifying performance. In the race he crashed after Johnny Parsons spun in front of him, taking both cars into the wall.

The team spent the early part of the season stiffening the chassis, and improving the car. "Fabricating a single-piece carbon underwing alone made the car two seconds a lap faster when we tested at Mid-Ohio," Cicale says. "It was exactly the same profile as the original multi-part aluminum honeycomb wing, but was just one piece, reasonably skinned."

With Newman-Haas's modifications, Mario put the car on the pole at Cleveland in July, then won from the pole at Elkhart Lake later in the month. He was second at Mid-Ohio, won again at Las Vegas, and finished second in the year's last two races at Laguna Seca and Phoenix. A strong second half to the year netted him an impressive third in the championship.

The T700 had become a good road racer and a reasonable oval-track car. "It started in a shaky situation but ended on a positive note," Mario remarks. Mario's son Michael, who was on his way to winning the 1983 Formula Atlantic championship (then known as Formula Mondiale), also would drive the T700 for his maiden run in an Indy car. He was planning to compete in a couple of end-of-season CART races to prepare for his first full season in 1984, so the moment was perfectly timed.

"Michael loved it," Mario says. "I was testing and the car was really good. Michael jumped in it and his lap times came right down to a competitive level. In retro-

in points in his rookie year in CART with Maury Kraines's Kraco team.

"Winning that championship was the fruit of insisting on Nigel Bennett coming on as Lola's chief designer," Mario says. "I fought hard for Nigel because he'd been there from the beginning of the ground effect era with Lotus. He did a very good job with the T800, so it was incredibly rewarding to win the championship. We achieved what we hoped and expected to do, so it was very satisfying for everyone involved."

Sullivan proved how good the Lola T800 was by winning three races that year for Doug Shierson's team driving the first "customer" T800 (i.e., not run by the factory team). Sullivan's successes helped Lola attack March's dominance of CART's customer-car market, but with Lola's primary effort going into building more cars, the development of the 1985 car lagged, allowing March to close the gap.

Mario's 1985 season began with a victory in Long Beach for the second year in a row and two wins in the next three races. He led the championship chase from the start of the year through Michigan in July. When the green flag waved for the Michigan 500, he was twenty points ahead of the Unsers, Al Sr. and Al Jr., only to have one of the worst crashes of his career when a wheel came off while running third with eight laps remaining.

"Right away the car headed straight for the wall," Mario recalls. "I knew it was going to hurt." He suffered a broken hip, collarbone, and four ribs. For the first time in his career, Mario was forced to miss the next race. Alan Jones, the 1980 F1 World Champion, substituted for him at Elkhart Lake. "That injury was really painful because of the hip and the clavicle. The shoulder belt comes right across your clavicle when you're strapped into the car.

"I had been lucky as hell. The only other time I visited a hospital before that was in 1974, when I crashed at Ontario testing the new Firestone radials." On that occasion he had been knocked out but came around in the hospital an hour later and tested a Formula 5000 car at Riverside the next day.

"I really thought he was going to be out for quite a while, but he only missed one race," Haas says. "When he came back at Pocono, he was still hurting. Mario always had a lot of determination. He didn't let pain stand in the way."

Mario returned to action at Pocono for 500 miles on the notoriously bumpy superspeedway, located midway between his home in Nazareth and "Open Woods" to the north. On the morning of the race, Michael and Kraco teammate Kevin Cogan narrowly escaped injury when their helicopter crashed.

"That was really an emotional race for me. I was hurting so bad. Then to play more on my emotions, Michael had that helicopter crash that morning while trying to leave 'Open Woods' for the track. Then a wheel came off his car while he was leading the race." Michael was not hurt in either incident, but Mario endured serious physical discomfort in finishing the race.

"Every time the car bottomed it was like someone was shooting a knife right through my hip. I finished seventh, but I finished, and I was so emotionally drained that I just grabbed Dee Ann and cried like a kid for about half an hour. I felt I had to just get it all out of me. Then I felt better. It was one of those days where I thought, 'If I can just get through this one, I can conquer the world.' But I felt really good about myself that I got through it. I figured after this, anything else had to be a piece of cake."

But in the year's remaining six races, Mario was utterly luckless, finishing only at Phoenix in October, when he was third behind championship leaders Al Unser Sr. and Al Jr. By season's end Mario had tumbled to fifth in the championship behind the Unsers, Rahal, and Sullivan.

At the end of 1985 Cicale was lured away from Newman/Haas by March's Robin Herd and Pat Patrick. Mario was very disappointed about Cicale's departure. "Tony was a guy with a fresh approach to things. He was a very articulate individual who would go back after we had our debrief and come back the following day and be able to reason things out. He had patience and total focus. He didn't worry about going to dinner. He didn't worry about what time it was. He worried about doing the job, and I loved that. He gave me that confidence and an even keel."

Aove: At Long Beach in 1985, Mario leads into first turn on the way to his second straight win in the California streets. He's chased here by Bobby Rahal, Al Unser Jr., Geoff Brabham, Emerson Fittipaldi, Bruno Giacomelli, Jacques Villeneuve Sr., Roberto Guerrero, Danny Sullivan, Jim Crawford, Michael Andretti, Al Unser Sr., and the rest of the field. (Paul Webb) Opposite: Pulling on his gloves, Mario prepares for his qualifying run at Milwaukee in June, 1985. He went on to win the pole and the race, beating Tom Sneva, Rick Mears, and that year's Indy 500 winner, Danny Sullivan, who had joined the Penske team the previous winter. At this stage of the season Mario seemed on course to repeat as CART champion. (Paul Webb)

Chapter 18

More Wins, More Disappointments

Englishman Mo Nunn joined Newman/Haas racing as Tony Cicale's replacement for the 1986
season. Nunn had run his own Formula One team
during Mario's F1 days and had come to the United
States in 1984 as an engineer for George Bignotti
and Dan Cotter's team and driver Roberto
Guerrero. Where Mario and Cicale had been very
much in sync, Mario and Nunn quickly discovered
they couldn't work together.

Above: Mario runs side by side with Michael in the 1986 Phoenix season-opener.
The 1986 Lola wasn't a very good car and was clearly outpaced by Adrian Newey's
latest March. (Dan Boyd) **Opposite:** Mario's 1986 season would end on a downbeat
note at Tamiami Park in suburban Miami, where he qualified fifth and struggled
home eleventh. He finished the year fifth in points, and won just two races at Portland and Pocono. It was his weakest season since joining Newman/Haas four years
earlier. (Paul Webb)

Mario says: "Mo was more effective for a guy who comes in and says, 'What should we do?' I'm more of a guy who says, 'This and that should be done, and what do you think?' We had a tough time with that because Morris had his own ideas.

"In his mind, I wasn't explaining enough to him for him to fully respond. He didn't like the fact that I would dictate and tell him what I wanted. Mo didn't have confidence in me. With Tony if I said, 'Hey, let's polish the car.' He would say, 'OK.' But Mo would always say, 'Are you sure, Mario? Let's do this or that to the set-up.' That was the big difference."

Nunn readily agrees. "I didn't have much satisfaction working with Mario. He was so experienced that he didn't have the confidence in me to let me do the job. The way I work is I tell the driver what changes I'm making and ask for his comments. It was different with Mario. It was his team, and he was used to running things and doing what he wanted."

Despite their differences and relatively mediocre year together, Nunn has great respect for Mario and likes to tell a story about a preseason tire test at Laguna Seca. Mario was trying to negotiate the first turn (which at that time was a very quick, left-hand kink) without lifting, but couldn't do it. A new, wider front tire was fitted, so he tried again.

"On the third lap with that tire he'd built up the courage to take it flat," Nunn says. "Suddenly we saw the car way up in the air and an explosion of dust. We jumped in the rental car and raced down to turn one. The first thing I saw was the gearbox, then an engine. Further around the turn the chassis was laying in the middle of the road, and Mario was standing up with his back to us.

"He was trying to put his watch band back into place, and his hands were shaking. The car was spread all over the place, but he didn't have a scratch on him. I said, 'Are

you OK?' He said, 'Yeah, and by the way, Morris, turn one's still not flat.' It didn't faze him at all."

Once the season was under way it became clear that the new Lola T86/00 couldn't match the latest, Adrian Newey-designed March, nor was its reliability very good, particularly in the year's second half. "We got the pole at Phoenix and Mid-Ohio, and the engine let us down," Nunn recalls. "We were the first to run Bosch's new fuel management system, and something broke."

Mario won two races in 1986, at Portland when Michael ran out of fuel on the last lap, and the Pocono 500 in mid-summer, the only time Mario was able to win his local 500-mile race.

"I was happy that he won the one race he'd been trying to win and never had," Nunn says. "In those days people didn't do much with shock absorbers, and I think we were ahead of the game with what we did on that bumpy oval. He locked 'em up in the pits one time and had to go 'round again, and he still won the race. I think we had a super car there."

Mario again finished fifth in the championship. Michael finished second, scored his first CART wins, and battled down to the wire with Bobby Rahal, who won the championship for the first time.

During 1985 and '86, Haas had more on his mind than Newman/Haas Racing. He had sold Beatrice Foods on a spectacular sponsorship deal for both CART and Formula One and started his F1 team in 1985 with Alan Jones running the last four races of the year in a Lola-built car. Haas hired former McLaren men Teddy Mayer and Tyler Alexander to run the team, which ran the full schedule in 1986 with Patrick Tambay joining Jones in a second car.

Team Haas planned to build its own F1 car for 1987, and Newey was hired by Haas to design it. But after Beatrice was taken over in a leveraged buyout, new owners Kohlberg, Kravis, Roberts began to dismantle the company, and the racing program died. "Beatrice paid the contract," Mario says. "It worked out very well for Carl. He made a lot of money from that."

With F1 team manager Alexander and designer Newey out of work, Haas put them to work at Newman/Haas. The only problem was that Haas had forgotten he had agreed to bring Cicale back as Mario's race engineer. That left Cicale in January looking ahead to the new season without a job.

Above: Leading Roberto Guerrero, Mario heads toward his third CART win and fourth overall victory on the Long Beach street course. By 1987, many of the racers in CART were twenty years younger than Mario, but at forty-seven he remained as competitive as ever. (Bob Tronolone) Opposite: At the start of the Meadowlands race in 1986, Mario gets the jump on the pole winner, Michael, who is chased by Al Unser Jr., Roberto Guerrero, Roberto Moreno, Danny Sullivan, and the rest of the field. Neither Mario nor Michael finished the race. Sullivan won, with Emerson Fittipaldi second and Bobby Rahal third. (Dan Boyd)

Newey was thrilled to team with Mario. "I could have gone off and been a race engineer in Formula One, but the opportunity came up to be a race engineer for Mario for a year, so I jumped at it. Obviously, for any young engineer, the chance to work with Mario was something pretty special, and straight away we struck up a good rapport."

For 1987 the team switched to Ilmor Engineering's new Chevrolet engine, which had been developed the previous year by Roger Penske. But the winter testing program was set back by an accident at Laguna Seca, remarkably similar to the previous year's crash in tire testing.

"Mario had a big accident when the rear wing came apart," Newey says. "It was a very salutary lesson for me. We hadn't had time to install a radio because the car was prepared at the last minute and, as he came past the pits, we could see the wing was cocked over to one side. But by the time we saw it, he was past us and, having no radio, we couldn't tell him to slow down. When we heard the bang at turn one, it was a pretty sickening feeling."

Like Nunn had the year before, Newey jumped into his rental car and raced down to the first turn. "We saw the gearbox and two rear wheels," Newey says. "Then we saw the car. It was a huge accident, and Mario was standing there tapping his watch, saying, 'At least my watch still works!' Considering the size of the accident, that was pretty amazing."

At Long Beach Mario dominated the season-opening weekend, qualifying on the pole and running away with the race to score his fourth win on the California streets. He was on the pole at Phoenix, and pulled out to a big lead before an engine mount bent, dropping him to fifth. "There was a massive crossweight in the car, so it became very oversteery," Newey says. "It was a great tribute to Mario that he kept soldiering on. Many drivers would have either pulled in the pits and said it was too

dangerous or stopped trying and finished twentieth."

Then came the month of May and possibly Mario's most dominant performance ever at the Speedway. "I had them covered at Indianapolis that year," he says. "There wasn't a single day when I was on the track that anybody went faster than me. Every day that I practiced, I was quickest. Every single day. On race day, I was just gone. I led every single lap."

For most of the race he babied the car and was running 400 rpm below the normal redline when the ominous sound of a broken valve spring signaled an agonizing end to Mario's race with twenty laps to go. Later dyno testing at Ilmor revealed a harmonics problem at the lower rpm Mario had been running.

"We had one of the original computer systems on that car," Mario recalls. "When they downloaded the data and simulated the rev range that I'd been running, the engine broke within a minute or so of the time I had actually broken in the race. Instead of running in fifth gear, I should have been running fourth gear, even though I didn't need to. That was just a killer for me to realize. I would have loved to run fourth gear and just gone for it, but it is all part of the Indianapolis saga."

Newey emphasizes how dominant Mario was that year. "Generally, we were packing up early every day, trying to finish by five o'clock and not bothering with Happy Hour," Newey says. "Everything went really well. In the race, it was just too easy. And, ultimately, that was our downfall from revving the engine too low. It was pretty sickening for everybody."

Alexander had won the Indy 500 twice before with Johnny Rutherford and the McLaren team, but was as disappointed as everyone else at Newman/Haas when Mario's engine failed. "We led the whole damn race, and the thing went onto seven cylinders with fifteen minutes left," Alexander says with a grimace. "Having been quick every single day for a month, that was not nice. Adrian and I didn't cry, but we came close. And Mario as well."

Indianapolis journalist Robin Miller recalls how impressed he was by Mario when he faced the media that afternoon. "He was *two laps* ahead of everybody, and his engine blew up," Miller says. "After this horrible moment, he stood there in the garage and talked to us for twenty or thirty minutes. He said, 'You know, they knew I was here today. We did the best we could.'

"I don't care how much money or fame you've got; that just had to tear his heart out. This guy should have won the Indy 500 about six times, and he ended up winning it once. That was an example of where he was still a man to beat, still on the

Left: Accelerating out of the pits at Indy, Mario is followed at a distance by Tom Sneva and Bobby Rahal. Mario reduced his rpm to cruise to the finish, but his engine failed with twenty laps remaining. Incredibly, later analysis by Ilmor engineers revealed that Mario's engine would have gone the distance had he run maximum power. (Pete Biro) **Opposite:** Mario leads Rahal at Cleveland in 1987. "The engine was very well matched to that car," Mario says, "and the fact that I had Adrian Newey with me was a big factor in my being competitive everywhere. The reliability of the Chevy/Ilmor wasn't there for the long races, but we were tough in the shorter races. It was a year too early for that engine." (Dan Boyd) **Following Pages:** The Newman/Haas crewmen execute a perfect pit stop for Mario as he blows away the field at Indianapolis in 1987. He built up a huge lead while running his engine well below the normal rpm redline. This was Mario's most dominant performance at Indianapolis: the only laps he did not lead were during pitstops. (Pete Biro)

top of his game, and he had that race ripped out of his hands."

At Milwaukee the following weekend, Mario qualified third. "It was a mark of Mario, and the team, that we picked up and were doing very well at Milwaukee," Newey says, "until we had another rear wing failure. This time the pylon broke." Mario spun into the wall in turn one, suffering several cracked ribs. "It hurt him more than he let on," Newey says. "He was in a lot of pain the next few races. He was able to get it up for qualifying, but he was struggling in the races with a lot of physical discomfort."

The next four races were all on physically demanding tracks—Portland, Cleveland, the Meadowlands, and Toronto. Still, Mario finished second to Bobby Rahal at the Meadowlands after a fierce battle, and scored an excellent win from the pole at Elkhart Lake at the end of August. "I was screaming at Mario over the radio to save fuel," Alexander says, "and he says in that classic, laid-back accent of his, 'Ah, shut up. I'm doing that!' You remember things like that."

"He was very strong at Elkhart," Newey adds. "But we had a lot of reliability problems with the engine that year." Indeed, Mario didn't finish six of the last eight races as engines failed him time and again. He took his seventh of eight poles that year at Laguna Seca in October and appeared a likely winner until he was robbed by another blown engine.

"It was a tremendously frustrating season for all us because of all the engine failures," Newey recalls. "I think it's fair to say that if he hadn't had all those engine failures he would have won the championship. But at the same time it was a mark of Mario that he never got upset over it and threw his toys overboard. He didn't allow it to affect his driving."

For 1988 Newey joined the March/Leyton House team to begin his F1 career in

Above: Mario and Aldo pose with their sons Jeff, Michael, and John at the Newman/Haas motorhome during the Phoenix race weekend in 1988. Jeff was just a few days short of his twenty-fourth birthday and was racing Indy Lights and IMSA GTP cars. John was twenty-five and had made his CART debut at Elkhart Lake the previous year. He ran his first full Champ car season in 1988. (Jutta Fausel) Opposite: Leading Darrell Waltrip at Mid-Ohio, Mario finished eighth. Mario scored his best result of the '87 IROC series—sixth place—at Watkins Glen. (Dan Boyd)

earnest, and Cicale returned to Newman/Haas after spending the second half of the 1987 season with Rick Galles's team engineering Geoff Brabham's car. Nigel Bennett had left Lola after the 1987 Indy 500 and agreed to work for Roger Penske to produce the PC17, which became the car to beat. That gave Bruce Ashmore the opportunity to take over as Lola's chief Champ car designer. Ashmore's T88/00 was a steady development of the T87/00, but it was no match for the new Penske, and Newman/Haas secretly rolled out a T87/00 for the year's three 500-mile races.

Mario started the 1988 season in good form, winning the first race at Phoenix after pole-winner Mears broke. Aboard the team's T87/00 Mario qualified fourth behind the Penskes at Indianapolis, but a transmission bearing broke in the race. Back in a T88/00 he scored a memorable win at Cleveland, beating Rahal and Danny Sullivan.

"To save some time we decided to change only the right-side tires in the last pit stop because there was only a small amount of fuel to put in," says Alexander. "We told him what we were going to do, and he gave us the usual, 'Yeah, yeah, yeah.' Laconic and to the point as always. That put us ahead of Rahal and Sullivan, and instead of fighting with them he just drove the shit out of the car the rest of the race."

At the Michigan 500 the car's fuel cell came apart in the race, and at the Pocono 500 the car was destroyed in a huge accident in the third turn with Dick Simon, who drove into Mario and Sullivan's path. All three drivers were lucky to emerge unscathed.

Back in a T88/00, Mario finished second to Emerson Fittipaldi at Mid-Ohio and scored a string of thirds at Elkhart, Nazareth, and Laguna. He was fifth yet again in the championship, this time behind Sullivan, Al Jr., Rahal, and Mears, and one place ahead of Michael.

For the first time since 1983, Mario and Michael also raced at Le Mans in 1988. They were joined by Aldo's son John in a factory Porsche 962 and finished sixth after threatening to win. "We were on five cylinders from the beginning of Sunday morning," Mario says. "What saved us was there was a lot of rain, and it didn't hurt us that much in the wet."

A restricted amount of fuel had been allotted to each team for the race, and rationing that supply to last 24 hours was critical. Before the engine problem, the Andretti Porsche had the other leaders thoroughly beaten on fuel mileage. "The Jaguar was already thirty-six liters in arrears, and both the other Porsches were already twenty liters over their allotment," Mario says. "We were just riding along, and all of a sudden something went wrong with one of the injectors. But we still finished sixth. The Jaguar won that year, but we would have won that race so easily."

Running Le Mans that year was part of a plan for Mario to leave Newman/Haas at the end of 1988 and move with Michael to Al Holbert's new Porsche CART team. Mario had started talking to Holbert and Porsche about the idea in 1987.

"Al Holbert was the driving force," Mario says. "The Porsche people really had faith in him, and I went to Germany with him for some secret meetings. But they were a bit obstinate about ground effects. They were developing the car without a moving ground plane in the wind tunnel. I told them that might work with a sports car, but it won't with a single-seater because you've got exposed wheels, and the air takes a totally different direction as the wheels are turning. I said, 'You're going to get totally erroneous readings,' which they did.

"I tried to tell them, but they had to pursue their own thing. I almost begged them not to debut the car with Big Al at Laguna. I said 'You're going to be embarrassed.'"

The Porsche Champ car was big and bulky, and when Al Unser Sr. drove it at

Laguna Seca he discovered a host of other flaws. It not only lacked horsepower and downforce, it also handled poorly and had a slow-shifting gearbox. Holbert, a four-time IMSA champion, tried the car himself at the final race of the season at Miami, but withdrew after a miserable practice period.

Holbert's team ran a Porsche-powered March for Teo Fabi in 1988, and Mario's doubts were corroborated when Fabi had a tough year. Fabi's best finish was fourth at Nazareth near the end of the year.

Cicale also had been talking with Porsche. "Mario and I agreed that I would go to Porsche in 1989 and get things steered in the right direction, and Mario would stay at Carl's in 1989 and come to Porsche in 1990. That was kind of the plan. Al Holbert more or less agreed to that plan and we were all looking forward to that."

Mario adds: "I was really excited about it because Al and I were really striking a very close friendship. We had a lot of the same objectives, and we did a lot of talking. One time at Mid-Ohio we went out into the woods after practice and talked for three hours, and he wrote everything down. The whole idea was that as soon as Al got it exactly the way we wanted, then I would join. We had Tony all juiced up to go as well, which he did, of course."

But Holbert was killed on September 30, 1988, in the crash of his own light plane. "When Al died, a big part of that program died with him," Mario says. "The Germans weren't aware of many of the things that Al and I had talked about. I didn't feel like we were on the same page in any way, so I just let it drop. It would have been interesting if Al had not died. I've said many times that it's impossible to imagine how much of a difference this one individual made to that program. Without him I saw a huge void.

"I had tremendous respect for [Porsche's racing boss] Norbert Singer, and I think Norbert had some idea of what Al and I were planning, but nobody else knew what the ultimate intentions were. So the whole thing just fizzled."

Left: Mario scored the fiftieth Champ car victory of his career at Phoenix. He beat Roberto Guerrero with Michael finishing third. Mario never qualified lower than sixth in 1988 and was on the front row six times. The amazing thing was that he was totally competitive on road courses, the only man of his generation still capable of that performance level. (Jutta Fausel) Opposite: At Le Mans in 1988, Mario shared a factory Porsche 962 with Michael and nephew John. They finished sixth despite running on five cylinders in the race's final eight hours. Porsche's racing boss Norbert Singer told them, "Let Stuck and Wollek use up their fuel fighting among themselves, and you'll quietly go into the lead." Adds Mario: "We stayed on schedule, and that's exactly what was happening until we lost a cylinder." (LAT Photographic)

Chapter 19

The Best of All Worlds

After the Porsche dream had deflated, Mario refocused his attention on turning Newman/Haas into a two-car team to accommodate his son Michael in 1989. "I never believed Carl could handle two cars," Mario says, "but after Holbert died and I had decided to stay with Carl, I started talking to him about Michael. I told him that with Michael he could pick up more sponsorship money and that I thought the team would gain new status and dimension. I also

Above: The 1989 season heralded a new era for both Mario and Newman/Haas as the team expanded to run two cars for Mario and Michael. Mario believed the move would be good for himself, the team, and Michael, and says he shared information with Michael more openly than he could have with any other teammate. (Jutta Fausel) **Opposite:** Mario and Michael run side by side in the Michigan 500 on the superfast Michigan Speedway. They qualified one-two for this race, with Mario taking his first pole in five years, but neither ran the distance as their engines gave out well before the finish. (Dan Boyd)

Costa Del Mar
BFGoodrich
Miller
HIGH LIFE
BFGoodrich
BOSCH
BBS
Hella

thought it would be great for me to have a young guy there to measure where I was at that age, and I thought it would be good for Michael's career. So I pushed for that. Having Michael was the best of all worlds."

In his first five years racing Champ cars with the Kraco team, Michael won seven races. He was second and third in the championship in 1986 and '87, both times to title-winner Rahal. Michael and his father had battled hard on the race track. Now they would do so as teammates.

Early in the 1989 season, Mario received another call from Enzo Ferrari, whose F1 driver, Gerhard Berger, had crashed in the San Marino GP at Imola, Italy. He was burned in the accident and would have to miss the Monaco GP two weeks later. "Would you replace Berger at Monaco?" Ferrari inquired. Mario was interested but knew that there was not enough testing time to become familiar with the techniques required by the car's new technology. "I would have needed a week to get used to the semi-automatic transmission," Mario says. "But there was no time. I said, 'I can't do you justice.'"

By that point in the Champ car season, it had become clear that once again the latest Lola couldn't quite measure up to Nigel Bennett's new Penske. The 1989 championship would be fought between the Roger Penske and Pat Patrick teams, which were both equipped with Penske PC18 chassis. Emerson Fittipaldi won the Indy 500, four other races, and the championship aboard Patrick's Marlboro-sponsored PC18, while Rick Mears was second in the standings with three wins for Penske. Danny Sullivan added two more wins, so PC18s won ten of the year's fifteen races.

Mario had a new race engineer, Brian Lisles, who replaced Porsche-bound Tony Cicale. Lisles had worked with Ken Tyrrell's Formula One team for ten years and was a rookie to oval tracks. Lisles learned a tremendous amount about ovals that year from Mario and from Tyler Alexander, who left to rejoin McLaren following the 1989 Indy 500.

"We went to Indy, and I could see right away this was Mario Andretti territory," Lisles says. "Mario loved being there. He loved the tradition. He loved the finesse you needed to get the best out of the car. He loved chasing the day as the conditions changed and being able to keep the car on top of the conditions.

"Mario would drive out of the pits and go 'round and do two or three warmup laps to get the oil warm," Lisles adds. "Then he'd stand on it, and his first lap would be around 220 mph, and he'd probably never do a lap any slower than that. He had a tremendous understanding of ovals and knew what the car was capable of and was willing to let it do the work for him. I could see very clearly how Mario could carry a car on a superspeedway better than most."

At Pocono in 1989, Lisles learned more about the Andretti family dynamic. Mario raced with new shock absorbers that sprang leaks and lost all their oil during the race, and he struggled to stay on the lead lap. Michael was leading the race when a yellow flag caught Mario directly in front of his son.

"The restart happened," Lisles recalls, "and there was no way the old man was going to let Michael go by and put himself a lap down. They fought tooth and nail for ten or fifteen laps with Michael calling over the radio saying, 'Why doesn't Dad let me go by? I'm leading the race!' And there was total silence from Mario. In the end, Michael gave up, and Mario managed to finish on the lead lap with no dampers in the car. There was no quarter asked or given on the track."

"I certainly never had to coach him," Mario recalls, "but working and talking together was beneficial to him and to me. That was because we were totally honest with each other, and that's something you can't be with another teammate of different blood. That honesty could sometimes shed light in areas of doubt that was huge for your confidence. Michael was good for me, but I'm sure I was good for Michael as well. I was never a good teacher. I think he benefited more from some of the driving school instructors early in his career. With me there was never any

Above: Mario pits on his way to fourth place in the 1989 Indy 500. New race engineer Brian Lisles had come from Formula One and says he could not have had a better oval-racing tutor than Mario. "I was really lucky in my first year to work with Mario," Lisles says. "I learned an incredible amount from him about the ovals."(Jutta Fausel)
Opposite: Before the CART season began Mario fulfilled an obligation to his late friend Al Holbert by driving one of Holbert's Porsche 962s with Michael (shown in car) in the Daytona 24 Hours. Holbert's team had been disbanded, but the car was prepared and run by Holbert's former crew chief, Kevin Doran, for Jim Busby's team. About a third of the way into the race the brakes failed on Mario and Michael's car. (LAT Photographic)

direct teaching such as, 'Sit down, Michael. We're going to go through this.' "

Mario thinks the honest communication inside the team contributed to his son's successful, fiery style. "Michael had that youth and exuberance working for him," Mario says. "He was getting away with a lot of banzai moves. Normally I would have fought harder, but I was so happy to see him doing so well. I almost didn't want to upstage him, not that I could have."

That first season together Michael led ten races for more than 400 laps and finished a fighting third in the 1989 championship behind Fittipaldi and Mears, while Mario finished sixth. Michael scored his first win for Newman/Haas in Toronto in July, then won the Michigan 500 two weeks later with Mario third, the first time they'd shared the podium as teammates.

Mario had finished second to Fittipaldi at Cleveland and second to Mears in the Laguna Seca season-closer, but for the first time in his career he did not score a win. "I never counted individual victories," Mario says, "but I always wanted to make sure at the end of the year: did I have a victory? And that was the first year I couldn't count one." Mario was unfazed, however, and with the approach of his fiftieth birthday in February of 1990 believed his age had no effect on his performance.

At the end of the year Cicale left the struggling Porsche Indy program and rejoined the team to engineer Mario's car. Lisles moved over to work with Michael. For the next two seasons, Michael's performance continued to improve while Mario's seemed stuck, unable to rise above the second level of the podium.

In 1990 Michael scored five wins and finished second in the championship behind a steady Al Unser Jr. Mario had two second-place finishes, at Portland and Mid-Ohio, both times behind Michael, and was seventh in points. Mario was winless for the second year in a row. "It drove a lot of it home to me where I was dropping off," he says. "I realized I was getting worse, and he was getting better. The handwriting was on the wall."

Michael's 1991 performance was even better. At Indianapolis he was beaten by Speedway maestro Mears, who won his fourth Indy 500 after a superb duel to the flag as they passed and repassed each other with daring outside moves. At Milwaukee the next weekend, Michael scored his first win of the season with cousin John second and Mario third. Aldo's son John had started racing Champ cars in 1987 and drove for the Porsche team beside Teo Fabi in 1990, then joined Jim Hall's team and won the first race of the 1991 season at Surfers Paradise, Australia.

The unprecedented family sweep at Milwaukee was a prelude to a dominant year for Michael as he won eight of seventeen races and led 965 laps, almost 600 more than anyone else. He also took eight poles and beat Rahal to the title with a record 234 points to Rahal's 200. At the final round at Laguna Seca, Mario finished third behind Al Unser Jr. so he was able to stand next to his son during the championship celebrations.

Mario led 102 laps and finished in the top three four times in 1991, but was again winless. Remarkably, every time he was on the podium with the other top finishers he was up there with Michael as they finished one-two in Toronto, one-three at Elkhart Lake and Laguna Seca, and one-two-three with John between them at Milwaukee.

"When Michael started going by me regularly, I felt, 'Thatta boy Michael!' At the same time it pissed me off, but I felt like a bit of me was riding with him, so I

Above: Mario confers with Jeff, whose career was derailed by his terrible accident in the 1992 Indy 500. (Dan Boyd)
Opposite left: The start at Portland in 1989. The pole winner, Teo Fabi, leads from Emerson Fittipaldi and Mario while Michael charges down the inside, trying to pass Arie Luyendyk, Sullivan, Mears, and Rahal. This type of thrusting start was characteristic of Michael's aggressive style, which made him a serious championship contender in each of the next three years. (Dan Boyd) **Opposite middle:** At Laguna Seca in 1990, Mario started from the outside pole next to pole-winner Danny Sullivan with Rick Mears and Al Unser Jr. on the second row. Mario's car broke early in the race while Sullivan went on to win from Unser and Michael, who had started fifth. (Bob Tronolone) **Opposite right:** Mario, Michael, and Bobby Rahal lined up on the second row of the grid on the pace lap prior to the start at Indianapolis in 1990. The family's atrocious luck at the Speedway continued, as neither Mario nor Michael finished. Mario blew an engine after 150 miles, while Michael pulled out later in the race because of an incurable and unmanageable vibration. (Dan Boyd)

"That's what drove me through all of my career: sheer passion and a love for the sport. I think I squeezed and squeezed as much as I could out of it."

still felt good about it. I never felt shame about growing old. I figured it wasn't my fault. It happens to all of us. You've got to be realistic, be able to analyze it, admit it, and accept it.

"You realize that you reach a certain point that, no matter how much your mind wants to do it, there's a part of nature that says it doesn't work. You can only push that envelope so far. You can't go against nature. I think I pushed that envelope as far as I could out of sheer passion and desire. That's what drove me through all of my career: sheer passion and a love for the sport. I think I squeezed and squeezed as much as I could out of it."

At the end of the year Cicale decided the time had come to end his long association with Mario and Newman/Haas. "Michael was extremely quick at that stage of his career," Cicale says. "Mario, on the other hand, was kind of in his twilight, starting to go down a little bit, and I think he really didn't want to accept that. He wanted to say he was as quick as Michael and there was no reason why he couldn't be as fast as Michael. He believed that if he wasn't as fast as Michael he wasn't getting good enough engineering support, and he started to copy what Michael was doing. I believed he should stop mimicking Michael. They had totally different styles, and they both had certain things they liked.

"I felt at the end of that year that I'd lost my influence with Mario," Cicale adds. "I don't want to stay with anyone I'm not helping. There was a little bit of conflict, and I thought I was losing some of my ability to impart confidence, so consequently I didn't put up any fight. I thought it was the right thing for me to leave and the right thing for Mario to have somebody else. So it was best that I go."

Mario does not disagree. "I think Tony's correct in the sense that I thought maybe I'd go faster, or because Michael was faster that I needed his set up. I was influenced by that, and I should have been more confident in myself and pursued more my own thing with Tony."

After Cicale left, Peter Gibbons, who had been with Penske the previous three years and had worked with Michael in the Kraco days, came in to engineer Michael's car in 1992. Brian Lisles switched back to Mario's side of the team.

In 1992 Ford introduced the new Ford/Cosworth XB engine, which Mario and Michael had begun testing in the fall of '91. The XB engine was powerful and much smaller than the existing Ilmor/Chevy or Judd engines, and its size allowed for a sleeker aerodynamic profile as well as a slight reduction in the center of gravity. At the same time, Bruce Ashmore had developed the 1991 and '92 Lolas to the point that they were competitive with the other chassis.

Characteristically, Mario was in his element working with Ford engineers to develop the new engine. "I always loved to try something different," Mario says, "to bring on new technology that was beyond the status quo despite what you pay for it in the interim because you have to do the development. It might have been detrimental to potential results for me at different times, but I liked the idea of working hard on something that nobody else had."

In 1992 Michael was clearly the man to beat as he set a record by leading 1,136 laps and led the opening lap of all but two races. Inevitably, the new engine lacked reliability, resulting in too many failures for Michael to beat Rahal to the championship. Although Michael won five races, Rahal drove a Lola-Chevy to his third title in his first year as a team owner, beating Michael by just four points, 196 to 192.

The 1992 season was a trying time for Mario, exacerbated by an accident during the Indianapolis 500 in which he suffered broken toes on both feet. The race was run in uncommonly cold weather, and many drivers crashed, Penske teammates Fittipaldi and Mears included. Mario had pitted under caution and left the pits without doing the customary burn-out to clean and heat the tires. When the race restarted, he charged below a couple of cars in turn four only to discover that his cold tires didn't have the grip he needed.

"My accident wasn't a big deal," Mario says with a shrug. "I had some broken bones and toes on my left foot, plus the big toe was squashed on my right foot as well. But with Jeff's situation, that was the devastating part of that day for me."

Twenty-five laps after Mario's wreck, his younger son, Jeff, hit the wall in a heavy crash. It was his second start at Indianapolis. Jeff had started racing cars in 1983 and was quite successful in Formula Fords and Super Vees before racing Indy Lights for three years. In his first full CART season the year before, he was named both CART and Indy 500 Rookie of the Year. The leg and foot injuries Jeff suffered were much more serious than Mario's and would confine him to a hospital for three months.

"I don't know if they were treating Emerson or somebody else, but they put me on ice, literally," Mario recalls from his hospital experience. "They put my feet in ice and said, 'Wait for your turn.' So I was waiting and licking my wounds, and all of a sudden I heard a commotion. There was that murmur that something was wrong.

Opposite: Mario leads Eddie Cheever, Scott Pruett, Scott Goodyear, Danny Sullivan, and John Andretti at Surfers Paradise in 1992. Mario finished the race in seventh place to beat everyone in this group except for his nephew, John, who finished in sixth place. (Michael C. Brown)

"Then I heard the name Jeff mentioned, and I didn't even want to ask. I knew he was still alive because he was there at the hospital, but I was bracing myself. It was the worst feeling I ever experienced in my entire life."

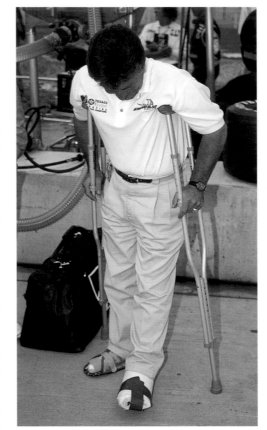

"Then I heard the name Jeff mentioned, and I didn't even want to ask. I knew he was still alive because he was there at the hospital, but I was bracing myself. It was the worst feeling I ever experienced in my entire life. I was so helpless. It was one of those moments that you hope is just a terrible dream, and everything will be all right when you wake up.

"At that point I realized they weren't going to get to me for a while. I was in pretty good pain. My feet and legs started to ache, and they made sure I was full of morphine and iced me up again with big packs of ice. I was so doped up I couldn't keep my eyes open. I was falling asleep."

With his father and brother in the hospital, Michael proceeded to run away with the race until his engine coughed and died, its fuel pressure gone just twelve laps from the finish. The family's apparent Speedway curse was never more evident than on that day.

"One of the doctors kept on coming over and giving me the thumbs up that Michael was still leading the race," Mario says. "I was half awake, praying, 'Thank God. Come on Michael. Bring it home.' Then they assured me that Jeff's injuries were very serious but not life-threatening. I kept thinking of Ronnie Peterson, and I said, 'Please do the right thing.' They said, 'Don't worry. We're on top of it.' Then I dozed off, and when I woke up it was four o'clock. The race was over, and I said to myself, 'Nobody has come to congratulate me.'

"A nurse was sitting there and I asked, 'Is the race over?' She said, 'Oh, yes.' I asked, 'Well, who won?' And she said, 'Do you really want to know?' She was right. I didn't want to know.

"That was by far the worst day of my career because of Jeff's injuries first and foremost. I didn't know how that was going to work out, but I had full confidence in [Dr.] Terry Trammell and the team at Methodist Hospital. If anybody could do the right thing, it was them. The other thing I felt was, 'Poor Michael.' I said, 'If we get through this one, guys, we're in good shape for the rest of our lives.'"

For only the second time in his career, Mario was forced to miss the next race, which was Detroit. He was back in action less than four weeks after his Indy accident.

"When I came back for Portland, that was very painful," he says. "I had a pin, just like a shish kabob, holding my toes together on my left foot, and on the way to Portland I stopped in Indianapolis to have Dr. Trammell pull those pins to allow me to race."

Incredibly, Mario qualified eighth. "I remember toward the end of the race the ripples at turn one before the chicane were really getting to me," Mario recalls with a grimace. "At the end of the race my left boot was full of blood because the stitches were pretty well stretched out." He finished the race in sixth place despite immense pain in his feet. After the race he sat in the team's motorhome for an hour, both feet wrapped in bags of ice while Michael celebrated his first win of the year.

As Michael went on to lead a record number of laps in 1992, Mario drove himself back into shape. Except for the Michigan 500, he finished every other race he ran that year and showed his prowess by taking the pole at Michigan with a new track record just over 230 mph. Mario finished the year in style with second place at Laguna Seca behind Michael. By then Michael had decided he was leaving Newman/Haas and Champ cars to go to Formula One with McLaren in 1993, so the one-two finish in California was a triumphant way for father and son to conclude their years together as teammates.

"Sharing the podium with Michael and starting on the front row together, those were unbelievable moments and treasures I will always hold dear," Mario says, the emotions still evident in his voice. "All told, we started together on the front row ten times, and we were on the podium together fifteen times. Really, that's unbelievable."

Adds Michael: "Those were things that were priceless, and we'll never be able to repeat. I believe those years will stay with both of us for the rest of our lives."

Michael admits that being Mario's son was difficult in some ways. "I think I always knew that I would be overshadowed by Dad's accomplishments, and I just accepted that," he says. "I almost preferred it that way. I'm not one who really likes to be known too much, so it actually worked out well for me. No matter what, I'm third on the all-time winners list, but I will always be known as Mario Andretti's son. It was fantastic to race with him, and to beat him gave me tremendous satisfaction because I knew I was beating the best."

Above: Michael won his fifth race in 1992 at Laguna Seca, the last event of the season. But Rahal's four wins and more consistent finishes were enough to win him the championship by just four points. Mario finished second at Laguna. (Michael C. Brown) **Opposite:** 1992 saw Mario miss a race because of injuries for only the second time in his career. After breaking toes on both feet in a crash at the Indy 500, he sat out the Detroit race two weeks later. Teo Fabi was his substitute driver. (Art Flores)

Chapter 20

Arrivederci, Mario

Michael Andretti's absence was just one of several
changes at Newman/Haas for 1993. Jim McGee replaced Ed Nathman as team manager after
spending a successful year helping Bobby Rahal's
new team win the 1992 CART title. Most signifi-
cantly, Haas had signed the controversial English
driver Nigel Mansell to be Mario's new teammate.
Incredibly quick when he was at the top of his
game, Mansell was also a moody and sometimes

Above: Mario drove a faultless race at Phoenix in 1993 to score his first win since
Cleveland in 1988. He beat Raul Boesel by a full lap to take the 52nd Champ car
victory of his career. At fifty-three, he also became the oldest man to win a Champ
car race—almost five years older than Johnny Rutherford, the next in line. (Michael
C. Brown) **Opposite:** At Long Beach in 1993 Mario qualified sixth and moved up in the
race, passing teammate Mansell who had qualified on the pole and was challenging for
the lead. Mario was convinced he had Mansell beaten and believed he could have run
down eventual winner Paul Tracy, but was stopped in his tracks by an engine failure.
(Bob Tronolone)

obstreperous man who had won the 1992 F1 world championship with the Williams team, then had a falling out with team boss Frank Williams over details of their contract negotiations. One of the many disagreements between the two men concerned the number of free hotel rooms the team would provide Mansell's entourage. Williams finally threw up his hands in disgust, which left Mansell in a position to accept Haas's offer to race Indy cars.

Mario and Mansell's careers briefly had overlapped in 1980, when Mansell was a test driver for Lotus during Mario's last year with the team. Mansell competed in two Grands Prix for Lotus in 1980 as a third-string driver beside Mario and Elio de Angelis, and from those early days a simmering disdain bubbled between the two very dissimilar characters.

Coming from the tough world of F1, in which distinctions between number one and number two drivers had become increasingly important, Mansell was a master at working a team to his advantage. Using his considerable charm and charisma as the current world champion, Mansell warmly embraced both the team and CART officials, and for the first time in his career Mario found himself treated as a number two driver.

"The biggest disappointment of Mansell's arrival was how the team rallied around him and let me kind of sit," Mario says. "Nigel had the charm when he needed it. He was buying gifts for the mechanics, just the guys on his car. I would never buy for half the team. I don't blame the mechanics, but it was a typical Nigel tactic, and that's destructive. I couldn't respect the guy as a person. I understand that you need to be selfish, but what I didn't like was that he was so busy undermining all the time."

McGee knew Mario better than anyone in racing and recognized how difficult Mansell's arrival was for him. "Mansell came in at the top of his game, and Mario was on the downside," McGee says. "At the ovals Mario was still pretty competitive, but Mansell was a special guy. He came over from Formula One, and he was full of confidence, and he just drove the hell out of the car, not knowing the limits

most of the time, while Mario, let's face it, was no longer at the top of the curve.

"Nigel was thirty-nine years old, and Mario was fifty-three. I think he was asking a lot of himself to compete at that level. He did a good job, but he was in an awkward position. He was the guy who more or less put Carl in business. He was the leader of the team and had been with them forever, and here comes this guy from the outside. Not many guys could handle that. Mario is a take-no-prisoners type of guy, and naturally all the press was on Mansell because he was new and he was a showman, and that just irked the hell out of Mario. I think it really played with his head."

Mario struggled with the latest, state-of-the-art Ohlins shock absorbers that were a pet project of Newman/Haas's chief engineer, Peter Gibbons, who engineered Mansell's car in 1993 and '94. "They were nice, trick shocks, but there was too much adjustment," Mario says. "I did not understand them, and I did not understand the car. Only Peter Gibbons understood them. I was totally confused. The shocks had more effect than you could imagine because I had no faith in them, and Peter believed in them 100 per cent."

Mario's relationship with Mansell was the opposite of the one he had enjoyed with Michael. "He would not ever want to sit down and debrief together," Mario says. "He knew he had the advantage with Peter Gibbons, and I found myself totally left out. I felt very betrayed by the team."

Mansell caused a stir by qualifying on the pole and winning the first race of the season in Surfers Paradise, while Mario qualified sixth and finished fourth. Mansell's mastery of CART's officials was revealed at this race when he served a stop-and-go penalty for a pit violation during a pit stop rather than as a separate, time-consuming black-flag visit to the pits as specified in the rule book. Had the penalty been applied in the proper fashion, Mansell would not have won the race.

At Phoenix two weeks later Mansell crashed massively in practice, breaking the retaining wall and suffering a back injury. Mario qualified second for the race, led the opening laps, then went on to win after leaders Paul Tracy and Emerson Fittipaldi both crashed in separate accidents in the last forty laps. It was Mario's first victory since Cleveland in 1988.

"It was a fairly lucky win," Mario says. "It was one of those races where I wasn't

Opposite: The first oval race of 1993 was on the one-mile Phoenix oval. Mansell was lucky to survive a crash during practice when he lost control of the car and smacked hard into the first turn wall. His car's transmission case punched a large hole in the wall and its gearbox oil created a flash fire. (Michael C. Brown) Above: Mario outqualified Mansell at Milwaukee, the pair of Newman/Haas Lolas starting fifth and seventh respectively. They ran together for a while in the race but Mansell then started moving up, going on to score the first oval victory of his career while Mario fell back with a whole host of problems, eventually finishing many laps behind in eighteenth place. (Dan Boyd)

"I got such a sour taste that I wasn't enjoying doing it anymore. So I thought maybe it was time to retire, and after I made the decision, quite honestly, I had some second thoughts."

strong at any point in particular, but I was there at the right spot."

Mansell returned to take the pole at Long Beach two weeks later. He faded in the race, but a slew of late race retirements moved him up to third by the finish. Paul Tracy qualified second to Mansell and led most of the race to score the first win of his career, while Mario qualified fifth and got up to third before he was stopped by ignition failure with ten laps to go.

Mario was especially upset because he had been compelled to race an engine he was sure was failing. He had tested the engine at Phoenix, thought there was a problem, and asked the team to check it on a dyno. The test revealed no problems. "They said, 'It's all in your head.' There was a miss for sure, but they said the data didn't show any problem. So they put that in as my race engine for Long Beach, and I went out in the morning warmup, and it had a miss." The problem Mario sensed was revealed to all when the ignition trigger on the flywheel broke, ending his race.

At Indianapolis Mario was among the quickest through the first week of practice while Mansell remained at his home in Florida having his injured back tended to. Pole day was billed as a shootout between Mario and Arie Luyendyk, but hot, humid weather turned it into a fiasco. Mario was second in the qualifying line and the first to run four qualifying laps. Conditions were bad enough that five of the next six drivers to attempt a qualifying run came in or waved off their attempts because their speeds were too slow.

Mario won the provisional pole with a bold drive that dispensed with the warmup lap and used the tires to their full potential in miserable, slippery conditions. Luyendyk, who had waved off his qualifying attempt earlier in the day, returned around five o'clock, when the weather had cooled, and was able to beat Mario's time to win the pole.

That year's 500 may have been the most competitive in history. Mario led 72 laps, twice as many as Mansell or anyone else, and no fewer than ten cars were in the hunt at the final restart. For most of the race Mario was dominant, despite a stop-and-go penalty from USAC for entering a closed pit. Fortunately, that penalty came during a caution period, so he didn't lose many places. But the tires Mario took on his last pit stop didn't work as expected, and in the final sprint to the flag he was shouldered back to fifth, finishing just over five seconds behind winner Emerson Fittipaldi and only half a second behind teammate Mansell in third.

As the year wore on Mario was overshadowed by Mansell, who won seven poles and five races on his way to capturing the championship. Relations between the two grew frostier all summer, and Mario was delighted to beat his teammate to the pole at the Michigan 500, and establish another new world closed-course speed record of 234.275 mph.

"All that Saturday morning before qualifying, he kept taking wing out and taking wing out," Brian Lisles recalls. By reducing the angle of the wings, Mario was reducing both the amount of downforce the car could generate, which made the car faster, and its aerodynamic drag, which made the car more difficult to control. "He was getting me scared to hell. There was no wing on it at all," Lisles says. And he took even more out for qualifying and did a very fast time and put it on the pole. It was his last pole and probably very fitting that it was at a superspeedway.

"I said, 'How did you know you could take that amount of wing out?' He said, 'You have to be absolutely scared on Saturday morning because the air is always dirty. But when you go out to qualify on your own, the air is nice and clean, so you always have a lot more downforce than you expect. It doesn't matter if you scare yourself on Saturday morning because you should be fine in qualifying.' A very brave man."

The pair of Newman/Haas Lolas dominated the race, finishing one-two and lapping the field. Mario led the opening twenty-seven laps before Mansell took over, on his way to winning by ten seconds. In victory circle Mansell feigned exhaustion, stumbling around and apparently looking for sympathy, and Mario was visibly disgusted with Mansell's performance. "That was one of the greatest pieces of acting I've ever seen," Paul Newman said later.

That kind of behavior was deeply antithetical to Mario's personal conduct. He believed a racing driver should never complain of pain or discomfort in public and had carried himself stoically from his earliest racing injuries through his broken feet at Indianapolis in 1992. The combination of Mario's personal distaste for Mansell and frustration with his reduced role in the team set him to thinking about retirement.

"I got such a sour taste that I wasn't enjoying doing it anymore. So I thought maybe it was time to retire, and after I made the decision, quite honestly, I had some second thoughts."

Nevertheless, Mario made up his mind that 1994 would be his final year racing open-wheel cars. "I surprised Dee Ann because I surprised myself. I never consulted her, and she reminds me of it to this day. Dee Ann said to me she resents the fact that I didn't discuss it with her, and I should have, no question. I know I would have gotten good advice, and maybe I would have even stayed a couple years longer. My decision wasn't well thought-out. I was acting on pure emotional disappointment. But I made the decision, and I wasn't going to go back on it."

Top: Mario and Mansell have a serious conference in the pits at the Milwaukee Mile. Mansell was asserting himself in the team, using his on- and off-track skills to pull the team around him while Mario's role and influence in the team began to dissipate. After ten years with Newman/Haas it was a difficult change for Mario to accept. (Dan Boyd)

Bottom: Mario took the 67th and last pole of his Champ car career at Michigan in 1993, setting a world closed course record of 234.275 mph. Here he poses with car owner Carl Haas and teammate Nigel Mansell, who shared the front row with him. (Art Flores)

Dee Ann minces no words in confirming her displeasure with the way Mario made his decision. "Oh, yes, I remember it well," she says. "I was furious. I had always been involved in all the decisions. I learned about it from a news media person, and I just laughed in his face and said, 'Yeah, sure, that'll be the day.' Little did I know the truth, and yes, I resented that a lot."

Was Mario's retiring at the end of 1994 a mistake? "Definitely, definitely," Dee Ann says. "He had a couple of good years left. I don't know if he was still going to be number one, but he still would have been in there." She believes it was all because of Mansell. "I definitely think jealousy took over from thinking rationally," Dee Ann says.

In fact, the 1994 season was as tough on Mansell as it was for Mario. Roger Penske produced the triple-shock PC23, which dominated the year, winning twelve races in the hands of Al Unser Jr., Emerson Fittipaldi, and Paul Tracy. Unser won the championship from Fittipaldi and Tracy.

In the face of that year's Penske steamroller, Mansell gave up. First, he grumbled incessantly that the Lola T94/00 was no match for the Penske. Then he refused to test and actually pulled out of two races, Toronto and Nazareth, because his car wasn't competitive. Although he managed to win three poles and finish second twice, Mansell never came close to winning in 1994 and finished eighth in the championship, a mere shadow of his 1993 season.

"When he really had to fight for it, he didn't have the stomach for it," Mario says. "He was very good when he had a clear advantage, but he didn't have the strength of character to soldier on when things weren't the best. When it didn't go right for him, he would blame everybody else.

"It was typical Nigel. He was a terrible influence on the team all around. Those were the most miserable two years of my career."

Mario's season was equally bad. His best race was the season-opener at Surfers

Paradise, where he finished third and shared the podium for the last time with Michael, who had won on his return to CART with Chip Ganassi's team following a rough year in F1. Mario produced his best qualifying performance of the year—fourth—in round two at Phoenix. At Indianapolis he qualified ninth but dropped out after just 23 laps because of a fuel system failure.

Mario's only good result the rest of the season was fourth place in Toronto. There was some small satisfaction in his final race, at Laguna Seca in October, when he outran Mansell until his gearbox broke. "Arrivederci, Mario," as the season was dubbed by his publicists, was anything but an ideal retirement year.

"I just wanted to get it over with," Mario says. "I didn't want that year to end, and yet I did. There were so many emotions. It was so much of a roller coaster. If I could have read the situation differently and known that Michael was going to come back to Newman-Haas, I would have never retired. I would have stayed active two more years, but by then it was done."

Lisles believes Mario's final year was underrated. "I think a lot of people were saying, 'Oh, he should have retired some time ago.' But to be fair to him, as I remember his last race at Laguna, I think he was going to be on the podium if the damn gears hadn't failed him.

"One of the very generous things Mario did after his last race at Laguna," Lisles adds, "was he got out of the car, took off his crash helmet, and gave it to his crew chief, John Simmonds. I would imagine there would be a lot of people who would die to have that helmet, but he gave it to the guy who had looked after his car for the last couple of years. That was a very nice gesture."

Lisles believes Mario chose the right time to retire. "I know he says he could have gone on for a few more years, but that's because he just loves driving cars. He used all of those skills he had learned and all the things that he understood. I think he was pulling all of the tricks out of the bottom drawer to stay where he needed to be. I think the reason he was able to go on like that was because he loved it so much. He didn't ever tire of it.

"Driving a racing car was such an important part of his daily activity, I think when he actually stopped, it took a lot to come off the habit. I'm sure his first year out of the car was pretty difficult for him."

Above: Mario in action at Laguna Seca on October 9, 1994—the last Champ car race of his career. He was running well in seventh place when he suffered a transmission failure, this time with only four laps left in the race. (Jutta Fausel) Opposite: Brian Lisles engineered Mario's cars during the last three years of his career. "Mario's career was built on a lot of hard work as well as God-given gifts," Lisles says. "He was always trying to think of the next little thing to make the car go faster." (Art Flores)

Mario admits it was a tough time in his life. "Oh, I missed it," he says. "It was a big change in my life because throughout my adult life I always had in mind a certain discipline. Even in the short off-season you never really let yourself go. You always maintain a certain physical discipline because you want to be in shape.

"As much as I now felt like I could have that extra glass of wine, I missed that sense of purpose. Something really huge was missing in my life. I'd go to a race track on race morning and think I didn't have a big day and the potential result ahead of me. A lot of the sense of purpose went out of my life.

"That was the only routine I knew for forty years, and I missed it. But you can't go on forever. And when you're not as quick as you used to be you don't enjoy it anymore. But life is all about change and learning to deal with it."

Tony Cicale says Mario's motivation and effort never dwindled. "I think when he couldn't be competitive it wasn't because his effort was lacking or he wasn't physically capable of doing it. I think it was because he started to lose his sharpness to small degrees in his hearing, his eyesight, and memory. I think all those things started to trouble him a little bit, and it was much more difficult for him to remain confident in his ability because he sensed deep down that these things were slowly and naturally degrading. I think that's what caught him out because throughout his prime, his memory was just phenomenal. He could remember every detail of set-ups from ten years ago and how each change affected each individual set-up and relate those changes to what we were doing today. I think that was a key element in his excellence as a driver."

Because of Mansell, Jim McGee and Mario were not as close in 1993 and '94 as they might have been. "We've had our ups and downs and ins and outs, but that happens," McGee says. "But he won his first race when I was his chief mechanic and his last race when I was team manager. All in all, looking at the fact that he survived and walked away with all his bones, the lucky stars were shining on him.

But that was never a consideration. He always stood on the gas.

"I think he got out at the right time," McGee says. "I think he did it right. He didn't tarnish his image like Foyt and Rutherford did. To the people in racing, to his peers, Mario was still a competitive guy when he retired, and Foyt and Rutherford weren't. They were just hangers-on, and that was tough to see. He did it right."

Carl Haas agrees: "I think he made a wise decision retiring when he did. He was still a contender. I've always had the highest respect for Mario, not only his accomplishments, but his whole demeanor. He's definitely lived and breathed racing. He's a good spokesman for the sport, everything you look for. He was a great driver, very versatile, very optimistic, and definitely had an understanding of cars, which was helpful in getting them set up. I'm really proud to have been with him for so long."

Adds Lisles: "I only came to realize after working at Newman/Haas for a while what made Mario extra special and still probably makes him extra special. There are two things. One is his absolute love of driving a car, of driving anything mechanical, to use it, to make it work properly, and make it flow properly.

"He just has a love for the feel of the machinery—airplanes, cars, motorbikes, motorboats, anything—and making them operate properly and smoothly. He's very inquisitive mechanically. He wants to know how everything works and how it's going to affect him, and what he could change to make his life better.

"The second thing is, he's always optimistic that the next change is going to be the one that really makes the difference. And that optimism never, ever dies."

Lisles says Mario was at his best as a driver in two ways. "When the car's almost perfect and it just needs that last little touch, he knows exactly what he needs to do to make that happen. That's how you get pole positions. And the other thing is when the car is just awful, he'll never give up. He'll never say the car is hopeless and walk away. There's always something you can do to maybe make it better or maybe give you a clue as to which way to go.

"I think in Mario's view there probably really is no such thing as an ultimately bad racing car. If you work at it hard enough, you can get it to be competitive. And those are very unusual qualities in a racing driver. There are very few drivers who are willing to make that kind of intellectual effort to just never give up regardless."

Epilogue: Mario Today

Of course, Mario's "retirement" didn't include sports cars or Le Mans. The great French race is one of the few motor racing classics Mario has not won, and he raced at Le Mans in 1995, '96, '97, and again in 2000. His best result was in 1995, when he finished second co-driving a Courage-Porsche with Frenchmen Bob Wollek and Eric Helary.

"It was really an eleventh-hour deal," Mario says. "With Courage being right there in Le Mans, they were able to organize a one-day test for me on the short circuit just to get familiar with the car and get fitted. I liked the car right away."

But a wet track, bad luck, and operational mistakes would combine to deny Mario a victory in the race he had first run three decades earlier.

"A Kremer Porsche spun in a very weird spot, at the next corner after Indianapolis," he recalls. "I got the car cocked into a spin so I wouldn't hit him. I almost kept it off the wall. I went onto the grass and just nudged the back on the wall and, of course, it cracked the body and bent the lower wishbone. I drove it in, and there was a comedy of errors. The car didn't look like it was that bad so they kept it in the pit road, which meant only two mechanics were allowed to work on it. If they had backed it up and brought it in the garage, which was totally legal, the whole crew could have tackled it. They could have fixed the thing in ten, fifteen minutes at the most. Instead, it took twenty-five minutes."

Wollek, Helary, and Mario still made it back to second place despite a couple of bad tire-changing calls caused by language problems between Mario and team manager Dominique Peidades. "Dominique was very good, but we couldn't communicate very well. He spoke English only marginally. At one point I said make sure you tell Wollek that slicks are absolutely OK. There's a definite dry line for slicks. But they wouldn't hear of it. They put intermediates on, and Wollek went out, did two laps and came in for slicks. That stop alone cost us, because in the end we lost the race by fifty-one seconds."

With Le Mans the only outlet for the passion to race that had shaped his entire life, Mario found that retirement not only brought a drastic change in lifestyle, but physical withdrawal symptoms as well. "I've picked up some allergies and problems I never had before because all of a sudden I didn't have a constant flow of adrenaline going through my body," Mario says.

"I went to the University of Pennsylvania to make sense out of what was happening to me. They said my body was so attuned to such a rigorous approach, going to the maximum physically all the time, and always had that adrenaline rush going. They said it would take a long time to adjust, and it *has* taken a long time to adjust. I suppose I'm not alone, but each individual reacts differently."

But Mario's life in retirement does resemble his racing days in terms of its variety. Just as the racer of the 1960s and '70s was constantly juggling a multitude of circuits, teams, and cars, Mario today divides his time among a wide range of professional and personal projects. His business interests include three auto dealerships and two car washes in Pennsylvania, and a chain of gas stations in California. He works in various capacities with a number of companies, most notably Texaco, Firestone, TRW, Market Scan, and Infineon Technologies.

While nothing has replaced his passion for racing, Mario's greatest source of pride is the Andretti Winery, a fifty-three-acre parcel located in California's Napa Valley. Established in 1996, the winery estates recreate the look and feel of the Tuscany region of Italy. Today it bottles about 18,000 cases a year and attracts wine lovers and race fans alike.

Mario's professional commitments continue to keep him almost constantly in motion. "I'm on the road twenty days a month," he says. "There are times when I look at my schedule and think I'm going to have a nice little break from traveling, but then those free days get filled in. This year I have only one weekend off from the beginning of May right through the summer, but I enjoy being productive like that."

Off the road, Mario's time at home in Nazareth centers on his family (which

Above: Mario motors along the country roads of eastern Pennsylvania near Nazareth in his Lamborghini Diablo. (Gary Gold) **Opposite:** Mario tested but didn't race this TWR-based Porsche prototype at Daytona early in 1995. Here Bob Wollek is at the wheel, while Mario contemplates the car's front end. "I helped do some testing with that car and I should have raced it because it won two years in a row," Mario says. "I just thought it was too underdeveloped and wouldn't finish. I totally misjudged that one." (Hal Crocker)

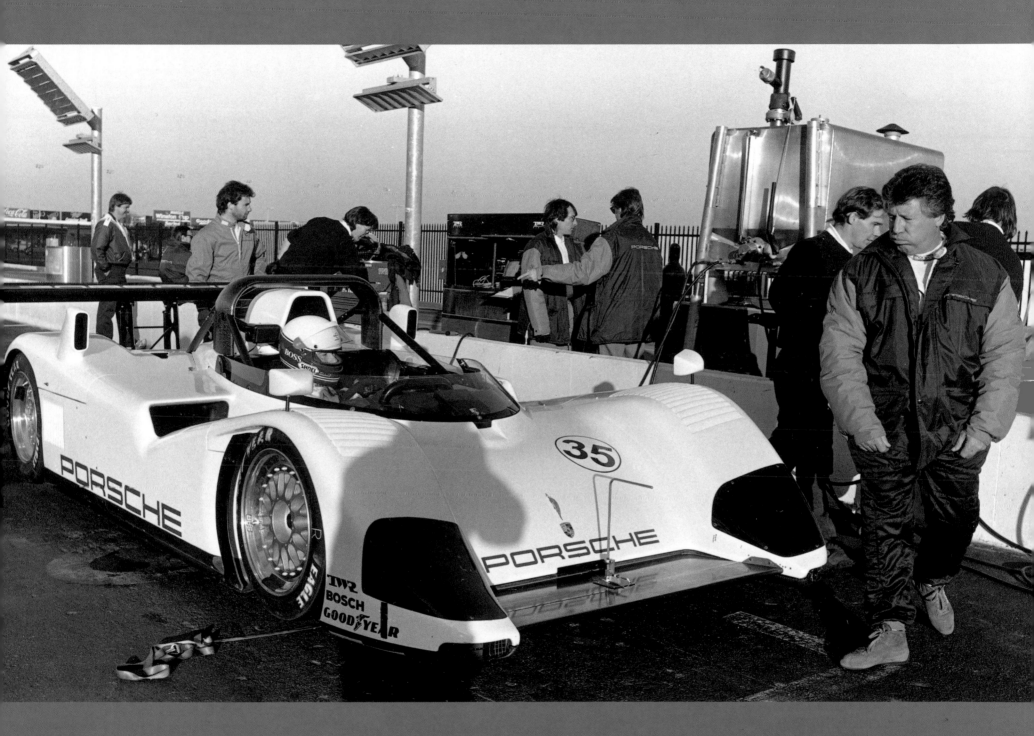

now includes five grandchildren) as well as a host of outdoor activities. "It's still pretty much the same outdoor recreation that I've always done," he says. "A lot of it takes place at 'Open Woods', because it's close and easy to have ready—the tennis courts and all the water sports and four-wheeling and flying my ultra-light. In the winter it's snowmobiling."

Nearly forty years after launching his professional career and more than five years since

its end, Mario Andretti's stature in the history of motorsports remains unparalleled. Despite his roots in Italy and its racing tradition, Mario is regarded by many as the greatest American driver ever. He won races and championships in a more diverse range of cars than anyone else and survived competitively at the top level of the sport for thirty years, much longer than any of motor racing's other great superstars. His accomplishments speak for themselves: four-time USAC and CART champion, the 1978 F1 World Champion, the 1967 Daytona 500 winner, the 1969 Indy 500 winner, three-time Indy 500 pole winner, three-time Sebring 12 Hours winner; 1969 Pike's Peak winner, 1974 USAC dirt-car champion, and 1979 IROC champion.

In forty-one years as a driver, Mario started more than 900 races and won more than 130 of them in a dozen different categories. His 52 Champ car wins ranks second on the all-time list after A. J. Foyt, and he holds the all-time record for Champ car poles (67) and laps in the lead with 7,587.

In addition to being the only person named Driver of the Year by a panel of racing journalists in three different decades (for 1967, 1978, and 1984) Mario was designated Driver of the Quarter Century in 1992 by a panel of past Drivers of the Year and racing writers. And along with the new millennium, the Driver of the Century title was again bestowed upon him—first by a vote of Associated Press sportswriters in December 1999, then by the readers of *Racer* magazine in its January 2000 issue.

Robin Miller, who followed Mario's career as a fan and then as a journalist, sums up Mario's place in racing history: "No one else has done the things he's done. Al and Bobby Unser were great drivers, and Foyt was a great driver, but they were great on one continent. Mario won races all around the world in all types of cars. He's done it all."

But Mario's seemingly endless catalog of victories, titles, and records are more than just the result of his immense natural gifts as a driver. For Mario, doing it all always included making whatever extra effort was needed to compete on or off the track, whether it meant testing new equipment, re-engineering a problematic car, or studying a new track or his fellow drivers.

Tony Cicale witnessed this first hand during his years as Mario's engineer at Newman/Haas. "When I look back at all the great drivers I've worked with, I still have to put Mario at the top of the list," he says. "He was certainly the most complete driver I've ever worked with. He was so fast in qualifying, such a good racer, and a good motivator. In the early years of Newman/Haas, he was so much better than anybody else out there, and he made anybody look good who was associated with him. He was truly in a class by himself."

Nigel Roebuck remembers fellow racing writer Denis Jenkinson summarizing Mario's stature more succinctly: "Jenks always used to say, 'He's the only real professional in the whole field. The rest are just boys.'"

A key factor in Mario's longevity as a racer was his ongoing fascination with the technology of motorsports, which changed dramatically over his four decades on the track. "To me, technological progress is what motor racing at the highest level is all about. It's the criterion that is solid, measurable, and has value," he says. "I don't think I could have remained motivated in the sport unless I had the continuous developments to look forward to each year.

"I was fortunate enough to come on the scene right at the time that a very interesting evolution was taking place, starting with the development of racing tires,

Above: After a two-year break, Mario returned to Le Mans in 2000 with Don Panoz's team, driving a Ford-powered Panoz LMP with regular drivers David Brabham and Jan Magnussen. They ran fourth behind the factory Audi team until debris from a wrecked Porsche badly damaged the car. After repairs there were more problems with a blown tire and seized gearbox, and the car limped home sixteenth. (Peter Brock) Opposite: This is one of the many wood-paneled trophy cases that line the entrance to Mario's home, Villa Montona. Mario's forty-one year career has yielded perhaps the most complete and diverse trophy collection of any driver. (Gary Gold)

"I've always been an optimist, even when faced with a lot of negatives. And, quite honestly, that attitude has helped me tremendously."

also acknowledges the impact that even the smallest changes in circumstance might have had on his record. "Years ago, during one of my long flights from South Africa after a race at Kyalami, I calculated that, but for five gallons of fuel, I would have won four more championships, three Formula One races, and five Champ car races. You can't imagine how many small things would have a big difference in my career. But it all came together, in spite of all the bad luck and the negatives."

And even in some of his toughest losses, such as his recurring misfortune at Indianapolis, Mario insists that consistently competing at the top of his ability was its own reward. Win or lose, he says, "They knew I was there. For all of the years I raced at Indy, from the very beginning until my last year, I was competitive. And that's the part that's important to me."

And in a sport where bad luck too often carries a price far greater than the loss of a race or title, Mario says he maintained enough perspective to count his blessings: "After a disappointment, I would think, 'I'm still able to go out and run the next race. I didn't get hurt. I still have all my faculties, all my limbs. What happened was bad, but I can recover from that. I can go out and race again.'"

Above all, Mario still marvels at how fortunate he was to have lived out a dream born nearly a half century ago as two young brothers cheered Alberto Ascari at Monza. "The biggest satisfaction that I've derived from my career is that I attained more goals—and I had set ambitious goals for myself—than I ever expected," he concludes. "When you've put a lifetime's effort into something that you love so much, and you can compare your achievements to the drivers who have been your inspiration, that brings an enormous sense of satisfaction and accomplishment.

"The bottom line for me, the ultimate reason I was able to succeed and maintain a high level of motivation, was that driving was my absolute love and passion."

which were then just six inches wide and made of hard compounds. A few years later chassis dynamics were revolutionized by the move from front-engine to rear-engine designs, followed by new suspension geometries and braking systems. Then with an understanding of aerodynamics, cars evolved from a pure cigar shape to sprout chin spoilers, then wings, then the total ground-effect package that became too efficient and had to be cut back. Now the more we restrict aerodynamics the more efficient the designers and engineers become in compensating for those losses. That's technology and progress."

But Mario also admits that being at the leading edge of racing technology could sometimes work against him: "Many times I spearheaded the development of new engines, often to my detriment and perhaps at the cost of championships. But I felt that that progress was necessary, and perhaps my spirit of innovation was good for the sport."

Mario takes a similarly philosophical view of the role that luck—both good and bad—played throughout his career. For all of his successes, many believe his record would be even more prodigious had he not received more than the average share of mechanical failures and other setbacks.

"I've always been an optimist, even when faced with a lot of negatives. And, quite honestly, that attitude has helped me tremendously," he maintains. But he

Above: A portrait of Mario at Le Mans in 1996. (Michael C. Brown) *Opposite:* Mario's aggressive driving style and commitment were undiminished at the end of his Champ car career. Here he clips an apex by running over the curbing at Surfers Paradise in 1994. He drove a superb race that day, coming through the field from nineteenth on the grid to finish a spectacular third behind Michael and Emerson Fittipaldi. (Michael C. Brown)

Index

Page numbers in italics refer to photographs and captions

Mario celebrates his sensational back-to-back wins in the two-race non-championship Questor Grand Prix at Ontario Motor Speedway in 1971. (Richard George)

Wms Grove 10-5-63